Microsoft Planner Essentials

Organize Your Work, Achieve Your Goals

Kiet Huynh

Table of Contents

CHAPTER I
Introduction to Microsoft Planner

1.1 Overview of Microsoft Planner

1.1.1 What is Microsoft Planner?

Introduction to Microsoft Planner

Microsoft Planner is a versatile task management tool within the Microsoft 365 suite, designed to help individuals and teams organize their work, track progress, and collaborate effectively. It provides a simple yet powerful interface that allows users to create, assign, and manage tasks in a visual manner, making it easy to stay on top of projects and deadlines.

Understanding the Core Concept

At its core, Microsoft Planner is based on the concept of organizing work into plans. Each plan is a container for tasks related to a specific project, goal, or initiative. Within a plan, tasks can be organized into buckets, which are customizable categories that help break down work into manageable segments. This structure makes it easier to focus on different aspects of a project, ensuring that nothing falls through the cracks.

User Interface and Design

The user interface of Microsoft Planner is intuitive and user-friendly. The primary workspace is the Planner Hub, where users can view all their plans at a glance. Each plan is represented by a tile, and clicking on a tile opens up the plan's detailed view. Here, tasks are displayed in columns (buckets), and each task is represented by a card that can be clicked to reveal more details, such as due dates, assignees, attachments, and comments.

The design philosophy behind Microsoft Planner is simplicity and accessibility. Unlike more complex project management tools, Planner is designed to be easy to use without requiring extensive training or technical knowledge. This makes it an ideal choice for teams of all sizes, from small groups to large enterprises.

Integration with Microsoft 365

One of the key strengths of Microsoft Planner is its seamless integration with other Microsoft 365 apps. Planner is deeply integrated with tools like Microsoft Teams, Outlook, SharePoint, and OneDrive, enabling users to collaborate more effectively across different platforms. For example, tasks in Planner can be linked to conversations in Microsoft Teams, deadlines can be synchronized with Outlook calendars, and files from OneDrive can be attached directly to tasks.

This level of integration ensures that Planner fits naturally into the existing workflows of organizations that use Microsoft 365. Users don't have to switch between different tools to manage their tasks and can access everything they need in one place.

Task Management Features

Microsoft Planner offers a range of features designed to simplify task management. Some of the key features include:

1. Task Creation and Assignment: Users can create tasks within a plan and assign them to specific team members. Each task can include details such as a title, description, due date, and priority level.

2. Buckets for Organization: Tasks can be grouped into buckets, which are customizable categories that help organize work. For example, buckets could represent different phases of a project, different departments, or different types of tasks.

3. Labels and Filters: Planner allows users to add labels to tasks for easy categorization and filtering. Labels are color-coded and customizable, enabling teams to create a system that suits their specific needs.

4. Task Dependencies: While Planner does not have advanced dependency management features like Microsoft Project, users can still manually track dependencies by noting related tasks and setting appropriate deadlines.

5. Comments and Collaboration: Each task in Planner includes a comments section, where team members can discuss the task, ask questions, and provide updates. This fosters collaboration and ensures that everyone is on the same page.

6. File Attachments: Users can attach files to tasks directly from OneDrive, SharePoint, or their local device. This is particularly useful for keeping all relevant documents in one place and accessible to the team.

7. Checklist and Subtasks: For tasks that require multiple steps, users can create checklists or subtasks within a task card. This feature helps break down complex tasks into smaller, more manageable actions.

8. Task Progress Tracking: Each task has a progress indicator, allowing users to mark tasks as Not Started, In Progress, or Completed. This provides a quick overview of the status of each task within a plan.

9. Planner Hub and My Tasks: The Planner Hub provides a central location where users can view all their plans and tasks across different plans. The My Tasks view consolidates all tasks assigned to a user, making it easier to manage workload.

Collaboration and Communication

Microsoft Planner is designed to enhance collaboration within teams. By providing a shared space where tasks are visible to all team members, Planner ensures transparency and accountability. Team members can see who is responsible for each task, track progress, and collaborate through comments and file sharing.

The integration with Microsoft Teams further enhances collaboration. Teams can add Planner as a tab within a channel, making it easy to access plans directly from the Teams interface. This integration allows teams to discuss tasks in real-time, share updates, and work together more efficiently.

Use Cases for Microsoft Planner

Microsoft Planner is versatile and can be used in a wide range of scenarios. Here are some common use cases:

1. Project Management: Planner is ideal for managing small to medium-sized projects. Teams can create a plan for each project, organize tasks into phases or workstreams, and track progress from start to finish.

2. Event Planning: For teams involved in organizing events, Planner can be used to manage all aspects of event planning, from logistics to marketing to follow-up. Tasks can be assigned to different team members, ensuring that everything is covered.

3. Marketing Campaigns: Marketing teams can use Planner to manage campaigns, track content creation, and monitor the progress of different marketing initiatives. Buckets can be used to represent different stages of the campaign, such as planning, execution, and review.

4. Product Development: Development teams can use Planner to organize tasks related to product development, from ideation to launch. Tasks can be categorized by feature, development stage, or priority.

5. Personal Task Management: Individuals can use Planner to organize their personal tasks and goals. For example, a user might create a plan for managing personal projects, tracking fitness goals, or planning a vacation.

6. Education and Training: Educators and trainers can use Planner to manage courses, track student assignments, and organize training materials. Tasks can be assigned to students or team members, and progress can be monitored throughout the course.

Limitations of Microsoft Planner

While Microsoft Planner is a powerful tool, it does have some limitations. It is designed for simplicity and ease of use, which means it may lack some advanced features found in more specialized project management tools. For example:

1. No Gantt Charts: Planner does not support Gantt charts, which are commonly used in project management to visualize task timelines and dependencies. Users who need this functionality may need to use Microsoft Project or another tool in conjunction with Planner.

2. Limited Task Dependencies: Unlike Microsoft Project, Planner does not have built-in support for complex task dependencies, such as setting tasks to start after the completion of another task. Users can manually track dependencies, but this requires extra effort.

3. Basic Reporting: Planner provides basic reporting features, such as progress charts and task lists, but it lacks advanced reporting and analytics capabilities. Teams that require detailed reporting may need to export data to other tools like Power BI.

4. Scalability: While Planner works well for small to medium-sized teams, larger organizations with complex projects may find it less suitable. For large-scale projects with hundreds of tasks and multiple dependencies, a more robust project management tool like Microsoft Project may be necessary.

Conclusion

Microsoft Planner is an accessible and user-friendly tool that empowers teams and individuals to organize their work, collaborate effectively, and achieve their goals. With its integration into the Microsoft 365 ecosystem, Planner offers seamless collaboration across different tools and platforms, making it a valuable asset for any organization. While it may have some limitations in terms of advanced project management features, its simplicity and ease of use make it an excellent choice for managing tasks and projects of varying complexity. Whether you're a team leader managing a project, a marketing professional planning a campaign, or an individual looking to organize your personal tasks, Microsoft Planner provides the tools you need to stay organized and productive.

1.1.2 Key Features of Microsoft Planner

Status		Bucket		Priority	

Status: 5 Tasks left

Not started	4
In progress	0
Late	1
Completed	0

Bucket chart: Backlog, Up next, In progres..., Blocked, Completed

Priority chart: Urgent, Important, Medium, Low

Members — Unassigned

Title	Assignment	Start date	Due date	Bucket	Progress	Priority
Assign tasks			8/16/2024	Backlog	Not started	Medium
Customize buckets			8/3/2024	In progress	Not started	Medium
Add new tasks			8/5/2024	Up next	Not started	Medium
Create a Plan			7/28/2024	Completed	Not started	Urgent
Add additional information to tasks			8/12/2024	Up next	Not started	Medium
+ Add new task						

Microsoft Planner is an intuitive, collaborative task management tool that allows teams to organize, assign, and track work efficiently. It is designed to be simple yet powerful, enabling teams of all sizes to plan and manage projects, tasks, and assignments. This section explores the key features that make Microsoft Planner a valuable tool for enhancing productivity and streamlining workflow.

1. Visual Task Management

One of the most distinguishing features of Microsoft Planner is its visual task management interface. Planner uses a kanban-style board to organize tasks into different categories, known as "buckets." Each task is represented as a card on the board, which can be moved between buckets as work progresses. This visual approach allows team members to quickly see the status of various tasks and projects at a glance.

- Buckets and Boards: Buckets are the core organizational structure within a plan. They allow you to categorize tasks based on different stages of a project, types of work, or any other criteria that fit your team's workflow. For example, a software development team might use buckets labeled "To Do," "In Progress," and "Completed" to track the stages of their work. Each plan has its own board where tasks are displayed in their respective buckets, offering a clear, real-time view of the entire project.

- Task Cards: Each task in Planner is represented by a card that contains detailed information about the task, including its title, description, due date, assigned team members, attachments, and more. Task cards can be easily moved between buckets to reflect progress, making it simple to track the flow of work from start to finish.

- Labels: Planner allows you to add color-coded labels to tasks, providing another layer of categorization. Labels can be customized to represent priorities, departments, types of work, or any other grouping that is important to your team. This visual categorization helps team members quickly identify and prioritize tasks.

2. Collaboration and Teamwork

Microsoft Planner is designed to facilitate collaboration and improve communication within teams. By bringing all project-related information and tasks into a single platform, Planner ensures that everyone on the team is on the same page and can contribute to the project's success.

- Task Assignment: Assigning tasks to team members is straightforward in Planner. Each task card has an "Assigned to" field where you can select one or more team members to take responsibility for the task. This feature ensures accountability and makes it easy for everyone to know who is responsible for what. Additionally, assigned tasks automatically appear in the assignee's "My Tasks" view, which consolidates all tasks they are responsible for across all plans.

- Comments and Conversations: Planner allows team members to comment on tasks, enabling ongoing discussions directly within the task card. This feature is particularly useful for clarifying requirements, providing updates, or asking for help without the need for separate email threads or meetings. All comments are visible to everyone involved in the task, ensuring transparency and keeping all relevant information in one place.

- Attachments and Links: Tasks in Planner can include attachments and links, making it easy to share relevant documents, files, or web pages with the team. Files can be uploaded directly to the task card, or links can be added to point to external resources. This centralizes all the necessary materials related to a task, reducing the time spent searching for information.

- Integration with Microsoft 365: Planner is tightly integrated with other Microsoft 365 tools, such as Teams, Outlook, and SharePoint. This integration allows for seamless collaboration across different platforms. For instance, you can discuss tasks in real-time via Microsoft Teams or schedule deadlines in Outlook, all while keeping the work organized in Planner. Documents from SharePoint or OneDrive can be easily attached to tasks, making it simple to collaborate on files without leaving the Planner environment.

3. Flexibility and Customization

Microsoft Planner offers a high degree of flexibility, allowing teams to tailor the tool to their specific needs. Whether you're managing a small project or a complex initiative, Planner can be customized to fit your workflow.

- Custom Buckets: The ability to create custom buckets is one of the most flexible features of Planner. You can set up buckets that align with your team's workflow, such as by project phase, task type, or priority level. This flexibility means that Planner can be used for a wide range of applications, from simple task tracking to complex project management.

- Custom Labels: In addition to custom buckets, Planner allows you to create custom labels for tasks. These labels can be color-coded and named according to your team's needs. For example, you might create labels for "High Priority," "Client Feedback," or "Needs Review." This feature makes it easy to visually organize tasks based on various criteria, helping team members focus on what's most important.

- Due Dates and Notifications: Planner enables you to set due dates for each task, ensuring that work stays on schedule. Team members receive notifications about upcoming deadlines, which helps keep the project on track. Notifications can be managed through the Microsoft Planner settings, allowing users to customize how and when they are alerted about task updates.

- My Tasks View: The "My Tasks" view in Planner is a personalized dashboard that consolidates all tasks assigned to a specific user across all plans. This feature is particularly useful for team members who are involved in multiple projects, as it provides a single place to see all their responsibilities. Tasks can be sorted by due date, plan, or priority, making it easy to manage workload and deadlines.

4. Progress Tracking and Reporting

Keeping track of progress and performance is crucial for successful project management. Microsoft Planner includes several features that help teams monitor progress, identify bottlenecks, and ensure that tasks are completed on time.

- Charts and Analytics: Planner includes built-in charts that provide a visual summary of the status of tasks within a plan. These charts show the distribution of tasks across different buckets, the progress of tasks (e.g., not started, in progress, completed), and the number of tasks assigned to each team member. This overview helps project managers and team members quickly assess the health of the project and identify areas that may require attention.

- Task Completion Status: Each task card includes a checkbox that team members can use to mark tasks as completed. This simple feature allows for easy tracking of task completion, both at the individual and project level. As tasks are completed, they move out of the active workflow, helping the team stay focused on what's still pending.

- Planner Hub: The Planner Hub provides a high-level overview of all your plans. From the Hub, you can see which plans are active, how many tasks are in each plan, and what the overall status of each plan is. This feature is particularly useful for managers or team leaders who oversee multiple projects, as it allows them to monitor the progress of each project at a glance.

- Exporting Data: For more detailed reporting, Planner allows you to export task data to Excel. This feature enables teams to create custom reports, perform deeper analysis, or integrate Planner data with other project management tools. Exported data includes task details such as start and end dates, assigned users, task status, and more, providing a comprehensive view of project progress.

5. Security and Compliance

Security is a critical consideration for any organization, and Microsoft Planner is built with robust security and compliance features to protect your data.

- Data Encryption: All data in Microsoft Planner is encrypted both at rest and in transit, ensuring that sensitive information is protected. This encryption helps safeguard your tasks, comments, and attachments from unauthorized access.

- Compliance with Industry Standards: Microsoft Planner is part of the Microsoft 365 suite, which is compliant with various industry standards and regulations, including GDPR, ISO/IEC 27001, and HIPAA. This compliance makes Planner a suitable tool for organizations that need to meet strict regulatory requirements.

- Role-Based Access Control: Planner leverages Microsoft 365's role-based access control (RBAC) to manage permissions. This means that access to plans, tasks, and data can be controlled based on user roles, ensuring that only authorized individuals can view or modify sensitive information.

- Audit Logs and Monitoring: Microsoft Planner integrates with Microsoft 365's auditing and monitoring tools, allowing organizations to track user activity and access logs. This feature is essential for maintaining security and compliance, as it provides a detailed record of how Planner is being used within your organization.

6. Accessibility Features

Microsoft Planner is designed to be accessible to all users, including those with disabilities. The tool includes several accessibility features that ensure everyone on your team can use Planner effectively.

- Keyboard Navigation: Planner supports full keyboard navigation, making it accessible to users who cannot use a mouse. All major actions, such as creating tasks, moving between buckets, and opening task details, can be performed using keyboard shortcuts.

- Screen Reader Support: Planner is compatible with screen readers, which read aloud the content on the screen. This feature is vital for visually impaired users, allowing them to navigate the Planner interface and interact with tasks and plans effectively.

- High Contrast Mode: For users with visual impairments, Planner supports high contrast mode. This mode enhances the visibility of text and interface elements by using a higher contrast color scheme, making it easier to read and navigate the application.

- Localization and Language Support: Planner is available in multiple languages, supporting teams around the world. The tool automatically detects the language settings of your Microsoft 365 account and adjusts the interface language accordingly.

Conclusion

The key features of Microsoft Planner make it an indispensable tool for teams looking to enhance their productivity, improve collaboration, and manage projects more effectively. Its visual task management, flexibility, robust security, and seamless integration with other Microsoft 365 tools provide a comprehensive solution for organizing work and achieving goals. Whether you're managing a small team or overseeing a large project, Microsoft Planner's features are designed to support your workflow and ensure your team's success.

1.1.3 Benefits of Using Microsoft Planner

Microsoft Planner is a versatile task management tool that has become an essential part of the Microsoft 365 suite. It provides a flexible, easy-to-use platform for organizing work, managing tasks, and collaborating with team members. Whether you are part of a large organization or managing a small project, Microsoft Planner offers numerous benefits that can help streamline your workflow and increase productivity. This section will explore the key advantages of using Microsoft Planner and how it can contribute to better project management and team collaboration.

1. Simplified Task Management

One of the primary benefits of Microsoft Planner is its ability to simplify task management. Planner allows you to create plans, organize tasks into buckets, assign tasks to team members, and set due dates and priorities. The drag-and-drop interface makes it easy to move tasks between buckets, ensuring that everyone on the team has a clear understanding of what needs to be done and when.

Tasks can also be broken down into subtasks, allowing for detailed planning and execution. This feature is particularly useful for larger projects that require multiple steps to complete. By organizing tasks in a hierarchical manner, team members can focus on specific aspects of the project without losing sight of the overall goal.

2. Enhanced Collaboration and Communication

Microsoft Planner is designed to enhance collaboration and communication within teams. Each plan is a shared space where team members can see the progress of tasks, add comments, and share files. This centralization of information ensures that everyone is on the same page and reduces the need for constant back-and-forth communication.

The integration with Microsoft Teams further enhances collaboration. Teams can be linked directly to Planner, allowing members to discuss tasks in real-time, hold meetings, and share updates without leaving the Planner environment. This seamless integration ensures that communication is streamlined and that important information is easily accessible to everyone involved.

3. Visual Project Tracking

One of the standout features of Microsoft Planner is its visual project tracking capabilities. Planner provides a clear and intuitive way to track the progress of tasks and projects through visual tools such as charts and graphs. The Planner Board displays tasks in a Kanban-style view, allowing you to see the status of each task at a glance.

The Charts view provides a more detailed overview of the project's progress, displaying the number of tasks in different stages (Not Started, In Progress, and Completed). This visual representation helps project managers quickly identify bottlenecks, redistribute workloads, and ensure that the project stays on track.

The use of color-coded labels also adds to the visual appeal, making it easy to categorize tasks by priority, department, or any other criteria that suit your needs. This visual aspect of Microsoft Planner makes it an excellent tool for those who prefer a more graphical approach to project management.

4. Flexibility and Customization

Microsoft Planner is highly flexible and can be customized to fit the needs of any team or project. Plans can be tailored with different buckets to represent stages of a project, departments, or any other organizational structure that makes sense for your team. You can also customize the task cards by adding attachments, links, and checklists, providing all the information needed to complete the task in one place.

Moreover, the ability to create templates for recurring plans saves time and ensures consistency across similar projects. This feature is particularly useful for teams that frequently manage projects with similar workflows, such as marketing campaigns or product launches. By using templates, teams can quickly set up new plans without having to start from scratch each time.

5. Integration with Microsoft 365 Ecosystem

As part of the Microsoft 365 suite, Planner integrates seamlessly with other Microsoft tools such as Outlook, SharePoint, and OneDrive. This integration allows for a more cohesive workflow, where tasks can be synced across different platforms and accessed from various devices.

For example, tasks in Planner can be linked to your Outlook calendar, ensuring that you stay on top of deadlines. Files stored in OneDrive or SharePoint can be easily attached to tasks in Planner, providing quick access to relevant documents. This level of integration eliminates the need to switch between different apps, saving time and reducing the risk of missing important information.

Additionally, Microsoft Planner integrates with Microsoft Power Automate, enabling users to automate repetitive tasks and create workflows that connect Planner with other applications. This automation capability can significantly increase efficiency by reducing manual work and ensuring that tasks are completed consistently.

6. Improved Accountability and Transparency

Microsoft Planner promotes accountability and transparency within teams. By assigning tasks to specific team members, it is clear who is responsible for each aspect of the project. This clarity reduces confusion and ensures that tasks are not overlooked.

Planner's transparency also extends to the visibility of progress. Team members and managers can see the status of tasks at any time, which helps in identifying potential delays and addressing issues before they escalate. The ability to add comments and updates to tasks further enhances transparency, as all communications related to a task are stored in one place.

This level of accountability and transparency fosters a collaborative environment where everyone is aware of their responsibilities and can contribute to the project's success.

7. Scalability for Teams of All Sizes

Microsoft Planner is designed to scale with your team and projects. Whether you are managing a small team of a few people or coordinating a large, cross-functional project, Planner can handle it. The ability to create multiple plans, each with its own set of tasks and buckets, allows for the management of several projects simultaneously without confusion.

For large organizations, Planner can be used in conjunction with Microsoft Project, another project management tool in the Microsoft 365 suite, to handle more complex projects. This scalability makes Microsoft Planner a suitable tool for teams of all sizes, from small startups to large enterprises.

8. User-Friendly Interface and Accessibility

One of the key strengths of Microsoft Planner is its user-friendly interface. The design is intuitive, with a clean and straightforward layout that makes it easy for users to navigate and manage their tasks. Even those who are new to project management tools will find Planner easy to use, thanks to its minimal learning curve.

Planner is also accessible across multiple devices, including desktops, tablets, and smartphones. The mobile app ensures that team members can stay connected and manage tasks on the go, providing flexibility in how and where work is done. This accessibility is crucial in today's dynamic work environment, where remote work and flexible hours are becoming the norm.

9. Cost-Effective Project Management Solution

For organizations already using Microsoft 365, Microsoft Planner is a cost-effective project management solution, as it is included in most Microsoft 365 plans at no additional cost. This makes Planner an attractive option for businesses looking to enhance their project management capabilities without incurring extra expenses.

Compared to other project management tools that require separate subscriptions, Microsoft Planner offers a robust set of features at a fraction of the cost. Its integration with other Microsoft 365 tools further enhances its value, providing a comprehensive project management solution within the Microsoft ecosystem.

10. Continuous Updates and Improvements

Microsoft Planner is continuously updated with new features and improvements, ensuring that it stays relevant and competitive in the ever-evolving landscape of project management tools. Microsoft regularly collects feedback from users and incorporates it into Planner's updates, making the tool more user-centric and responsive to the needs of its users.

These updates are automatically applied, meaning that users always have access to the latest features without needing to install new software or perform manual upgrades. This continuous improvement ensures that Microsoft Planner remains a cutting-edge tool that evolves alongside the needs of its users.

11. Supporting Remote and Hybrid Work Environments

In the era of remote and hybrid work, Microsoft Planner has proven to be an invaluable tool for keeping teams connected and productive, regardless of their physical location. Planner's cloud-based platform ensures that all team members can access plans and tasks from anywhere, at any time. This is especially important for distributed teams that rely on digital tools to collaborate and stay organized.

Planner's integration with Microsoft Teams and other collaboration tools further supports remote work by providing a central hub for communication and project management. Team members can discuss tasks, share files, and track progress without the need for in-person meetings, making Planner an essential tool for modern, flexible work environments.

12. Data Security and Compliance

As part of the Microsoft 365 suite, Microsoft Planner benefits from the robust security and compliance features that Microsoft offers. Data in Planner is encrypted both in transit and at rest, ensuring that sensitive information is protected from unauthorized access. Microsoft also complies with various global standards and regulations, such as GDPR, HIPAA, and ISO/IEC 27001, providing peace of mind for organizations that handle sensitive data.

Moreover, Planner's integration with Azure Active Directory (AAD) allows for advanced security configurations, such as multi-factor authentication and conditional access policies.

These features ensure that only authorized users can access your organization's plans and tasks, further enhancing the security of your data.

13. Streamlined Onboarding and Training

For organizations looking to implement Microsoft Planner, the onboarding process is straightforward. Because Planner is part of the Microsoft 365 suite, users who are already familiar with other Microsoft tools will find it easy to adapt to Planner. The interface is consistent with other Microsoft applications, reducing the learning curve.

Microsoft also provides extensive resources for training and support, including online tutorials, documentation, and community forums. These resources make it easy for new users to get up to speed with Planner and start managing tasks and projects effectively. The availability of templates and best practices further supports users in quickly adopting Planner for their specific needs.

14. Supporting Agile Project Management

Microsoft Planner is well-suited for teams that follow Agile project management methodologies. The Kanban-style board in Planner aligns closely with Agile practices, allowing teams to visualize work in progress, manage backlogs, and conduct sprints. Tasks can be easily moved between different stages of completion, making it ideal for iterative work processes.

Planner's flexibility also supports Scrum practices, with the ability to create sprint plans, assign tasks to team members, and track progress against sprint goals. This makes Planner a valuable tool for Agile teams looking to manage their work in a structured yet adaptable manner.

15. Facilitating Knowledge Sharing and Documentation

In addition to task management, Microsoft Planner can serve as a repository for project-related knowledge and documentation. Files, links, and notes can be attached to tasks, ensuring that all relevant information is stored in one place. This feature not only makes it easier to complete tasks but also facilitates knowledge sharing within the team.

By centralizing project information in Planner, teams can reduce the time spent searching for documents and ensure that everyone has access to the same resources. This documentation can also be valuable for future projects, as it provides a reference for best practices and lessons learned.

Conclusion

Microsoft Planner offers a comprehensive set of benefits that make it an indispensable tool for task management and team collaboration. From simplifying task management to enhancing communication, providing visual project tracking, and supporting remote work environments, Planner is designed to meet the needs of modern teams. Its integration with the Microsoft 365 ecosystem, user-friendly interface, and continuous updates make it a powerful tool for organizations of all sizes. Whether you are managing a small team or coordinating large-scale projects, Microsoft Planner can help you stay organized, improve productivity, and achieve your goals.

1.2 Getting Started with Microsoft Planner

1.2.1 Accessing Microsoft Planner

Introduction

Accessing Microsoft Planner is the first crucial step in leveraging its project management capabilities. Microsoft Planner is a part of the Microsoft 365 suite, and as such, it integrates seamlessly with other Microsoft tools, enhancing your ability to manage tasks, collaborate with teams, and streamline project workflows. This section will guide you through the process of accessing Microsoft Planner across different platforms, including web access, desktop applications, and mobile devices. We will also cover the necessary prerequisites and potential issues you might encounter during the access process.

Prerequisites

Before diving into accessing Microsoft Planner, ensure the following prerequisites are met:

1. Microsoft 365 Subscription: Microsoft Planner is available only with certain Microsoft 365 plans. Ensure your subscription includes Microsoft Planner. Typically, it's available with Microsoft 365 Business Essentials, Business Premium, and Enterprise plans. Personal or Family subscriptions might not include Planner.

2. Microsoft Account: You need a valid Microsoft account associated with your Microsoft 365 subscription. If you don't have an account, you will need to create one through the Microsoft website or sign up for a Microsoft 365 plan.

3. Permissions: Ensure you have the necessary permissions to access Planner within your organization. If you're using a work or school account, your administrator needs to have enabled Planner for your account.

Accessing Microsoft Planner via Web Browser

Microsoft Planner can be accessed through any modern web browser. Here's a step-by-step guide:

1. Open Your Web Browser: Launch your preferred web browser (e.g., Google Chrome, Microsoft Edge, Mozilla Firefox, or Safari).

2. Navigate to Microsoft Planner: Type `https://tasks.office.com` into the address bar and press Enter. This URL redirects you to the Microsoft Planner web application. Alternatively, you can access Planner via the Microsoft 365 homepage by logging into `https://www.office.com` and selecting the Planner tile.

3. Sign In: If you are not already signed in, you will be prompted to enter your Microsoft 365 credentials. Enter your username and password associated with your Microsoft 365 account.

4. Explore the Planner Interface: Upon successful login, you will be directed to the Planner dashboard. Familiarize yourself with the layout:

  - Left Navigation Pane: Contains links to your plans, charts, and other Planner tools.

  - Plan Dashboard: Displays your active plans and tasks.

  - Toolbar: Includes options to create new plans, access settings, and more.

Accessing Microsoft Planner via Desktop Application

While Microsoft Planner does not have a standalone desktop application, it can be accessed through the Microsoft 365 desktop suite. Here's how you can add it to your taskbar or start menu for quicker access:

1. Using Microsoft Edge (Windows 10/11):

  - Open Microsoft Edge and navigate to `https://tasks.office.com`.

  - Click on the three-dot menu in the top right corner of Edge and select "Apps" > "Install this site as an app". This will create a shortcut on your desktop or taskbar.

2. Pinning to Taskbar or Start Menu:

  - Open Planner in your web browser.

  - Click on the Planner icon in your browser tab and drag it to your taskbar for easy access. Alternatively, right-click on the tab and select "Pin to Start" to add it to your Start Menu.

Accessing Microsoft Planner via Mobile Devices

Microsoft Planner is available as a mobile app for both iOS and Android devices, offering the flexibility to manage your tasks on the go. Here's how to access Planner on mobile devices:

1. Download the Mobile App:

  - For iOS: Go to the App Store on your iPhone or iPad, search for "Microsoft Planner," and tap "Get" to download and install the app.

  - For Android: Go to the Google Play Store on your Android device, search for "Microsoft Planner," and tap "Install".

2. Sign In: Open the Microsoft Planner app and sign in using your Microsoft 365 credentials. If prompted, grant the necessary permissions for the app to function correctly.

3. Navigate the Mobile Interface: The mobile app interface is optimized for touch interactions and may differ slightly from the web version. Familiarize yourself with key features such as:

- Plans View: Access your existing plans and create new ones.

- Tasks: View and manage tasks, including assigning them, setting due dates, and updating progress.

- Notifications: Receive updates and alerts about task changes and deadlines.

Accessing Microsoft Planner via Microsoft Teams

If your organization uses Microsoft Teams, you can integrate Microsoft Planner into your Teams environment for a more unified experience:

1. Open Microsoft Teams: Launch the Microsoft Teams application on your desktop or mobile device, or access it via a web browser at `https://teams.microsoft.com`.

2. Navigate to a Team: Select the team where you want to add Planner. Click on the "+" icon at the top of the channel or team page to add a new tab.

3. Add Planner: From the list of available apps, select "Planner". You can either create a new plan or add an existing one to the Teams channel.

4. Access and Manage Plans: Once added, Planner will be available as a tab within the selected channel. You can manage your tasks and plans directly from Microsoft Teams, enhancing team collaboration and productivity.

Troubleshooting Access Issues

Despite following the correct procedures, you might encounter issues accessing Microsoft Planner. Here are some common problems and their solutions:

1. Access Denied or Missing Planner Tile:

  - Verify that your Microsoft 365 subscription includes Planner.

  - Check with your IT administrator to ensure Planner is enabled for your account.

  - Try accessing Planner from a different browser or clearing your browser's cache and cookies.

2. Sign-In Issues:

  - Ensure you are using the correct Microsoft 365 credentials.

- If you've forgotten your password, use the Microsoft password reset tool.

- Check if there are any ongoing issues with Microsoft 365 services by visiting the Microsoft 365 Service Status page.

3. Sync Problems:

- Ensure your internet connection is stable.

- Refresh the Planner page or restart the app.

- Check for any updates or patches for your browser or mobile app.

Conclusion

Accessing Microsoft Planner is a straightforward process that involves navigating through web, desktop, and mobile platforms. By understanding these methods, you can choose the one that best fits your workflow and ensures you're equipped to manage tasks and projects efficiently. With Planner's integration into the broader Microsoft 365 ecosystem, you can enhance your productivity and collaborate more effectively with your team.

This section has covered the basics of accessing Microsoft Planner and provided troubleshooting tips to handle common issues. In the next section, we will delve into creating your first plan and exploring the core functionalities of Microsoft Planner.

1.2.2 Creating Your First Plan

Introduction

Accessing Microsoft Planner is the first crucial step in leveraging its project management capabilities. Microsoft Planner is a part of the Microsoft 365 suite, and as such, it integrates seamlessly with other Microsoft tools, enhancing your ability to manage tasks, collaborate with teams, and streamline project workflows. This section will guide you through the process of accessing Microsoft Planner across different platforms, including web access, desktop applications, and mobile devices. We will also cover the necessary prerequisites and potential issues you might encounter during the access process.

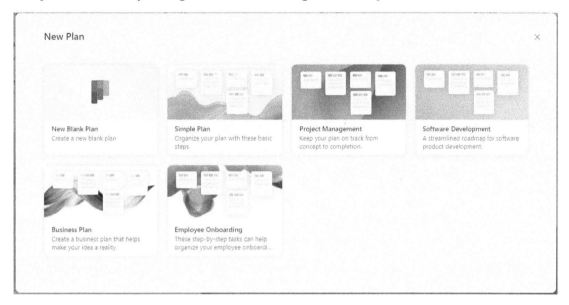

Prerequisites

Before diving into accessing Microsoft Planner, ensure the following prerequisites are met:

1. Microsoft 365 Subscription: Microsoft Planner is available only with certain Microsoft 365 plans. Ensure your subscription includes Microsoft Planner. Typically, it's available with Microsoft 365 Business Essentials, Business Premium, and Enterprise plans. Personal or Family subscriptions might not include Planner.

2. Microsoft Account: You need a valid Microsoft account associated with your Microsoft 365 subscription. If you don't have an account, you will need to create one through the Microsoft website or sign up for a Microsoft 365 plan.

3. Permissions: Ensure you have the necessary permissions to access Planner within your organization. If you're using a work or school account, your administrator needs to have enabled Planner for your account.

Accessing Microsoft Planner via Web Browser

Microsoft Planner can be accessed through any modern web browser. Here's a step-by-step guide:

1. Open Your Web Browser: Launch your preferred web browser (e.g., Google Chrome, Microsoft Edge, Mozilla Firefox, or Safari).

2. Navigate to Microsoft Planner: Type `https://tasks.office.com` into the address bar and press Enter. This URL redirects you to the Microsoft Planner web application. Alternatively, you can access Planner via the Microsoft 365 homepage by logging into `https://www.office.com` and selecting the Planner tile.

3. Sign In: If you are not already signed in, you will be prompted to enter your Microsoft 365 credentials. Enter your username and password associated with your Microsoft 365 account.

4. Explore the Planner Interface: Upon successful login, you will be directed to the Planner dashboard. Familiarize yourself with the layout:

  - Left Navigation Pane: Contains links to your plans, charts, and other Planner tools.

  - Plan Dashboard: Displays your active plans and tasks.

  - Toolbar: Includes options to create new plans, access settings, and more.

Accessing Microsoft Planner via Desktop Application

While Microsoft Planner does not have a standalone desktop application, it can be accessed through the Microsoft 365 desktop suite. Here's how you can add it to your taskbar or start menu for quicker access:

1. Using Microsoft Edge (Windows 10/11):

  - Open Microsoft Edge and navigate to `https://tasks.office.com`.

  - Click on the three-dot menu in the top right corner of Edge and select "Apps" > "Install this site as an app". This will create a shortcut on your desktop or taskbar.

2. Pinning to Taskbar or Start Menu:

  - Open Planner in your web browser.

  - Click on the Planner icon in your browser tab and drag it to your taskbar for easy access. Alternatively, right-click on the tab and select "Pin to Start" to add it to your Start Menu.

Accessing Microsoft Planner via Mobile Devices

Microsoft Planner is available as a mobile app for both iOS and Android devices, offering the flexibility to manage your tasks on the go. Here's how to access Planner on mobile devices:

1. Download the Mobile App:

   - For iOS: Go to the App Store on your iPhone or iPad, search for "Microsoft Planner," and tap "Get" to download and install the app.

   - For Android: Go to the Google Play Store on your Android device, search for "Microsoft Planner," and tap "Install".

2. Sign In: Open the Microsoft Planner app and sign in using your Microsoft 365 credentials. If prompted, grant the necessary permissions for the app to function correctly.

3. Navigate the Mobile Interface: The mobile app interface is optimized for touch interactions and may differ slightly from the web version. Familiarize yourself with key features such as:

   - Plans View: Access your existing plans and create new ones.

   - Tasks: View and manage tasks, including assigning them, setting due dates, and updating progress.

   - Notifications: Receive updates and alerts about task changes and deadlines.

Accessing Microsoft Planner via Microsoft Teams

If your organization uses Microsoft Teams, you can integrate Microsoft Planner into your Teams environment for a more unified experience:

1. Open Microsoft Teams: Launch the Microsoft Teams application on your desktop or mobile device, or access it via a web browser at `https://teams.microsoft.com`.

2. Navigate to a Team: Select the team where you want to add Planner. Click on the "+" icon at the top of the channel or team page to add a new tab.

3. Add Planner: From the list of available apps, select "Planner". You can either create a new plan or add an existing one to the Teams channel.

4. Access and Manage Plans: Once added, Planner will be available as a tab within the selected channel. You can manage your tasks and plans directly from Microsoft Teams, enhancing team collaboration and productivity.

Troubleshooting Access Issues

Despite following the correct procedures, you might encounter issues accessing Microsoft Planner. Here are some common problems and their solutions:

1. Access Denied or Missing Planner Tile:

  - Verify that your Microsoft 365 subscription includes Planner.

  - Check with your IT administrator to ensure Planner is enabled for your account.

  - Try accessing Planner from a different browser or clearing your browser's cache and cookies.

2. Sign-In Issues:

  - Ensure you are using the correct Microsoft 365 credentials.

  - If you've forgotten your password, use the Microsoft password reset tool.

  - Check if there are any ongoing issues with Microsoft 365 services by visiting the Microsoft 365 Service Status page.

3. Sync Problems:

  - Ensure your internet connection is stable.

  - Refresh the Planner page or restart the app.

  - Check for any updates or patches for your browser or mobile app.

Understanding the Purpose of Your Plan

Before diving into the technical steps, it's crucial to understand the purpose of your plan. A well-defined plan helps ensure that tasks are organized efficiently, deadlines are met, and team members are aligned. Consider the following questions to clarify the purpose of your plan:

- What is the main objective of the plan? Is it for a specific project, a recurring task, or a personal goal?

- Who will be involved? Identify the team members or stakeholders who will participate in this plan.

- What are the key deliverables? Outline the major milestones and outputs expected from this plan.

Step-by-Step Guide to Creating Your First Plan

1. Accessing Microsoft Planner

1. Open Microsoft Planner:

   - Navigate to the Microsoft Planner app via Office 365 or Microsoft 365.

   - You can access Planner directly through the Office 365 app launcher or by visiting tasks.office.com.

2. Sign In:

   - Use your Microsoft account credentials to sign in.

   - Ensure you have the necessary permissions and licenses to access Microsoft Planner.

2. Creating a New Plan

1. Start a New Plan:

   - On the Planner homepage, click on the "New Plan" button.

   - You'll find this option in the left navigation pane or under the "Plans" tab.

2. Name Your Plan:

   - Enter a descriptive name for your plan that reflects its purpose.

   - Keep the name concise but informative, making it easy for team members to understand the plan's objective at a glance.

3. Choose Privacy Settings:

- Public Plan: Anyone within your organization can view and join the plan.

- Private Plan: Only invited members can access the plan.

- Select the option that best fits your project's confidentiality requirements.

4. Add a Plan Description:

  - Provide a brief description of the plan's goals, scope, and important details.

  - This helps team members understand the plan's context and objectives.

5. Create the Plan:

  - Click "Create Plan" to finalize the setup.

  - You will be redirected to the Planner interface where you can start organizing your plan.

3. Setting Up Buckets

Buckets help categorize and organize tasks within your plan. They act as containers for grouping tasks by stage, category, or priority.

1. Add Buckets:

  - Click on the "Add new bucket" button.

  - Enter a name for the bucket, such as "To Do," "In Progress," or "Completed."

  - You can create multiple buckets to represent different stages or categories relevant to your project.

2. Organize Tasks into Buckets:

  - Drag and drop tasks into the appropriate buckets.

  - This visual organization helps track progress and manage workflow more effectively.

4. Adding Tasks

Tasks are the core components of your plan. Each task represents an actionable item that needs to be completed.

1. Create a Task:

   - Click on "+ Add task" within the bucket where you want to place the task.

   - Enter a task name and description, if needed.

2. Assign Tasks:

   - Assign the task to one or more team members by selecting their names from the drop-down menu.

   - Ensure that the right people are responsible for each task to ensure accountability.

3. Set Due Dates and Priority:

   - Assign due dates to tasks to keep track of deadlines.

   - Set priorities (e.g., Urgent, Important, Medium, Low) to indicate the task's importance.

4. Add Task Details:

   - Include additional details, such as checklists, attachments, and comments, to provide more context.

   - Checklists help break tasks into smaller, manageable steps, while attachments support file sharing.

5. Save and Update Tasks:

   - Click "Save" to add the task to your plan.

   - You can update task details, move tasks between buckets, or adjust due dates as needed.

 5. Inviting Team Members

1. Add Members to Your Plan:

   - Click on the "Members" tab or "Add members" button.

   - Enter the email addresses of the team members you want to invite.

   - Select "Add" to include them in the plan.

2. Set Roles and Permissions:

- Decide if team members should have editing permissions or view-only access.

- Ensure that everyone involved has the necessary access to collaborate effectively.

6. Customizing the Plan View

1. Choose a View:

 - Microsoft Planner offers different views, such as "Board" (default), "Charts," and "Calendar."

 - Switch between views to find the one that best suits your project management needs.

2. Filter and Sort Tasks:

 - Use filters to view tasks by priority, due date, or assigned member.

 - Sort tasks to focus on the most urgent or important ones.

3. Color Code Tasks:

 - Use labels to color-code tasks based on categories or themes.

 - This visual aid helps in quickly identifying tasks with similar attributes.

7. Monitoring and Updating the Plan

1. Track Progress:

 - Regularly review the progress of tasks and buckets.

 - Use the "Charts" view to see an overview of task completion and upcoming deadlines.

2. Update Tasks:

 - As tasks progress, update their status and move them to the appropriate buckets.

 - Communicate with team members through comments to provide updates or seek clarifications.

3. Review and Adjust:

 - Periodically review the plan to ensure it remains aligned with project goals.

- Make adjustments to tasks, buckets, or team assignments as needed.

Best Practices for Creating and Managing Plans

- Be Clear and Specific: Define clear objectives and detailed task descriptions to avoid confusion.

- Communicate Effectively: Use comments and updates to keep all team members informed.

- Regularly Review and Update: Keep the plan dynamic by regularly updating tasks and reviewing progress.

- Utilize Integrations: Leverage integrations with other Microsoft tools to enhance functionality and streamline workflows.

- Seek Feedback: Gather feedback from team members to improve the plan's effectiveness and address any issues promptly.

Conclusion

Creating your first plan in Microsoft Planner is just the beginning. With the foundational steps outlined above, you are now equipped to set up and manage plans that drive productivity and achieve your goals. As you become more familiar with Microsoft Planner, you'll discover additional features and techniques that can further enhance your project management capabilities.

1.2.3 Understanding the Planner Interface

Introduction to the Interface

Microsoft Planner is designed with a user-friendly interface that facilitates efficient task management and team collaboration. The Planner interface is divided into several key areas, each serving a specific function to help users organize and track their work.

Understanding these components will enhance your ability to navigate Planner effectively and maximize its features.

1. Dashboard Overview

Upon logging into Microsoft Planner, you are greeted with the Dashboard. The Dashboard serves as the central hub where you can view all your plans and access various functionalities. Here's a breakdown of its main components:

1.1. Navigation Pane

Located on the left side of the screen, the Navigation Pane provides access to different areas of Planner. It includes:

- My Tasks: A personalized view of tasks assigned to you across all plans. It helps you track your individual workload.

- Planner Hub: A consolidated view of all plans you are a part of, allowing quick access to any plan.

- Favorites: A section where you can pin your most frequently accessed plans for easy access.

- Groups: Displays the Office 365 groups associated with your plans, allowing you to view and manage related group tasks.

1.2. Plan View

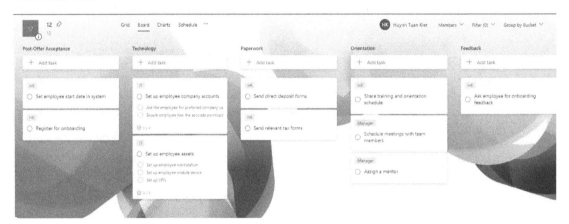

The Plan View is the main workspace where you interact with your plans. It consists of several key elements:

- Plan Title: At the top of the Plan View, you'll find the title of your plan. This area allows you to rename or change plan settings.

- Buckets: Buckets are columns within the plan that help you categorize and organize tasks. You can create, rename, or delete buckets as needed.

- Tasks: Each bucket contains tasks, which are represented as cards. These cards include essential information such as task title, due date, and assignee.

1.3. Task Details

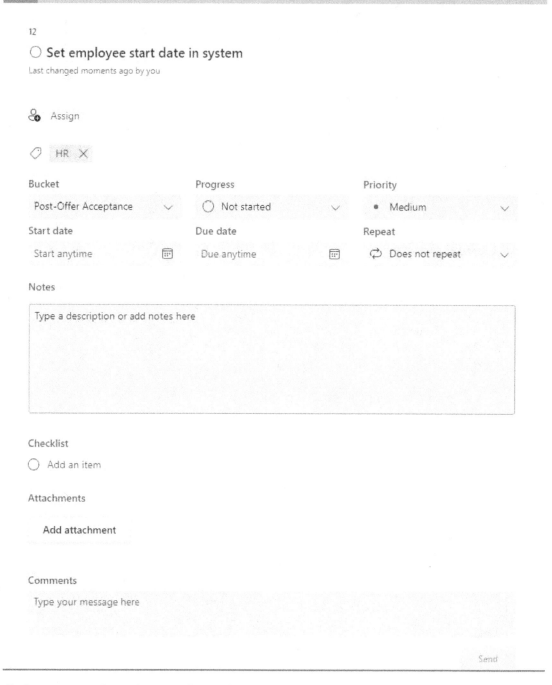

12

○ **Set employee start date** in system

Last changed moments ago by you

⚘ Assign

🏷 HR ✕

Bucket	Progress	Priority
Post-Offer Acceptance ⌄	○ Not started ⌄	● Medium ⌄

Start date	Due date	Repeat
Start anytime 🗓	Due anytime 🗓	↻ Does not repeat ⌄

Notes

Type a description or add notes here

Checklist

○ Add an item

Attachments

Add attachment

Comments

Type your message here

Send

Clicking on a task card opens the Task Details pane, which provides a deeper view of the task's information. This pane includes:

- Task Title and Description: The title of the task and a detailed description of what needs to be done.

- Assignee: The person responsible for completing the task. You can assign or reassign tasks to team members here.

- Due Date: The deadline for completing the task. You can set or modify the due date from this section.

- Priority: An option to mark the task's priority level as low, medium, or high.

- Checklist: A list of subtasks that need to be completed as part of the main task. Check off items as they are completed.

- Attachments: Upload files or add links related to the task.

- Comments: A discussion thread where team members can communicate about the task.

2. Views and Filters

Microsoft Planner offers several views and filters to help you manage and visualize your tasks effectively:

2.1. Board View

The Board View is the default view that displays tasks in columns (buckets). This visual representation allows you to easily drag and drop tasks between buckets as their status changes.

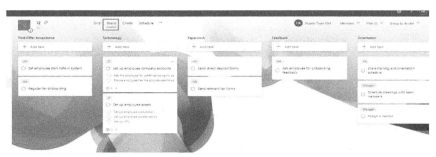

2.2. Charts View

The Charts View provides a visual summary of task progress across your plan. It includes:

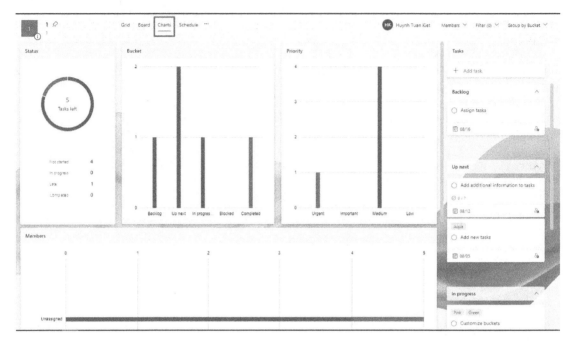

- Progress Charts: Displays the percentage of tasks that are not started, in progress, or completed.

- Status Breakdown: Shows the distribution of tasks by status and priority.

- Assignee Distribution: Visualizes the number of tasks assigned to each team member.

2.3. Schedule View

The Schedule View offers a calendar layout where you can see tasks organized by due dates. This view helps you plan and manage deadlines more effectively.

3. Customizing the Interface

Microsoft Planner allows for various customizations to tailor the interface to your needs:

3.1. Customizing Buckets

You can add new buckets, rename existing ones, or rearrange them to fit your workflow. To add a new bucket, click the "Add new bucket" button. To rename or delete a bucket, click the three dots (ellipsis) next to the bucket name.

3.2. Filtering Tasks

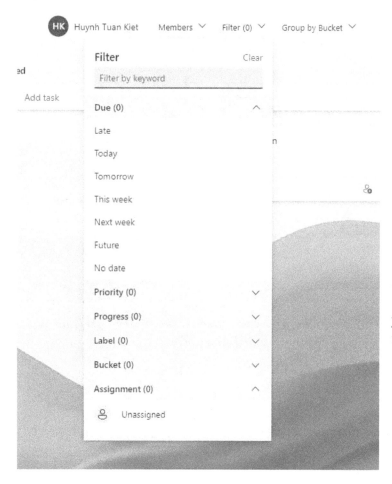

Use the Filter options to narrow down the list of tasks based on criteria such as due date, priority, and assignee. Click the "Filter" button to access these options.

3.3. Sorting Tasks

Tasks can be sorted by different parameters such as due date, priority, or title. Click the sort icon to select your preferred sorting method.

4. Integration with Other Microsoft 365 Apps

Microsoft Planner integrates seamlessly with other Microsoft 365 applications, enhancing its functionality and streamlining your workflow:

4.1. Integration with Microsoft Teams

You can add Planner tabs to Microsoft Teams channels, allowing team members to view and interact with plan details directly within Teams. This integration provides a unified workspace for project management and team communication.

4.2. Integration with Microsoft Outlook

Planner tasks can be synchronized with your Outlook calendar, making it easier to track deadlines and manage tasks alongside your email and meetings.

4.3. Integration with Microsoft To Do

Tasks assigned to you in Planner appear in Microsoft To Do, allowing you to manage your personal and professional tasks in one place. This integration helps you maintain focus and prioritize tasks across different platforms.

5. Accessibility and Mobile Experience

Microsoft Planner is designed to be accessible on various devices, including desktops, tablets, and smartphones:

5.1. Desktop Application

The Planner desktop application provides full functionality and access to all features. It's ideal for in-depth task management and planning.

5.2. Mobile App

The Microsoft Planner mobile app allows you to manage tasks on the go. While it offers a more streamlined experience compared to the desktop application, it provides essential functionalities such as viewing tasks, updating statuses, and adding comments.

5.3. Accessibility Features

Planner includes accessibility features to support users with disabilities. These features include keyboard shortcuts, screen reader compatibility, and high-contrast modes to ensure an inclusive user experience.

Conclusion

Understanding the Microsoft Planner interface is crucial for effectively managing your tasks and projects. By familiarizing yourself with the Dashboard, Plan View, Task Details, and various customization options, you can streamline your workflow and enhance team collaboration. Integration with other Microsoft 365 applications further amplifies Planner's capabilities, making it a powerful tool for organizing work and achieving goals.

With this comprehensive guide to the Planner interface, you are well-equipped to leverage its features and optimize your productivity.

1.3 Planner vs. Other Microsoft Tools

1.3.1 Planner vs. Microsoft To Do

When it comes to task and project management within the Microsoft ecosystem, Microsoft Planner and Microsoft To Do are two prominent tools that serve different purposes. Understanding the distinctions between these tools can help users select the right solution for their needs, and leverage the strengths of each to improve productivity and organization.

Overview of Microsoft To Do

Microsoft To Do is a task management application designed for individual use. It enables users to create, manage, and prioritize personal tasks with ease. Key features include:

- My Day: This feature allows users to focus on tasks they want to accomplish today by selecting items from their various lists.

- Task Lists: Users can create multiple task lists to organize their to-dos, such as work tasks, personal tasks, or shopping lists.

- Reminders and Due Dates: To Do supports setting reminders and due dates for tasks to help users stay on track.

- Recurring Tasks: Users can create tasks that repeat on a daily, weekly, or custom schedule.

- Integration with Microsoft 365: To Do integrates seamlessly with other Microsoft 365 apps, such as Outlook and Microsoft Teams.

Overview of Microsoft Planner

In contrast, Microsoft Planner is designed for team-based project management. It provides a more robust solution for tracking tasks within a collaborative environment. Key features include:

- Plans and Buckets: Users can create plans for different projects and organize tasks into buckets for better categorization.

- Task Assignment: Tasks can be assigned to team members, complete with due dates, labels, and priority levels.

- Boards and Charts: Planner provides visual boards and charts to track project progress and task completion.

- Task Dependencies: Users can set dependencies between tasks to reflect the sequence of work.

- Integration with Microsoft Teams and Outlook: Planner integrates with Microsoft Teams for real-time collaboration and with Outlook for email notifications.

Key Differences

1. Purpose and Scope

   - Microsoft To Do: Primarily aimed at individual users for personal task management. It is ideal for managing daily tasks, personal projects, and maintaining individual productivity. The focus is on simplicity and ease of use for personal organization.

   - Microsoft Planner: Designed for team collaboration and project management. It is suited for managing complex projects involving multiple people and tasks. Planner provides a more comprehensive approach to tracking and organizing work across teams and departments.

2. Task Organization

   - Microsoft To Do: Tasks are organized into lists, which can be customized by the user. Each list can contain tasks with due dates, reminders, and notes. The organization is linear and list-based.

   - Microsoft Planner: Tasks are organized within plans, and each plan can be divided into buckets. This bucket-based approach allows for categorizing tasks by different phases, types, or priorities within a project. Tasks can be moved between buckets as they progress.

3. Collaboration Features

- Microsoft To Do: Limited collaboration features. It primarily supports personal task management, although users can share lists with others. Collaboration is more about sharing information rather than managing joint projects.

- Microsoft Planner: Built for team collaboration. It allows users to assign tasks to team members, track task progress, and communicate within the platform. Teams can collaborate on tasks through comments, attachments, and real-time updates.

4. Visual Tracking

- Microsoft To Do: Lacks advanced visual tracking. Tasks are listed in a simple, linear fashion, with limited visual representation of progress.

- Microsoft Planner: Provides visual boards and charts, including a Kanban-style board for tasks, a progress chart, and a schedule view. These visual tools help teams monitor project status and task completion.

5. Integration with Other Tools

- Microsoft To Do: Integrates with Microsoft Outlook, allowing tasks to sync with Outlook's task list and calendar. It also integrates with Microsoft Teams and other Microsoft 365 apps for a unified experience.

- Microsoft Planner: Integrates deeply with Microsoft Teams, making it easy to create and manage Planner tasks directly within a team chat. It also integrates with Outlook, allowing tasks to appear in the calendar and be managed through email notifications.

6. Task Dependencies and Advanced Features

- Microsoft To Do: Does not support task dependencies. It is focused on managing tasks without complex project requirements.

- Microsoft Planner: Supports task dependencies, allowing users to define the order in which tasks must be completed. This feature is essential for managing projects with sequential workflows and interrelated tasks.

Use Cases and Recommendations

- Microsoft To Do: Best suited for individuals who need a simple and effective way to manage their personal tasks and daily activities. It is ideal for users who want to keep track of their to-do lists, set reminders, and organize their work without the need for complex project management features.

- Microsoft Planner: Recommended for teams and organizations that need a collaborative platform for managing projects. It is useful for tracking tasks, assigning work, and visualizing project progress. Planner's features are designed to handle multiple tasks and team collaboration efficiently.

Integration and Workflow

Both Microsoft To Do and Microsoft Planner integrate with Microsoft 365, allowing users to create a seamless workflow. For example, tasks from Planner can be viewed and managed in Outlook, while personal tasks from To Do can be shared or integrated with Planner for a comprehensive view of all work.

Conclusion

While Microsoft To Do and Microsoft Planner are both valuable tools within the Microsoft ecosystem, they serve different needs. Microsoft To Do is perfect for individual task management, offering simplicity and ease of use. Microsoft Planner, on the other hand, is designed for team-based project management, providing robust features for collaboration and project tracking. By understanding the strengths of each tool, users can select the right one for their specific requirements and use them effectively within their personal and professional lives.

1.3.2 Planner vs. Microsoft Project

Microsoft Planner and Microsoft Project are both powerful tools offered by Microsoft for managing projects, but they cater to different needs and complexities. Understanding the distinctions between these two tools is crucial for selecting the right one based on your project management requirements. This section provides an in-depth comparison of Microsoft Planner and Microsoft Project, focusing on their features, use cases, and benefits.

Overview of Microsoft Project

Microsoft Project is a comprehensive project management tool designed for more complex and detailed project planning. It offers robust features that cater to project managers who need to handle large-scale projects with intricate timelines, dependencies, and resource management.

Key Features of Microsoft Project:

- Gantt Charts: Microsoft Project's Gantt charts are essential for visualizing project timelines, dependencies, and critical paths. They provide a detailed view of tasks, start and end dates, and task relationships.

- Resource Management: The tool includes advanced resource management features, allowing users to allocate resources, track their availability, and manage workload and costs. It supports resource leveling to address overallocation issues.

- Project Scheduling: Microsoft Project offers extensive scheduling capabilities, including task dependencies, constraints, and milestones. This allows project managers to create detailed schedules and adjust them as needed.

- Financial Tracking: The software supports budget management and cost tracking. It provides tools to monitor project expenditures, compare budgeted vs. actual costs, and manage financial forecasts.

- Custom Reports: Microsoft Project enables users to generate custom reports and dashboards, which can be tailored to specific project needs and stakeholders. This feature is crucial for tracking progress and communicating with teams and executives.

Overview of Microsoft Planner

Microsoft Planner, on the other hand, is a more lightweight and intuitive project management tool aimed at simplifying task and project management for teams. It is ideal for managing smaller projects and day-to-day tasks within an organization.

Key Features of Microsoft Planner:

- Task Boards: Planner uses a Kanban-style task board with buckets to organize tasks. This visual approach makes it easy for team members to see task status and progress.

- Task Management: Users can create tasks, assign them to team members, set due dates, and attach files. Tasks can be organized into buckets and labeled for better categorization.

- Simple Scheduling: Planner offers basic scheduling tools, such as due dates and reminders. It integrates with Microsoft Outlook to synchronize task deadlines and calendar events.

- Team Collaboration: Planner emphasizes team collaboration, with features like comments, file sharing, and notifications. It integrates seamlessly with Microsoft Teams for enhanced communication.

- Charts and Analytics: While not as advanced as Microsoft Project's reporting capabilities, Planner provides simple visual charts to track task progress and team performance.

Comparative Analysis

Complexity and Use Case:

- Microsoft Project: Ideal for large-scale projects with complex scheduling, resource allocation, and financial tracking needs. It is suited for project managers who require detailed planning and control over all aspects of the project lifecycle. Examples include construction projects, large IT implementations, and major event planning.

- Microsoft Planner: Best for smaller projects and task management within teams. It excels in ease of use and quick setup, making it suitable for daily task management, team collaboration, and simple project tracking. Examples include marketing campaigns, team initiatives, and personal project management.

Integration and Compatibility:

- Microsoft Project: Integrates well with other Microsoft 365 tools, but its integration capabilities are more focused on project management and resource planning. It also integrates with Microsoft Power BI for advanced reporting and analytics.

- Microsoft Planner: Designed to work seamlessly with Microsoft Teams, SharePoint, and Outlook. It provides a more straightforward integration experience with these tools, enhancing team collaboration and communication.

User Experience:

- Microsoft Project: Requires a steeper learning curve due to its extensive features and complex interface. It is typically used by experienced project managers who are familiar with advanced project management methodologies.

- Microsoft Planner: Offers a user-friendly interface that is easy to navigate, making it accessible to all team members regardless of their project management experience. Its simplicity and visual task boards facilitate quick adoption and use.

Cost and Licensing:

- Microsoft Project: Generally comes with a higher price point and is available through different licensing plans, including standalone and subscription-based options. It is often included in enterprise-level Microsoft 365 plans.

- Microsoft Planner: Included as part of Microsoft 365 subscriptions at no additional cost. It is available to all Microsoft 365 users, making it a cost-effective solution for task and project management.

Reporting and Analytics:

- Microsoft Project: Offers advanced reporting features, including customizable reports and dashboards. It provides detailed insights into project performance, resource utilization, and financial status.

- Microsoft Planner: Provides basic visual analytics, such as charts and progress indicators. While it does not offer advanced reporting capabilities, it gives a high-level view of task progress and team workload.

Decision-Making Factors:

When choosing between Microsoft Planner and Microsoft Project, consider the following factors:

- Project Size and Complexity: For complex projects with intricate scheduling and resource needs, Microsoft Project is the better choice. For simpler projects and team collaboration, Microsoft Planner is more suitable.

- Team Collaboration Needs: If team collaboration and ease of use are top priorities, Microsoft Planner's integration with Microsoft Teams and its visual task boards make it an excellent option.

- Budget Constraints: Microsoft Planner offers a cost-effective solution as part of Microsoft 365 subscriptions, whereas Microsoft Project may involve additional costs depending on the licensing plan.

- Reporting Requirements: For detailed reporting and analytics, Microsoft Project provides advanced capabilities. If basic progress tracking suffices, Microsoft Planner's built-in charts and task views will meet your needs.

Conclusion

In summary, both Microsoft Planner and Microsoft Project offer valuable project management capabilities, each suited to different needs and scenarios. Microsoft Project excels in handling complex projects with detailed planning, resource management, and reporting. It is ideal for experienced project managers who require comprehensive control over project details. Microsoft Planner, on the other hand, provides a more straightforward and collaborative approach to task management, making it perfect for smaller projects and team-focused initiatives.

Choosing the right tool depends on your specific project requirements, team dynamics, and budget considerations. By understanding the strengths and limitations of each tool, you can make an informed decision and leverage Microsoft's project management solutions to enhance your productivity and achieve your goals.

1.3.3 Integrating Planner with Other Microsoft Apps

Integrating Microsoft Planner with other Microsoft applications enhances its functionality and provides a seamless experience across various tools. This integration is crucial for maximizing productivity, improving team collaboration, and streamlining project management processes. In this section, we will explore how Microsoft Planner interacts with key Microsoft tools, including Microsoft Teams, Outlook, SharePoint, and Power Automate.

1.3.3.1 Integrating Microsoft Planner with Microsoft Teams

a. Adding Planner Tabs to Teams Channels

One of the most effective ways to integrate Microsoft Planner is by adding Planner tabs to Microsoft Teams channels. This integration allows team members to access and manage their Planner tasks directly within the Teams interface, eliminating the need to switch between applications.

To add a Planner tab to a Teams channel:

1. Navigate to the Teams Channel: Go to the desired channel within your team.

2. Add a Tab: Click the "+" icon at the top of the channel.

3. Select Planner: Choose "Planner" from the list of available apps.

4. Create or Select a Plan: You can either create a new plan or select an existing one to link to the tab.

5. Configure Tab Settings: Name the tab and configure any additional settings as needed.

6. Save and Share: Click "Save" to add the Planner tab to the channel.

With Planner integrated into Teams, team members can view tasks, update statuses, and track progress without leaving the Teams environment. This integration fosters better collaboration and keeps everyone informed about project developments.

b. Using Planner with Microsoft Teams Meetings

During Microsoft Teams meetings, you can leverage Planner to track action items and project tasks discussed in the meeting. Integration with Teams allows you to:

1. Access Planner Tasks in Meetings: While in a Teams meeting, you can access Planner tasks using the "Apps" feature or directly from a Planner tab if it's already added to the channel.

2. Create Action Items: Quickly create new tasks or assign action items directly from the meeting chat or the Planner tab.

3. Track Progress: Use the Planner tab to monitor the progress of tasks related to the meeting.

This integration helps ensure that meeting discussions translate into actionable tasks and keeps everyone aligned on responsibilities.

c. Notifications and Updates

Microsoft Teams can be configured to provide notifications about Planner tasks. These notifications can be customized to alert team members about task assignments, due dates, and status changes. To configure notifications:

1. Go to Planner Settings: Open Microsoft Planner and navigate to the plan you want to manage notifications for.

2. Set Up Notifications: Configure how you want to receive updates (e.g., via email or Teams notifications).

3. Manage Notification Preferences: Adjust preferences for each plan and team to ensure that notifications are relevant and timely.

Integrating Planner with Teams enhances communication and ensures that team members stay updated on task-related activities.

1.3.3.2 Integrating Microsoft Planner with Outlook

a. Syncing Planner Tasks with Outlook Calendar

Microsoft Planner can sync with Outlook to display Planner tasks and due dates in your Outlook calendar. This integration helps users keep track of deadlines and manage their time effectively. To sync Planner tasks with Outlook:

1. Open Planner: Access your Planner and go to the plan you want to sync.

2. Connect to Outlook: Click on "..." (More options) and select "Add plan to Outlook calendar."

3. Follow Instructions: Follow the prompts to add the Planner calendar to your Outlook calendar.

4. View and Manage Tasks: Once synced, you can view Planner tasks and deadlines directly in your Outlook calendar.

This integration allows you to see all your commitments in one place, facilitating better time management.

b. Creating Planner Tasks from Outlook Emails

Another valuable integration is the ability to create Planner tasks from Outlook emails. This feature allows users to convert emails into actionable tasks, ensuring that important items are tracked and managed. To create a Planner task from an email:

1. Open Outlook: Access the email you want to convert into a task.

2. Select "More Actions": Click on the three dots in the email options.

3. Choose "Create Task in Planner": Select the option to create a task in Planner.

4. Fill in Task Details: Add relevant details such as task name, due date, and assignment information.

5. Save and Add to Planner: Click "Save" to add the task to your Planner.

This integration helps users manage tasks more efficiently by directly linking email correspondence to task management.

c. Using Planner with Outlook Tasks

If you use Outlook Tasks, you can integrate it with Planner to streamline task management across platforms. Tasks can be synced between Outlook and Planner, allowing for seamless tracking and updates. To sync Outlook Tasks with Planner:

1. Open Outlook: Access your Outlook Tasks.

2. Link to Planner: Use the integration options to connect Outlook Tasks with Planner.

3. Sync and Manage: Ensure that tasks are synchronized and manage them as needed.

This integration ensures that tasks are consistently updated across both platforms, improving productivity and task visibility.

1.3.3.3 Integrating Microsoft Planner with SharePoint

a. Adding Planner to SharePoint Sites

You can integrate Microsoft Planner with SharePoint by adding Planner as a web part to SharePoint sites. This integration allows you to display Planner tasks and project information directly on your SharePoint site, making it easier for team members to access and manage tasks. To add Planner to a SharePoint site:

1. Open SharePoint: Go to the SharePoint site where you want to add Planner.

2. Edit the Page: Click "Edit" to modify the site page.

3. Add a Web Part: Choose "+" to add a new web part and select "Planner."

4. Configure Planner Web Part: Select the plan you want to display and configure settings.

5. Save and Publish: Save your changes and publish the updated page.

By integrating Planner into SharePoint, you provide a centralized location for project management and enhance visibility across the organization.

b. Using SharePoint Lists with Planner

SharePoint Lists can be integrated with Planner to manage tasks and project information. This integration allows you to use SharePoint Lists as a data source for Planner tasks, providing additional customization options. To use SharePoint Lists with Planner:

1. Create a SharePoint List: Set up a SharePoint List to track project data or tasks.

2. Link to Planner: Use Power Automate to create a flow that links SharePoint List items to Planner tasks.

3. Manage Tasks: Manage tasks in Planner based on data from the SharePoint List.

This integration allows for advanced task management and customization by leveraging SharePoint's data management capabilities.

c. Document Management and Collaboration

SharePoint's document management features can be integrated with Planner to enhance collaboration on project documents. This integration allows you to attach SharePoint documents to Planner tasks and collaborate on files directly from within Planner. To integrate document management:

1. Attach Documents: When creating or editing a task in Planner, attach relevant SharePoint documents.

2. Collaborate on Files: Use SharePoint's collaboration tools to work on documents linked to Planner tasks.

3. Track Document Changes: Monitor changes and updates to documents associated with Planner tasks.

Integrating SharePoint's document management with Planner facilitates better collaboration and ensures that all project-related documents are easily accessible.

1.3.3.4 Integrating Microsoft Planner with Power Automate

a. Automating Task Creation with Power Automate

Microsoft Power Automate (formerly Microsoft Flow) can be used to automate task creation in Planner based on triggers from other applications. This automation streamlines task management and ensures that tasks are created automatically based on predefined conditions. To set up task automation:

1. Open Power Automate: Access the Power Automate portal.

2. Create a Flow: Set up a new flow and choose a trigger (e.g., new email, form submission).

3. Configure Actions: Add actions to create tasks in Planner based on the trigger.

4. Save and Test: Save the flow and test it to ensure tasks are created as expected.

By automating task creation, you reduce manual effort and ensure tasks are created consistently.

b. Syncing Tasks Between Planner and Other Apps

Power Automate can also be used to sync tasks between Planner and other applications, such as Microsoft To Do or external project management tools. This integration ensures that task updates are reflected across platforms. To set up task synchronization:

1. Open Power Automate: Access your Power Automate account.

2. Create Sync Flow: Set up a flow to synchronize tasks between Planner and the target application.

3. Configure Sync Rules: Define rules for how tasks should be synced (e.g., updates, deletions).

4. Test and Deploy: Test the synchronization flow and deploy it for use.

Syncing tasks across applications ensures that all task information is up-to-date and accessible from multiple platforms.

c. Generating Reports and Notifications

Power Automate can be used to generate reports and notifications based on Planner data. This integration allows you to create custom reports or receive notifications about task status, upcoming deadlines, and project progress. To set up reports and notifications:

1. Open Power Automate: Go to the Power Automate portal.

2. Create a Report Flow: Set up a flow to generate reports based on Planner data.

3. Configure Notifications: Set up notifications for task updates, deadlines, or progress.

4. Customize and Test: Customize the reports and notifications to meet your needs and test them to ensure accuracy.

Using Power Automate for reporting and notifications enhances visibility into project progress and ensures timely communication about task-related activities.

Integrating Microsoft Planner with other Microsoft apps enhances its functionality and provides a more cohesive project management experience. By leveraging these integrations, teams can streamline their workflows, improve collaboration, and effectively manage tasks and projects across various platforms.

CHAPTER II
Setting Up Your Plans

2.1 Creating and Customizing Plans

2.1.1 Creating a New Plan

Creating a new plan in Microsoft Planner is the first step in organizing your tasks, projects, or workflows. Whether you're managing a small team project or coordinating a large-scale initiative, Microsoft Planner provides the tools to structure your work effectively. In this section, we'll delve into the steps involved in creating a new plan, the key considerations to keep in mind, and how to set up your plan for success.

Understanding the Purpose of a Plan

Before you create a new plan, it's important to understand its purpose. A plan in Microsoft Planner acts as a container for tasks, resources, and deadlines associated with a specific project or objective. This structure allows you to break down large projects into manageable components, assign tasks to team members, and track progress over time. Understanding the scope and goals of your project will help you set up your plan in a way that aligns with your needs.

Steps to Create a New Plan

Step 1: Accessing Microsoft Planner

To begin, log in to your Microsoft 365 account and navigate to Microsoft Planner. You can access Planner directly from the Microsoft 365 app launcher, often referred to as the "waffle" menu, located in the top left corner of your screen. Once you click on the Planner icon, you'll be taken to the Planner Hub, where you can view all your existing plans or start a new one.

Step 2: Starting a New Plan

In the Planner Hub, click on the "New Plan" button, typically located in the upper right corner of the screen. A pop-up window will appear, prompting you to enter the details for your new plan.

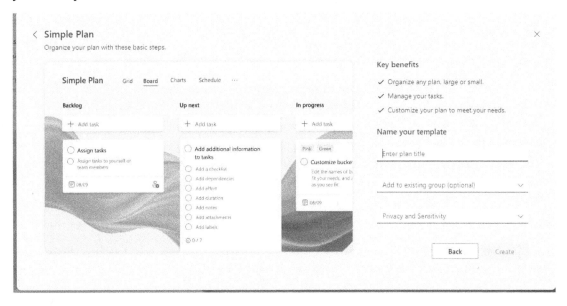

Step 3: Naming Your Plan

One of the first things you'll need to do is give your plan a name. Choose a name that clearly reflects the purpose of the plan. For example, if you're managing a marketing campaign, you might name your plan "Q3 Marketing Campaign." The name should be concise yet descriptive enough to convey the plan's objective to all team members.

Step 4: Choosing a Privacy Setting

After naming your plan, you'll need to select a privacy setting. Microsoft Planner offers two options: Public and Private.

- Public: If you choose the public option, anyone in your organization can see your plan and its contents. This setting is useful for plans that involve cross-departmental collaboration or when transparency is necessary.

- Private: A private plan is only visible to the team members you explicitly add to the plan. This setting is ideal for sensitive projects or when you need to control who can view and contribute to the plan.

Consider the nature of your project and your organization's culture when deciding on the privacy setting.

Step 5: Adding a Group (Optional)

If you're using Microsoft Planner within Microsoft Teams or Outlook Groups, you'll have the option to associate your plan with an existing group. This feature helps integrate your plan with other Microsoft 365 tools, streamlining communication and collaboration. If you're starting a plan for a new project, you can create a new group that will be associated with this plan, providing a dedicated space for team communication, file sharing, and more.

Step 6: Creating the Plan

Once you've named your plan and selected the appropriate privacy setting, click the "Create Plan" button. Microsoft Planner will generate a new plan, and you'll be taken directly to the plan's dashboard. Here, you'll begin to see the framework of your plan, including default sections like "To Do," "In Progress," and "Completed."

Customizing Your New Plan

Creating the plan is just the first step. Customization is key to ensuring that the plan meets your specific needs and that it aligns with your project's goals.

1. Setting Up Buckets

Buckets in Microsoft Planner allow you to categorize tasks into different stages, areas of responsibility, or types of work. By default, your plan starts with a single bucket named "To Do," but you can add more buckets to better organize your tasks.

To create a new bucket, click on the "Add new bucket" option on the plan dashboard. Name the bucket according to its function. For example, in a project management plan, you might have buckets like "Design," "Development," "Testing," and "Deployment." This categorization helps in visualizing the workflow and understanding the status of different parts of the project at a glance.

2. Assigning Tasks to Buckets

Once you've created your buckets, you can start assigning tasks to them. This process involves dragging and dropping tasks into the appropriate bucket. Assigning tasks to buckets not only keeps the plan organized but also makes it easier to track the progress of specific tasks or phases within the project.

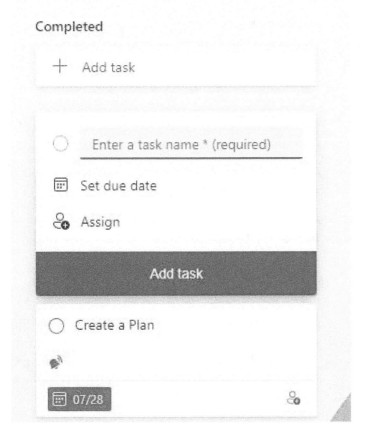

3. Using Labels for Categorization

Labels in Microsoft Planner are color-coded tags that you can apply to tasks to further categorize them. Labels are useful for indicating task types, priority levels, or specific themes. For instance, in a content creation plan, you might use labels like "High Priority," "Social Media," or "Email Campaign."

To create or apply a label, click on a task and select the "Add label" option. You can then choose from existing labels or create a new one. Each label can be renamed to match the specific needs of your plan.

4. Setting Up Task Details

Tasks in Microsoft Planner come with a range of customizable details that help clarify what needs to be done and by whom. When you click on a task, you can:

- Add a Task Description: Provide a brief summary of the task to give context and instructions to the assignee.

- Set a Due Date: Assign a deadline to ensure that tasks are completed on time.

- Attach Files or Links: Upload relevant documents or add links to resources that are necessary for completing the task.

- Add Comments: Use the comment section to communicate with team members directly within the task, ensuring that all discussions are kept in context.

These features allow you to ensure that each task is clearly defined and fully understood by the team members responsible for completing it.

5. Adding Team Members

Once your plan is set up, you can start adding team members. To do this, click on the "Members" section of the plan and type in the names or email addresses of the people you want to add. Microsoft Planner is integrated with your organization's directory, making it easy to find and add colleagues.

Assigning tasks to specific team members is crucial for accountability. Each task can be assigned to one or more people, ensuring that everyone knows what they are responsible for.

Best Practices for Creating Effective Plans

To ensure that your plan is effective and meets your project goals, consider the following best practices:

1. Start with Clear Objectives

Before creating tasks and assigning them to team members, make sure the objectives of the plan are clearly defined. This will help you determine what tasks are necessary and how they should be organized.

2. Keep the Plan Simple and Focused

While it's tempting to include every possible task in your plan, try to keep it as simple and focused as possible. Overloading your plan with too many tasks or details can make it overwhelming for team members and difficult to manage.

3. Regularly Review and Update the Plan

A plan is a living document that should evolve as the project progresses. Regularly review the plan to ensure it remains relevant and adjust tasks, deadlines, or priorities as needed. This keeps the plan aligned with the project's needs and helps prevent bottlenecks or delays.

4. Communicate Clearly with Team Members

Ensure that all team members understand their responsibilities and how their tasks fit into the overall plan. Use the communication tools within Microsoft Planner, such as task comments, to facilitate ongoing dialogue and collaboration.

5. Utilize Integrations with Other Microsoft 365 Tools

Microsoft Planner integrates seamlessly with other tools in the Microsoft 365 suite, such as Teams, Outlook, and SharePoint. Leveraging these integrations can enhance collaboration and make it easier to manage your project across different platforms.

6. Monitor Progress and Adjust as Needed

As your project moves forward, monitor the progress of tasks and the overall plan. Use the Planner's built-in charts and visualizations to track progress and identify any areas that may need additional attention or resources. If tasks are falling behind schedule, consider reallocating resources or adjusting deadlines to keep the project on track.

Common Challenges and How to Overcome Them

1. Incomplete Task Assignments

One common challenge in plan creation is the incomplete assignment of tasks. This can lead to confusion and delays in task completion. To avoid this, make sure that every task is clearly assigned to a team member and that they understand their responsibilities.

2. Overlapping Deadlines

Another challenge is managing overlapping deadlines, which can overwhelm team members. When setting due dates, be mindful of the workload of each team member and try to stagger deadlines when possible to prevent bottlenecks.

3. Lack of Engagement from Team Members

If team members are not engaging with the plan, it can hinder the project's progress. Encourage engagement by involving team members in the plan creation process and ensuring that they understand how the plan aligns with the project's goals.

4. Difficulty in Prioritizing Tasks

Prioritizing tasks within a plan can be difficult, especially in complex projects. Using labels, setting clear deadlines, and regularly reviewing the plan can help you maintain focus on the most important tasks.

Conclusion

Creating a new plan in Microsoft Planner is a foundational step in organizing your work and achieving your goals. By carefully setting up your plan, customizing it to fit your needs, and following best practices, you can create a powerful tool that will guide your project from start to finish. Remember, a well-structured plan is not just about listing tasks—it's about creating a roadmap that leads your team to success.

2.1.2 Setting Plan Details

When creating a new plan in Microsoft Planner, setting the plan details is a crucial step that ensures the plan is organized and aligned with the project's objectives. Properly setting the details not only helps in managing the tasks efficiently but also facilitates collaboration among team members. This section will guide you through the essential aspects of setting plan details, including naming your plan, defining objectives, setting privacy settings, adding members, and establishing timelines.

Naming Your Plan

The first step in setting plan details is choosing an appropriate name for your plan. The name should be descriptive enough to convey the plan's purpose at a glance. For example, if the plan is for a marketing campaign, a name like "Q3 Product Launch Campaign" would be more informative than just "Marketing Plan." A clear and specific name helps team members quickly understand the scope and focus of the plan.

When naming your plan, consider the following tips:

- Clarity: Ensure the name clearly reflects the project's objective or the specific task it represents.

- Consistency: Follow a consistent naming convention across all plans within your organization to avoid confusion.

- Avoid Acronyms: Unless universally understood within your team, avoid using acronyms that might be unclear to some members.

- Length: Keep the name concise, ideally within 3-5 words, to ensure it fits well in the interface and is easy to read.

After deciding on a name, it can be entered into the designated field when creating the plan. This name will be visible to all members and will be used to identify the plan in the Planner Hub and other integrated Microsoft 365 applications.

Defining Objectives and Goals

Once the plan is named, the next step is to clearly define the objectives and goals of the plan. This step is essential as it provides direction and purpose to the team members, ensuring that everyone understands the expected outcomes. The objectives should be specific, measurable, achievable, relevant, and time-bound (SMART).

Here's how to define effective objectives for your plan:

- Specific: Clearly define what needs to be accomplished. For example, instead of a vague objective like "Improve sales," specify "Increase Q3 sales by 20% through targeted email campaigns."

- Measurable: Include criteria for measuring progress. This could be in terms of numbers, percentages, or other quantifiable metrics.

- Achievable: Ensure the objectives are realistic given the resources and time available.

- Relevant: Align the objectives with the broader goals of the organization or the specific project.

- Time-bound: Set a clear timeline or deadline by which the objectives should be achieved.

By setting well-defined objectives, you provide a roadmap for your team, enabling them to focus on what truly matters and work towards achieving the desired results efficiently.

Setting Privacy Settings

Microsoft Planner offers flexibility in how you share your plans with others. During the plan creation process, you will be prompted to choose the privacy settings for your plan. You can choose between two options: Public or Private.

- Public Plans: A public plan is accessible to anyone within your organization who has a link to the plan. They can view the plan, see the tasks, and track the progress. Public plans are suitable for projects that require transparency and open collaboration across different departments or teams.

- Private Plans: A private plan is only accessible to the members you explicitly add to the plan. This setting is ideal for sensitive projects that involve confidential information or for teams that require focused collaboration without external input.

When setting the privacy of your plan, consider the nature of the project and the level of collaboration required. For example, if the plan involves strategic decisions or confidential client information, setting it as private would be more appropriate. Conversely, if the plan is for a company-wide initiative where open input is valuable, a public setting might be better.

You can change the privacy settings at any time after the plan has been created, which provides flexibility as the project evolves.

Adding Members

After setting the privacy, the next step is to add members to your plan. Adding the right people to your plan is crucial for ensuring that the tasks are handled by those with the appropriate skills and knowledge.

To add members:

1. Search for Members: Use the search bar to find people within your organization. You can search by name, email, or job title.

2. Add Members: Once you find the right person, click on their name to add them to the plan. You can add multiple members at once.

3. Assign Roles: While Microsoft Planner does not have role-based permissions, it's good practice to discuss roles and responsibilities with your team members as they are added to the plan. Clearly define who is responsible for what, to avoid any confusion.

Adding members at the outset of a project ensures that everyone is onboard from the beginning, which promotes better collaboration and accountability. It's also a good idea to regularly review the list of members and make adjustments as the project progresses, adding new members as needed and removing those who are no longer involved.

Establishing Timelines and Deadlines

Setting a timeline is a critical part of plan details, as it helps to map out the duration of the project and ensure that all tasks are completed within the specified period. A well-defined timeline keeps the project on track and allows team members to manage their time effectively.

To establish a timeline:

1. Set Start and End Dates: Determine the overall duration of the project by setting a start date and an end date for the plan. These dates should align with the project's objectives and the deadlines for key deliverables.

2. Break Down the Timeline: Divide the overall timeline into smaller phases or milestones. For example, if your plan is for a product launch, you might have phases like "Research and Development," "Marketing Preparation," and "Product Release."

3. Assign Deadlines: For each task within the plan, set specific deadlines. This ensures that tasks are completed in a timely manner and that the project progresses smoothly. Deadlines can be adjusted as needed, but having them in place from the start provides a clear schedule for the team to follow.

4. Consider Dependencies: Some tasks may depend on the completion of others before they can start. Identifying and managing these dependencies is key to setting a realistic timeline. Microsoft Planner allows you to visually organize tasks in a way that highlights these dependencies, making it easier to adjust timelines as needed.

Having a well-defined timeline helps in maintaining momentum throughout the project and reduces the risk of delays. It also allows team members to plan their workloads more effectively, ensuring that they can contribute to the project without being overburdened.

Setting Up Plan Descriptions and Notes

While Microsoft Planner does not have a specific field for detailed plan descriptions, it's a good practice to include a summary of the plan's purpose and key details in the "Plan Notes" section. This section can be used to provide an overview of the plan, outline the objectives, and include any important information that team members need to know.

When writing the plan description:

- Be Concise: Summarize the key points of the plan in a few sentences. Focus on the most important aspects, such as the overall goal and key deliverables.

- Include Context: Provide any necessary background information that will help team members understand the context of the plan.

- Highlight Important Details: Emphasize any critical information that team members need to keep in mind, such as key deadlines, dependencies, or special instructions.

Using the Plan Notes section effectively helps to ensure that everyone involved in the plan has a clear understanding of what the project entails and what is expected of them.

Establishing Plan Permissions and Access Levels

Although Microsoft Planner's permissions are relatively straightforward, ensuring that your team understands how to interact with the plan is important. As the plan creator, you will have full control over the plan, including the ability to add or remove members, edit tasks, and change plan details.

Here's a brief overview of permissions within Microsoft Planner:

- Plan Owner: The person who creates the plan is the owner and has full permissions to manage the plan.

- Members: Members added to the plan can view and edit tasks, add comments, and collaborate with other team members. However, they cannot change the plan's privacy settings or remove other members.

- Guest Members: If you add people from outside your organization (assuming your organization's settings allow this), they will have more limited access, typically restricted to viewing and editing tasks.

Understanding and managing these permissions ensures that the right people have access to the right information and that the project remains secure.

Utilizing Plan Labels and Tags

Labels and tags are powerful tools in Microsoft Planner that help in organizing and categorizing tasks within a plan. Setting up labels early in the plan creation process allows you to apply them consistently across all tasks, making it easier to sort and filter tasks later on.

To set up labels:

1. Define Categories: Determine the categories that will be most useful for your plan. For example, labels could represent task types, priorities, departments, or stages of completion.

2. Create Labels: Microsoft Planner allows you to create up to six color-coded labels per plan. Assign each label a meaningful name that corresponds to the category it represents.

3. Apply Labels: As you create tasks within the plan, apply the relevant labels to categorize them. This will help you and your team members quickly identify and group similar tasks.

Using labels effectively can significantly enhance the organization of your plan, making it easier to navigate and manage, especially as the number of tasks grows.

Customizing Plan Buckets

Buckets are another key feature in Microsoft Planner that help in organizing tasks within a plan. Each bucket represents a category or stage in the project, and tasks are placed into these buckets based on their status or type.

To customize buckets:

1. Determine Categories: Decide how you want to categorize your tasks. Common approaches include using buckets for stages in a workflow (e.g., "To Do," "

In Progress," "Completed") or for different project phases (e.g., "Design," "Development," "Testing").

2. Create and Name Buckets: Create new buckets by clicking the "Add new bucket" button and entering a name for each bucket. The names should be clear and indicative of the category they represent.

3. Organize Tasks: As you create tasks, place them in the appropriate bucket. This organization helps team members quickly see which tasks are at what stage and what needs to be done next.

Customizing buckets to fit your project's workflow is an essential step in ensuring that tasks are organized in a way that aligns with your team's processes and priorities.

Final Review of Plan Details

Before finalizing your plan, it's important to review all the details you've set. This includes checking the plan name, objectives, privacy settings, members, timelines, labels, and buckets. A thorough review helps to ensure that everything is correctly set up and that there are no oversights.

During the review, consider the following:

- Consistency: Ensure that the naming conventions and categorization methods are consistent throughout the plan.

- Accuracy: Double-check that all dates, names, and other details are accurate.

- Clarity: Make sure that all members understand their roles and the structure of the plan.

Once you're satisfied with the setup, you can start adding tasks and assigning them to team members, confident that your plan is well-organized and ready for action.

Setting plan details in Microsoft Planner is a foundational step in project management that requires careful thought and consideration. By following the steps outlined above, you can create a well-structured plan that supports effective collaboration, keeps your team aligned with project goals, and ensures that tasks are completed on time.

2.1.3 Customizing Plan Buckets

Introduction to Plan Buckets

In Microsoft Planner, a "Bucket" serves as a fundamental organizational tool within a plan. It allows users to categorize tasks into distinct groups, making it easier to manage workflows, track progress, and maintain a clear overview of ongoing projects. Buckets can be thought of as containers or segments within a plan, where related tasks are grouped together according to specific criteria, such as phases of a project, types of tasks, or departments involved.

Customizing Plan Buckets is an essential step in setting up your plan effectively. It ensures that tasks are organized in a way that aligns with your project's structure and goals, facilitating efficient task management and team collaboration.

The Importance of Customizing Plan Buckets

Customizing Plan Buckets provides several key benefits:

1. Enhanced Task Organization: By categorizing tasks into buckets, you can easily distinguish between different types of work or phases of a project. This organization helps in quickly identifying where a task belongs and understanding the scope of work within each category.

2. Improved Workflow Management: Customizing buckets according to the project's workflow stages, such as "To Do," "In Progress," and "Completed," allows teams to visualize the progress of tasks as they move through the pipeline. This approach aids in tracking task statuses and ensuring that nothing falls through the cracks.

3. Clearer Communication: When working with a team, well-defined buckets help in setting clear expectations regarding task assignments and deadlines. Team members can immediately see where their tasks fit within the broader project and understand the priorities.

4. Flexibility and Adaptability: Customizing buckets gives you the flexibility to tailor the plan to your project's unique requirements. Whether you're managing a simple to-do list or a complex project with multiple phases, you can create buckets that reflect the specific needs of your work.

Steps to Customize Plan Buckets

Customizing Plan Buckets in Microsoft Planner is a straightforward process, but it requires thoughtful consideration to ensure that the buckets align with your project's structure and objectives. Here's a step-by-step guide on how to customize plan buckets effectively:

1. Analyzing Your Project Structure

Before creating buckets, it's essential to analyze the structure of your project. Consider the following:

- Phases or Stages of the Project: If your project has distinct phases (e.g., Planning, Development, Testing, Launch), you may want to create buckets that correspond to these stages.

- Types of Tasks: Group tasks by their nature, such as "Research," "Design," "Development," or "Marketing." This approach is useful when tasks across different stages share similar characteristics.

- Departments or Teams: If multiple departments or teams are involved, consider creating buckets for each department (e.g., "Engineering," "Marketing," "Sales").

- Priority Levels: You can also organize tasks by priority (e.g., "High Priority," "Medium Priority," "Low Priority"), allowing the team to focus on the most critical tasks first.

2. Creating and Naming Buckets

Once you've analyzed your project's structure, follow these steps to create and name your buckets:

- Step 1: Open the Plan: Navigate to the plan where you want to customize the buckets.

- Step 2: Click 'Add New Bucket': In the Planner board view, you'll see the option to add a new bucket. Click on this option to create your first bucket.

- Step 3: Name the Bucket: Choose a name that clearly reflects the purpose of the bucket. For example, if you're creating a bucket for the initial phase of a project, you might name it "Initiation" or "Phase 1."

- Step 4: Repeat for Additional Buckets: Continue adding and naming buckets until you've created all the categories necessary for your plan.

Naming Conventions: Keep the bucket names concise and specific. Avoid vague terms like "Miscellaneous" or "General," as they can lead to confusion. Instead, use descriptive names that immediately convey the purpose of each bucket.

3. Reordering and Organizing Buckets

The order of your buckets can influence how easily you and your team can navigate the plan. Here's how to organize them effectively:

- Step 1: Drag and Drop Buckets: Microsoft Planner allows you to rearrange buckets simply by dragging and dropping them in the desired order. This feature is useful for arranging buckets in a sequence that aligns with your workflow or project timeline.

- Step 2: Prioritize Based on Workflow: If your project follows a linear progression, arrange the buckets from left to right in the order tasks need to be completed. For instance, you might start with "To Do" on the left and end with "Completed" on the right.

- Step 3: Group Related Buckets Together: If your plan includes buckets for different departments or task types, consider grouping similar buckets together to make it easier for team members to find relevant tasks.

4. Adding Tasks to Buckets

Once your buckets are set up, the next step is to populate them with tasks:

- Step 1: Create a Task: Click on the "+" sign under the bucket where you want to add a task.

- Step 2: Assign the Task: Enter the task name and details. Assign it to the appropriate team member, set a due date, and prioritize it based on its importance.

- Step 3: Drag and Drop Existing Tasks: If you have existing tasks that need to be reorganized, you can drag and drop them into the appropriate buckets.

5. Customizing Buckets Based on Feedback

As your project progresses, you may find that the initial bucket setup needs to be adjusted. Here's how to customize buckets based on team feedback and evolving project needs:

- Step 1: Gather Feedback: Regularly check in with your team to gather feedback on the bucket setup. Are the buckets clear? Is the organization working for everyone? Are there any new categories that need to be added?

- Step 2: Adjust Bucket Names: If a bucket's purpose has changed or needs to be clarified, you can easily rename it by clicking on the bucket name and typing in a new one.

- Step 3: Add or Remove Buckets: Depending on the feedback, you may need to add new buckets for additional phases or task types, or remove buckets that are no longer needed.

Best Practices: Ensure that any changes to the bucket structure are communicated to the entire team. Consistency is key to maintaining clarity and avoiding confusion.

Advanced Customization Techniques

For more advanced customization, Microsoft Planner offers several features that can help you optimize your buckets even further:

1. Using Labels within Buckets

Labels are color-coded tags that you can apply to tasks within buckets to add another layer of categorization. Here's how to use them effectively:

- Step 1: Create Labels: In the Planner board view, click on a task and select the "Labels" option. You can create up to six labels, each with a different color.

- Step 2: Apply Labels to Tasks: Assign labels to tasks within a bucket to signify certain characteristics, such as task priority, department, or status. For example, you might use a red label for "Urgent" tasks or a green label for tasks assigned to the marketing department.

- Step 3: Filter Tasks by Label: Once labels are applied, you can filter tasks within a bucket (or across the entire plan) by label, making it easier to focus on specific groups of tasks.

2. Utilizing Checklists within Buckets

For tasks that involve multiple steps or sub-tasks, consider using checklists within each task to break down the work:

- Step 1: Create a Task Checklist: Open a task within a bucket and add a checklist. Each item on the checklist can represent a sub-task or step that needs to be completed.

- Step 2: Track Progress: As each checklist item is completed, mark it off. This feature is particularly useful for tasks that require input from multiple team members or involve several stages of work.

- Step 3: Move Tasks Based on Checklist Completion: As checklist items are completed, you might move the task to a different bucket to reflect its progress (e.g., from "In Progress" to "Review").

3. Automating Bucket Management with Power Automate

For users seeking to automate aspects of bucket management, Microsoft Power Automate (formerly Microsoft Flow) can be integrated with Planner to streamline repetitive tasks:

- Step 1: Set Up a Flow: Use Power Automate to create workflows (flows) that automatically move tasks between buckets based on certain triggers, such as task completion, due dates, or label changes.

- Step 2: Define Triggers and Actions: For example, you could create a flow that automatically moves a task to the "Completed" bucket once all checklist items are checked off.

- Step 3: Test and Monitor: After setting up a flow, test it to ensure it works as intended. Monitor the flow's performance to ensure it continues to function correctly as the project evolves.

Examples of Effective Bucket Customization

To illustrate how bucket customization can vary depending on the project type, here are a few examples:

Example 1: Software Development Project

- Buckets: "Backlog," "To Do," "In Progress," "Code Review," "Testing," "Completed"

- Customization: Tasks move sequentially through each bucket as they progress through the development cycle.

Example 2: Marketing Campaign

- Buckets: "Content Creation," "Design," "Approval," "Publishing," "Promotion,"

"Analytics"

- Customization: Buckets are organized by the type of work, allowing different teams (e.g., content writers, designers) to focus on their specific tasks.

Example 3: Event Planning

- Buckets: "Planning," "Vendor Coordination," "Marketing," "Logistics," "Execution," "Post-Event Follow-Up"

- Customization: Tasks are grouped by the stage of event planning, with specific tasks assigned to team members responsible for each area.

Conclusion

Customizing Plan Buckets in Microsoft Planner is a crucial step in ensuring that your plan is organized, efficient, and tailored to the specific needs of your project. By thoughtfully analyzing your project structure, creating and naming buckets, organizing them effectively, and leveraging advanced customization techniques like labels, checklists, and automation, you can create a Planner board that not only enhances task management but also fosters better collaboration and communication within your team.

As you continue to use Microsoft Planner, revisit and refine your bucket setup to adapt to changing project requirements and team feedback. By doing so, you'll ensure that your plan remains a powerful tool for achieving your project goals and driving your team's success.

2.2 Adding and Managing Tasks

2.2.1 Creating Tasks

Creating tasks in Microsoft Planner is a fundamental aspect of managing your work effectively. Tasks are the building blocks of any project or plan, allowing you to break down larger objectives into manageable pieces, assign responsibilities, and track progress. This section will guide you through the process of creating tasks in Microsoft Planner, ensuring that you can set up your plans in a way that promotes productivity and clarity.

Understanding the Role of Tasks

Before diving into the mechanics of creating tasks, it's important to understand their role within Microsoft Planner. Each task represents a specific action or deliverable that needs to be completed as part of your overall plan. Tasks help in organizing your work by defining what needs to be done, who is responsible, and when it should be completed. By creating clear and actionable tasks, you can ensure that your projects move forward efficiently and that everyone on your team knows their responsibilities.

Step-by-Step Guide to Creating a Task

1. Accessing the Plan:

   - To create a task, first, ensure that you are within the correct plan where the task will be added. Navigate to the desired plan from the Planner Hub or directly from the Microsoft Teams interface if your Planner is integrated with Teams.

2. Adding a New Task:

   - Once you're in the correct plan, locate the "Add task" button. This button is typically found under the bucket where you want to place the task. Click on "Add task" to start the creation process.

3. Entering Task Details:

   - After clicking "Add task," you'll see a simple form where you can enter the basic details of the task. At a minimum, you'll need to provide the task's name. This should be a clear and concise title that describes the action or deliverable. For example, instead of "Meeting," a more descriptive task name would be "Schedule team meeting to review project milestones."

4. Setting a Due Date:

- Below the task name, you'll find an option to set a due date. The due date is critical for time management, helping ensure that tasks are completed on schedule. Click on the calendar icon and select the appropriate date. This will automatically create a visual deadline that can be tracked within the Planner's calendar view and charts.

5. Assigning the Task:

- Tasks can be assigned to specific team members responsible for their completion. This is done by clicking the "Assign" button and selecting the person from the list of plan members. If the person is not already part of the plan, you can invite them to join before assignment. It's possible to assign a task to multiple people, which can be useful for collaborative efforts. However, be clear about who is the primary owner of the task to avoid confusion.

Customizing Task Details

Once the basic task is created, you can further customize it to ensure that all necessary information is captured and easily accessible.

1. Adding a Description:

- Each task can have a detailed description that provides more context or specific instructions. To add a description, click on the task name to open the task details pane. Here, you'll find a text box labeled "Description." Use this space to elaborate on what needs to be done, including any important notes, links, or references. A well-written description can significantly reduce the need for back-and-forth communication, as it makes the expectations clear upfront.

2. Attaching Files and Links:

- Microsoft Planner allows you to attach files directly to tasks, making it easy to keep all relevant documents in one place. You can upload files from your computer, link to documents in OneDrive, or even add URLs that direct to external resources. Attachments are particularly useful for tasks that require review or action on specific documents, such as "Review project proposal" or "Edit marketing brochure."

3. Adding Comments:

 - The comments section within a task is a collaborative space where team members can leave notes, ask questions, or provide updates. Comments are timestamped and tagged with the commenter's name, making it easy to track discussions. This feature is especially useful for tasks that require ongoing input or decisions from multiple stakeholders. For example, "Please review the attached draft and provide feedback by the end of the day" can be a comment that prompts immediate action.

4. Using Labels for Categorization:

 - Microsoft Planner offers color-coded labels that can be applied to tasks for additional categorization. Labels can represent anything from priority levels, types of tasks, or specific themes within the project. To add a label, click on the "Label" button within the task details pane, select a color, and then name the label. For example, you might use labels such as "High Priority," "Client Feedback," or "Internal Review." These labels help in quickly identifying and sorting tasks within a plan.

Task Dependencies and Sequencing

In many projects, tasks are interdependent, meaning that one task must be completed before another can begin. While Microsoft Planner does not natively support Gantt charts or detailed dependency tracking like Microsoft Project, you can still manage dependencies by carefully sequencing tasks and using visual cues.

1. Using Buckets for Sequencing:

 - Buckets in Microsoft Planner can be used to group tasks in a sequential order. For instance, you could create buckets labeled "Phase 1," "Phase 2," and "Phase 3" to represent different stages of the project. Within each bucket, arrange tasks in the order they need to be completed. This manual sequencing provides a visual roadmap of the project's progression.

2. Creating a Checklist for Subtasks:

 - For tasks that involve multiple steps, you can create a checklist within the task details pane. Each checklist item acts as a subtask that can be checked off as completed. This is particularly useful for complex tasks that require detailed tracking but do not necessarily need to be broken down into separate tasks within the Planner. For example, a task labeled

"Prepare for product launch" might have a checklist that includes "Finalize product specs," "Create marketing materials," and "Schedule launch event."

3. Assigning Deadlines Based on Dependencies:

- When setting due dates, consider the dependencies between tasks. Ensure that tasks that need to be completed first have earlier due dates. Communicate clearly with your team about these dependencies so that they understand the importance of meeting deadlines to avoid delays in the overall project timeline.

Task Prioritization

Not all tasks are of equal importance, and prioritizing tasks is essential to ensure that critical work is completed on time. Microsoft Planner provides several tools to help you prioritize tasks effectively.

1. Using Labels to Indicate Priority:

- As mentioned earlier, labels can be used to signify priority levels. Create labels such as "High Priority," "Medium Priority," and "Low Priority" and apply them to tasks accordingly. This makes it easy to filter and focus on the most important tasks at any given time.

2. Reordering Tasks Within Buckets:

- Tasks within a bucket can be reordered by simply dragging and dropping them into the desired sequence. Place higher-priority tasks at the top of the bucket to ensure they receive attention first. This visual cue helps keep the team focused on what matters most.

3. Communicating Priorities with the Team:

- While labels and ordering provide visual cues, it's also important to communicate priorities verbally or in writing during team meetings or updates. Ensure that everyone understands which tasks are critical and why, and adjust priorities as needed based on the project's evolving requirements.

Reviewing and Editing Tasks

As your project progresses, tasks may need to be updated, reassigned, or even removed. Microsoft Planner provides the flexibility to review and edit tasks easily.

1. Editing Task Details:

- At any time, you can click on a task to open the details pane and make edits. This includes changing the task name, due date, assigned team members, and any other information. Frequent review and adjustment of tasks are important for keeping your plan accurate and reflective of the current project status.

2. Reassigning Tasks:

- If the responsibility for a task needs to change, you can reassign it to another team member. Simply click on the "Assign" button and select a new person. The original assignee will be notified of the change, and the new assignee will receive a notification of their new task.

3. Marking Tasks as Complete:

- Once a task is finished, mark it as complete by checking the box next to the task name. Completed tasks will be visually distinguished in the Planner, often moving to the bottom of the bucket or being hidden, depending on your settings. This action not only helps in tracking progress but also provides a sense of accomplishment for the team.

4. Archiving or Deleting Tasks:

- If a task is no longer relevant, you can either delete it or archive it for future reference. Deleting a task removes it from the plan entirely, while archiving (by marking it as complete) keeps it in the plan but out of the active view. Archiving is useful for maintaining a record of all work done without cluttering the active task list.

Best Practices for Task Creation

To maximize the efficiency and effectiveness of task management in Microsoft Planner, consider the following best practices:

1. Be Specific and Clear:

- Task names should be specific and descriptive. Avoid vague terms like "Work on project" in favor of more detailed actions like "Draft initial project proposal." Clear task names help team members understand exactly what is expected without needing further clarification.

2. Break Down Large Tasks:

- If a task seems too large or complex, break it down into smaller, more manageable subtasks or create separate tasks. This makes it easier to track progress and reduces the likelihood of missed steps.

3. Regularly Review and Update Tasks:

- Periodically review your plan and update tasks as needed. This includes revising due dates, reassigning tasks, and adding new tasks as the project evolves. Regular maintenance of your plan ensures that it remains an accurate reflection of the project's current status.

4. Leverage Collaboration Features:

- Encourage team members to use the comments, attachments, and checklists within tasks to collaborate effectively. The more information shared within the task itself, the less time will be spent on follow-up communications.

By following these steps and best practices, you can create and manage tasks in Microsoft Planner in a way that enhances organization, accountability, and project success. Tasks are more than just a to-do list; they are a central element of your project's workflow, enabling you to track progress, manage resources, and achieve your goals efficiently.

2.2.2 Assigning Tasks to Team Members

Assigning tasks effectively is one of the core aspects of using Microsoft Planner. It not only helps distribute work evenly among team members but also ensures accountability and transparency within a project. This section will guide you through the best practices for assigning tasks to team members, making sure that everyone knows their responsibilities, deadlines, and how their tasks contribute to the overall project goals.

Understanding the Importance of Task Assignment

Before diving into the technical aspects of assigning tasks, it's essential to understand why this process is critical to project management:

1. Clear Responsibility: Assigning tasks ensures that each team member knows exactly what is expected of them. This clarity helps in reducing misunderstandings and conflicts that can arise when responsibilities are unclear.

2. Balanced Workload: By carefully assigning tasks, project managers can ensure that the workload is distributed fairly among team members. This balance prevents burnout and increases overall productivity.

3. Accountability: When a task is assigned to a specific individual, that person is held accountable for its completion. This accountability is vital for tracking progress and ensuring that deadlines are met.

4. Enhanced Collaboration: Assigning tasks promotes collaboration as team members are aware of who is working on what. It encourages communication and cooperation, which are crucial for the successful completion of any project.

5. Visibility and Tracking: Microsoft Planner allows you to monitor who is assigned to each task. This visibility is helpful for project managers to track progress, identify bottlenecks, and make necessary adjustments to keep the project on track.

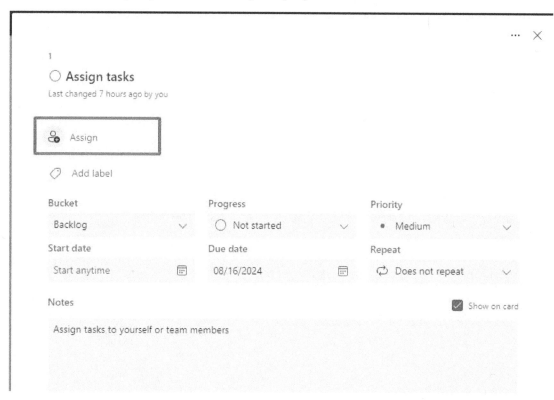

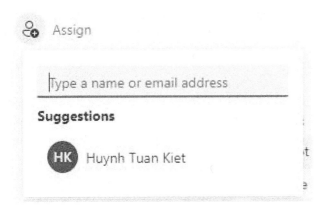

How to Assign Tasks in Microsoft Planner

Microsoft Planner makes task assignment straightforward and intuitive. Follow these steps to assign tasks to your team members:

1. Create or Select a Task: Start by creating a new task or selecting an existing one in your plan. If you're creating a new task, enter the task name and details as discussed in previous sections.

2. Locate the Assign Field: Once the task is created, locate the "Assign" field within the task details pane. This field is usually found under the task name or near the top of the task details.

3. Select Team Members: Click on the "Assign" field to open a drop-down list of all team members associated with the plan. You can either scroll through the list or start typing a team member's name to filter the results.

4. Assign the Task: Click on the team member's name to assign the task to them. You can assign a task to one or multiple team members, depending on the nature of the task. The assigned members will immediately receive a notification about their new task assignment.

5. Review and Save: After assigning the task, review the task details to ensure everything is correct. Once satisfied, save the task to confirm the assignment.

Best Practices for Task Assignment

Assigning tasks in Microsoft Planner goes beyond just selecting a name from a list. To maximize efficiency and ensure successful project outcomes, consider the following best practices:

1. Understand Your Team's Strengths and Weaknesses: Before assigning tasks, take the time to understand the strengths, weaknesses, and skill sets of your team members. Assign tasks based on their expertise to ensure that the right person is handling the right job.

2. Communicate Expectations Clearly: When assigning a task, ensure that the assignee understands what is expected of them. This includes the task objectives, deadlines, and any specific instructions. Use the task description field in Microsoft Planner to detail these expectations.

3. Assign Tasks Based on Availability: Always consider the current workload and availability of your team members. Assigning tasks to already overburdened team members can lead to delays and reduced quality of work. Use Planner's calendar view to gauge availability before assigning tasks.

4. Encourage Ownership: Encourage team members to take ownership of the tasks assigned to them. This ownership can be fostered by involving them in the task assignment process, allowing them to volunteer for tasks that align with their interests and skills.

5. Set Realistic Deadlines: Assign tasks with realistic deadlines that your team can meet without compromising quality. Overly ambitious deadlines can lead to stress and burnout, while overly lenient deadlines may result in procrastination.

6. Monitor Progress Regularly: After assigning tasks, regularly monitor progress to ensure that everything is on track. Use Microsoft Planner's progress tracking features to check in on task status and provide support where necessary.

7. Use Labels for Clarity: Utilize labels in Microsoft Planner to categorize tasks by type, priority, or department. Assigning tasks with clear labels helps team members quickly understand the nature of the task and its urgency.

8. Provide Feedback and Recognition: Once tasks are completed, provide feedback to the assignees. Positive feedback and recognition for a job well done can boost morale and encourage continuous improvement.

Assigning Tasks to Multiple Team Members

In some scenarios, a task might require the efforts of more than one person. Microsoft Planner allows you to assign a single task to multiple team members. Here's how you can effectively manage such tasks:

1. Define Roles Clearly: When assigning a task to multiple people, clearly define the roles and responsibilities of each team member. Use the task description field to specify who is responsible for what part of the task.

2. Encourage Collaboration: Tasks assigned to multiple people should encourage collaboration. Facilitate communication among the assignees to ensure they are working together effectively. Microsoft Planner's comment section can be useful for team members to discuss the task.

3. Monitor Joint Task Progress: Joint tasks can sometimes lead to confusion if roles are not clearly defined. Regularly monitor progress to ensure that all team members are contributing and that the task is moving forward as expected.

4. Use Subtasks for Clarity: If a task is too complex for joint ownership, consider breaking it down into smaller subtasks and assigning each subtask to a different team member. This approach provides clarity and ensures that all aspects of the task are covered.

Reassigning Tasks in Microsoft Planner

At times, you may need to reassign tasks due to changes in team composition, availability, or workload. Microsoft Planner allows for easy reassignment of tasks, ensuring flexibility in project management.

1. Open the Task: To reassign a task, start by opening the task details.

2. Remove Current Assignee(s): Click on the assigned team member's name and select the option to remove them from the task.

3. Select a New Assignee: Follow the standard task assignment process to select a new team member for the task.

4. Communicate the Change: After reassigning the task, communicate the change to both the previous and new assignee to ensure a smooth transition. Update the task description if necessary to reflect any changes in expectations or deadlines.

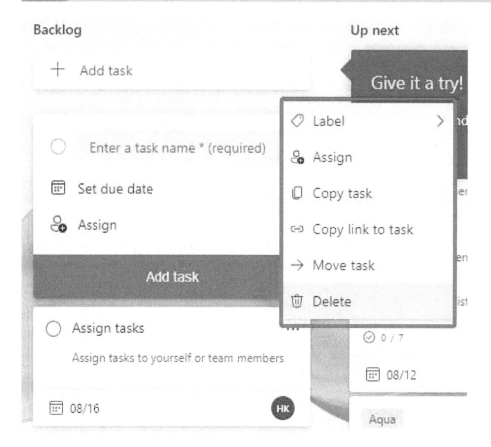

Handling Task Conflicts

Conflicts can arise when tasks are not clearly defined or when multiple team members are assigned to the same task without proper role delineation. Here's how to handle such situations:

1. Clarify Task Objectives: If conflicts arise due to unclear task objectives, revisit the task description and clarify the goals. Make sure all team members understand their specific roles and responsibilities.

2. Resolve Conflicts Promptly: Address task conflicts as soon as they are identified. Engage the involved team members in a discussion to resolve misunderstandings and find a mutually agreeable solution.

3. Reassign Tasks if Necessary: If a conflict cannot be resolved, consider reassigning the task to another team member who is better suited or available to complete it.

4. Document Changes: Keep a record of any changes made to task assignments, including the reasons for reassignment or role adjustments. This documentation can be helpful for future reference and for maintaining transparency within the team.

Using Microsoft Planner for Agile Task Management

Microsoft Planner is an excellent tool for teams using Agile methodologies. In Agile, tasks are often referred to as user stories, and they are managed in short cycles called sprints. Here's how to assign tasks in an Agile environment using Planner:

1. Create User Stories as Tasks: In Agile, user stories describe a feature or function from the end-user perspective. Create these user stories as tasks in Microsoft Planner.

2. Assign Tasks for Sprints: At the beginning of each sprint, assign user stories (tasks) to the relevant team members. Ensure that the tasks are manageable within the sprint duration.

3. Use Buckets as Sprints: Organize tasks by sprint using buckets. This setup helps you track which tasks are part of the current sprint and which are slated for future sprints.

4. Monitor Sprint Progress: Use Planner's progress tracking features to monitor the completion of tasks during the sprint. Adjust assignments as needed to ensure the sprint goals are met.

5. Retrospective and Feedback: At the end of each sprint, hold a retrospective meeting to review what went well and what could be improved. Use the feedback to refine task assignment practices in future sprints.

Conclusion

Assigning tasks to team members in Microsoft Planner is a crucial aspect of project management that ensures clarity, accountability, and efficiency. By following the best practices outlined in this section, you can create a productive and harmonious work environment where tasks are managed effectively, deadlines are met, and goals are achieved. Whether you're managing a small team or a large project, mastering task assignment in Microsoft Planner will enhance your ability to lead your team to success.

2.2.3 Setting Due Dates and Priorities

Effectively managing tasks in Microsoft Planner involves more than just creating and assigning them. Setting due dates and prioritizing tasks are critical steps that help ensure your projects are completed on time and with the appropriate focus. This section will delve into the processes of assigning due dates and prioritizing tasks, offering best practices to maximize productivity and efficiency in your work.

Understanding Due Dates in Microsoft Planner

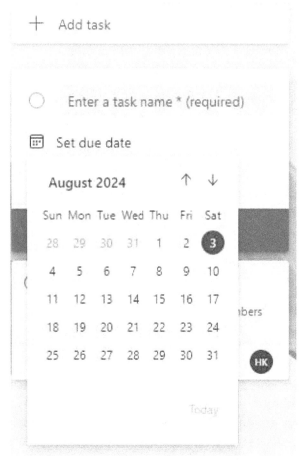

Due dates are a crucial element of task management. They serve as deadlines that guide team members toward timely completion of their responsibilities. Setting due dates in Microsoft Planner is straightforward, but understanding how to leverage them effectively requires a strategic approach.

When you set a due date for a task in Microsoft Planner, you're essentially setting a target date for the task's completion. This date becomes visible to all team members who have access to the plan, providing clear expectations and reducing the likelihood of tasks falling behind schedule.

How to Set Due Dates:

1. Creating a New Task:

   - Navigate to the specific plan where you want to create a task.

- Click on the "+ Add Task" button under the appropriate bucket.

- Enter the task name, and click on the calendar icon labeled "Due date."

2. Assigning a Due Date:

- Select the due date by clicking on the calendar icon. A calendar view will appear, allowing you to pick a specific date.

- Once you select the date, it will be saved automatically, and the due date will appear on the task card.

3. Modifying Due Dates:

- If you need to change the due date, click on the task to open its details, then click on the current due date. Choose a new date from the calendar, and the task will update accordingly.

4. Recurring Tasks:

- For tasks that repeat regularly, you can set up recurring due dates. Although Microsoft Planner doesn't directly support recurring tasks, you can create multiple tasks with the same name and set due dates at regular intervals.

Best Practices for Setting Due Dates:

- Align with Project Milestones: Ensure that task due dates align with overall project deadlines. This alignment helps maintain a steady workflow and prevents bottlenecks.

- Allow Buffer Time: Avoid setting due dates right before critical project milestones. Allow some buffer time for unexpected delays or additional review processes.

- Communicate Expectations: When assigning tasks with due dates, clearly communicate the importance of adhering to deadlines. This helps team members prioritize their work accordingly.

- Regularly Review and Adjust: As the project progresses, regularly review task due dates. Adjust them if necessary to accommodate changes in project scope or unforeseen delays.

Prioritizing Tasks in Microsoft Planner

Prioritization is essential for effective task management, especially when juggling multiple projects or tasks with varying levels of importance. Microsoft Planner allows you to prioritize tasks by categorizing them and using visual indicators to denote their urgency or importance.

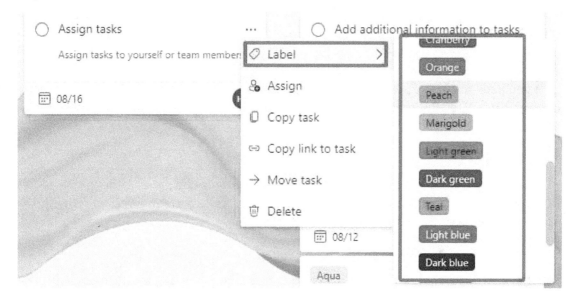

How to Prioritize Tasks:

1. Using Labels:

  - Microsoft Planner provides color-coded labels that can be used to prioritize tasks. You can assign labels to tasks based on their urgency or importance.

  - For example, you could use a red label for high-priority tasks, a yellow label for medium-priority tasks, and a green label for low-priority tasks.

2. Customizing Task Titles:

  - Include priority indicators directly in the task titles, such as adding "[High Priority]" or "[Urgent]" to the beginning of a task name. This makes it immediately clear to team members which tasks require immediate attention.

3. Grouping Tasks by Buckets:

- Buckets can also be used to organize tasks by priority. For instance, you can create separate buckets for "High Priority," "Medium Priority," and "Low Priority" tasks.

- This method is particularly useful for plans that involve a large number of tasks, as it visually separates tasks by their urgency.

4. Sorting Tasks:

- Within each bucket, you can manually sort tasks based on their priority. Drag and drop the most critical tasks to the top of the list, ensuring they are seen and addressed first.

Best Practices for Prioritizing Tasks:

- Identify Critical Path Tasks: In project management, the critical path refers to the sequence of tasks that must be completed on time for the project to be finished on schedule. Identify these tasks and prioritize them accordingly.

- Balance Priorities Across Team Members: Ensure that no single team member is overloaded with high-priority tasks. Distribute the workload evenly to maintain productivity and morale.

- Reassess Priorities Regularly: Project priorities can change as new information becomes available or as project scope evolves. Regularly reassess task priorities and adjust as necessary.

- Use Priority as a Planning Tool: During project planning, use task prioritization as a tool to sequence work effectively. Determine which tasks are dependencies for others and prioritize accordingly.

Integrating Due Dates and Prioritization for Effective Task Management

While setting due dates and prioritizing tasks are valuable on their own, their true power lies in their integration. Effective task management involves not only knowing when a task is due but also understanding its importance in the broader context of the project. By combining these elements, you can create a well-structured plan that drives your project forward efficiently.

Combining Due Dates and Prioritization:

1. Plan with Priority in Mind: Start by identifying high-priority tasks and setting due dates for them. Ensure that these tasks have reasonable deadlines that reflect their importance.

2. Sequence Tasks Logically: Once high-priority tasks are scheduled, sequence other tasks in a way that supports the overall project timeline. Lower-priority tasks can have more flexible due dates.

3. Monitor Progress: Use Microsoft Planner's chart view to monitor task completion rates. This view can help you identify if high-priority tasks are being completed on time or if adjustments are needed.

4. Communicate Clearly: Regularly update your team on task priorities and due dates. Use team meetings or updates within Microsoft Planner to keep everyone aligned.

Examples of Effective Task Management:

- Example 1: Product Launch Plan

 - In a product launch plan, tasks related to finalizing the product design and obtaining necessary approvals should be marked as high priority with firm due dates. Tasks like promotional content creation, while important, can have more flexible deadlines and be marked as medium priority.

- Example 2: Event Planning

 - For an event, tasks like booking the venue and confirming speakers are critical and should be prioritized with early due dates. Secondary tasks like creating event materials can follow, with deadlines closer to the event date.

Leveraging Microsoft Planner's Features for Enhanced Task Management

Microsoft Planner offers several features that can further enhance your ability to manage due dates and priorities effectively.

Planner Hub and My Tasks:

- The Planner Hub provides an overview of all your plans, allowing you to see due dates and task priorities across different projects. Use this view to monitor your workload and ensure that high-priority tasks are on track.

- The "My Tasks" view aggregates all tasks assigned to you from different plans, making it easier to manage your personal priorities and deadlines.

Notifications and Alerts:

- Set up email notifications or mobile alerts to remind you of upcoming due dates. Microsoft Planner allows you to customize notifications so that you're alerted to important deadlines without being overwhelmed by less critical updates.

Integration with Outlook and Teams:

- Integrate Microsoft Planner with Outlook to sync tasks with your calendar. This integration ensures that you're always aware of task deadlines and can plan your schedule accordingly.

- Use Microsoft Teams to discuss task priorities and deadlines in real-time with your team. Integration between Planner and Teams allows you to link tasks directly within your team's communication channels.

Conclusion: Mastering Due Dates and Prioritization

Setting due dates and prioritizing tasks in Microsoft Planner are fundamental skills for effective project management. By strategically assigning deadlines and understanding task importance, you can guide your team toward successful project completion. Remember, the key to mastering these skills lies in regular review, clear communication, and leveraging the full range of tools that Microsoft Planner offers.

Whether you're managing a complex project with multiple dependencies or simply organizing daily tasks, the principles outlined in this section will help you stay organized, meet your deadlines, and achieve your goals.

2.3 Organizing and Categorizing Tasks

Organizing and categorizing tasks within Microsoft Planner is crucial for maintaining clarity and focus in your project management workflow. Effective organization not only enhances productivity but also ensures that every team member is aligned with the project's objectives and timelines. In this section, we will explore how to effectively use labels for categorization, group tasks by buckets, and create task checklists. We'll start by delving into one of the most powerful features of Microsoft Planner: labels.

2.3.1 Using Labels for Categorization

Labels in Microsoft Planner provide a versatile way to categorize and visually distinguish tasks. By assigning labels, you can quickly filter and sort tasks based on their characteristics, priority, or status, thereby making it easier to manage complex projects with multiple moving parts.

Understanding the Purpose of Labels

Labels are essentially tags that you can assign to tasks within a plan to categorize them according to your needs. Each label can be customized with a name and a color, offering a visual cue that makes it easy to identify tasks at a glance. Labels are particularly useful for grouping tasks that share common attributes, such as:

- Task Priority: You might use labels to indicate the priority of tasks, such as "High Priority," "Medium Priority," and "Low Priority." Assigning labels based on priority helps ensure that team members focus on the most critical tasks first.

- Task Type: Labels can categorize tasks by type, such as "Design," "Development," "Testing," and "Documentation." This is especially useful in multi-disciplinary teams where different members are responsible for different types of work.

- Task Status: Although Planner provides basic status tracking (Not Started, In Progress, Completed), you can use labels for more detailed status tracking, such as "Awaiting Approval," "On Hold," or "Needs Review."

- Team or Department: If your project involves multiple teams or departments, you can label tasks according to the responsible team, such as "Marketing," "Sales," "Engineering," or "Finance." This way, team members can easily filter tasks relevant to their department.

Creating and Assigning Labels

To create and assign labels in Microsoft Planner, follow these steps:

1. Open the Task: Navigate to the task you want to label and click on it to open the task details pane.

2. Add a Label: On the task details pane, you will see a section labeled "Labels" with a series of color-coded buttons. Click on any of these buttons to select a label for the task.

3. Customize the Label: By default, the labels are unnamed and simply represented by colors. Click on the label color to rename it to something more meaningful for your project, such as "Urgent," "Bug Fix," or "Research."

4. Assign Multiple Labels: You can assign more than one label to a task if it fits into multiple categories. For example, a task might be labeled as both "High Priority" and "Development."

5. Save and Close: Once you've assigned and customized the labels, simply close the task details pane. The labels will now be visible on the task card within your plan.

Using Labels to Filter and Sort Tasks

Labels become even more powerful when you use them to filter and sort tasks in your Planner view. Here's how you can do it:

1. Filter by Label: In the plan view, click on the "Filter" button in the top-right corner. This will open a panel where you can filter tasks by various criteria, including labels. Select the label(s) you want to filter by, and Planner will display only the tasks that match those labels.

2. Sort by Label: While Microsoft Planner doesn't currently offer direct sorting by label, you can manually organize your tasks by dragging and dropping them into groups based on their labels. Alternatively, you can use the "Group by" feature to group tasks by different criteria, such as progress or due date, and then manually arrange them according to labels.

3. Combining Labels with Other Filters: You can combine label filtering with other filters, such as due date or assigned user, to create a highly customized view of your tasks. For example, you might filter tasks that are labeled "High Priority" and are due within the next week, providing a focused view of urgent tasks.

Best Practices for Using Labels

To make the most of labels in Microsoft Planner, consider the following best practices:

- Consistency is Key: Ensure that your team agrees on a consistent labeling system. For example, everyone should understand what each label color represents and use them accordingly. This consistency helps avoid confusion and ensures that labels are meaningful across the entire team.

- Limit the Number of Labels: While it might be tempting to create a label for every possible category, too many labels can lead to clutter and confusion. Aim to create a manageable number of labels (5-10) that cover the most important categories for your project.

- Regularly Review and Update Labels: As projects evolve, some labels might become obsolete, or new categories might emerge. Regularly review and update your labels to ensure they remain relevant and useful.

- Use Labels in Combination with Other Features: Labels are most effective when used in combination with other Planner features, such as buckets and checklists. For example, you might use buckets to organize tasks by phase and labels to categorize them by priority.

Common Challenges and Solutions

While labels are a powerful tool, they can present some challenges if not used properly. Here are some common issues and how to address them:

- Overlapping Categories: Sometimes, tasks might fall into overlapping categories, making it difficult to decide on a label. In such cases, use multiple labels but prioritize the most important category for filtering and sorting purposes.

- Inconsistent Label Use: Inconsistent use of labels can lead to confusion and miscommunication. Establish clear guidelines for when and how to use each label, and ensure that all team members follow these guidelines.

- Label Overload: Too many labels can make it difficult to quickly identify the most important tasks. To avoid label overload, periodically audit your labels and remove any that are no longer needed or are rarely used.

By using labels effectively, you can significantly enhance the organization of your tasks within Microsoft Planner, making it easier to manage projects and achieve your goals.

2.3.2 Grouping Tasks by Buckets

Grouping tasks by buckets in Microsoft Planner is a powerful way to organize workstreams, projects, and daily tasks. It allows teams to segment their work into meaningful categories, making it easier to manage complex projects, prioritize work, and ensure that nothing falls through the cracks. In this section, we will delve into the concept of buckets, explore their strategic importance, and provide a step-by-step guide on how to effectively use them to optimize task management.

Understanding Buckets in Microsoft Planner

Buckets in Microsoft Planner serve as containers for tasks. They are used to group tasks that share a common attribute, objective, or phase within a project. For example, in a marketing campaign, you might have buckets such as "Content Creation," "Design," "Social Media," and "Analytics." Each bucket contains tasks that fall under its respective category, allowing for better organization and oversight.

Buckets provide a visual way to manage tasks, enabling teams to see at a glance how tasks are progressing within each category. This feature is particularly beneficial in Agile project management, where tasks can be moved from one bucket to another as they progress through different stages of completion.

Strategic Importance of Grouping Tasks by Buckets

The strategic use of buckets goes beyond simple task categorization. It plays a crucial role in enhancing productivity, facilitating collaboration, and improving project visibility. Here's how:

1. Improved Task Organization: By grouping tasks into buckets, teams can avoid the chaos of having all tasks listed in a single, overwhelming to-do list. Buckets help in creating a structured approach to task management, allowing team members to focus on specific areas of a project without losing sight of the bigger picture.

2. Enhanced Focus and Prioritization: Buckets allow teams to prioritize tasks within a specific category. For example, in a software development project, critical bugs might be placed in a "High Priority" bucket, ensuring they are addressed before other tasks. This focused approach helps in managing workloads efficiently and ensures that high-priority tasks are completed on time.

3. Facilitating Collaboration: When working in teams, buckets can be used to assign tasks to different departments or individuals. For instance, in a product launch, you might have separate buckets for marketing, product development, and customer support. This clear delineation of responsibilities fosters better collaboration and communication among team members.

4. Visibility and Tracking: Buckets provide a high-level overview of the project's progress. By simply looking at the number of tasks in each bucket, project managers can gauge which areas of the project are on track and which ones require attention. This visibility is crucial for making informed decisions and keeping the project on schedule.

5. Adaptability and Flexibility: As projects evolve, tasks can be easily moved between buckets. For example, a task that was initially in the "In Progress" bucket can be shifted to the "Completed" bucket once it's finished. This flexibility allows teams to adapt quickly to changing priorities and project requirements.

How to Group Tasks by Buckets in Microsoft Planner

Now that we've explored the importance of buckets, let's walk through the process of grouping tasks by buckets in Microsoft Planner.

 Step 1: Create a New Plan Before you can group tasks into buckets, you need to have a plan in place. If you haven't already created a plan, follow these steps:

1. Open Microsoft Planner and click on "New Plan".

2. Enter a name for your plan and choose whether you want it to be public or private.

3. Click "Create Plan" to set it up.

Once your plan is created, you can start adding tasks and organizing them into buckets.

Step 2: Set Up Buckets

1. Navigate to Your Plan: Go to the plan where you want to set up buckets.

2. Add a Bucket: By default, Microsoft Planner creates a bucket named "To Do". To add a new bucket, click on the "+ Add new bucket" link on the right side of the "To Do" bucket. Enter a name for your new bucket that reflects the category or phase of the tasks it will contain.

3. Create Multiple Buckets: Repeat the process to create additional buckets for different categories of tasks. For example, in a content marketing plan, you might create buckets named "Content Ideas", "Writing", "Editing", and "Publishing".

Step 3: Assign Tasks to Buckets

1. Create a Task: Within your plan, create a task by clicking "+ Add task" under the appropriate bucket. Enter the task name, set a due date, and assign it to a team member if needed.

2. Move Tasks Between Buckets: If you've already created tasks and want to move them into a different bucket, simply drag and drop the task card into the desired bucket. This functionality allows for easy reorganization of tasks as the project progresses.

3. Edit Bucket Assignments: To change the bucket assignment of a task, click on the task card to open its details, then select a different bucket from the drop-down menu.

Step 4: Customize Buckets for Better Management

1. Prioritize Tasks Within Buckets: While buckets organize tasks by category, you can further prioritize tasks within each bucket by reordering them. Drag the task cards up or down within the bucket to reflect their priority.

2. Use Labels for Additional Categorization: To add another layer of organization, use labels to color-code tasks based on criteria such as urgency, department, or status. For example, you might use a red label for tasks that are urgent or a green label for tasks that are on track.

3. Set Up Custom Views: Use Microsoft Planner's custom views to filter tasks by bucket, due date, or label. This can help team members focus on specific tasks or buckets without distractions.

Step 5: Review and Adjust Buckets Regularly

1. Conduct Regular Reviews: Periodically review your buckets and the tasks within them to ensure that everything is on track. This is particularly important in Agile and iterative project management, where priorities may shift over time.

2. Adjust Buckets as Needed: As the project evolves, you may find that you need to add new buckets or reorganize existing ones. For example, as a project nears completion, you might add a "Final Review" bucket for last-minute checks. Alternatively, if a bucket becomes too crowded, consider breaking it down into smaller, more focused buckets.

3. Archive Completed Buckets: Once a bucket is no longer needed (e.g., all tasks within it are completed), consider archiving it to keep your plan uncluttered. While Microsoft Planner doesn't have a built-in archive function, you can move completed tasks to a "Completed" bucket or simply delete the bucket if it's no longer relevant.

Best Practices for Using Buckets in Microsoft Planner

To get the most out of buckets in Microsoft Planner, consider the following best practices:

1. Keep Buckets Simple and Focused: Avoid creating too many buckets, as this can lead to complexity and confusion. Aim for a balance between having enough buckets to organize your tasks effectively and keeping the structure simple enough to be manageable.

2. Align Buckets with Project Phases or Goals: When setting up buckets, consider how they align with your project's phases or goals. For instance, in a software development project, buckets might correspond to stages like "Requirements Gathering", "Design", "Development", and "Testing".

3. Regularly Update Buckets and Tasks: Ensure that buckets and their tasks are kept up to date. Regularly check for tasks that need to be moved to a different bucket or that require a change in priority.

4. Communicate Bucket Structure to the Team: Clearly communicate the purpose of each bucket to your team members. This helps ensure that everyone is on the same page and understands where tasks should be placed.

5. Use Buckets to Reflect Workflows: If your team follows a specific workflow or process, set up buckets that mirror these stages. For example, in a content creation workflow, you might have buckets for "Drafting", "Review", "Approval", and "Publication".

6. Combine Buckets with Labels and Filters: Enhance your task management by using buckets in conjunction with labels and filters. This combination allows for a more granular organization of tasks and makes it easier to focus on specific subsets of work.

7. Leverage Planner's Integration with Other Tools: Take advantage of Microsoft Planner's integration with other tools like Microsoft Teams and Outlook. For example, you can set up notifications in Teams for tasks in a specific bucket, or use Outlook to schedule time to work on tasks within a particular bucket.

Real-World Applications of Grouping Tasks by Buckets

Let's explore some real-world scenarios where grouping tasks by buckets in Microsoft Planner can be particularly beneficial:

1. Product Development: In a product development project, you might create buckets for "Research", "Design", "Prototyping", "Testing", and "Launch". This structure helps the team focus on different stages of development and ensures that tasks are completed in the correct sequence.

2. Event Planning: For event planning, buckets could include "Logistics", "Marketing", "Speakers", "Registrations", and "Post-Event Follow-Up". Each bucket contains tasks related to its specific aspect of the event, helping to keep the planning process organized and on track.

3. Sales and Marketing Campaigns: A sales and marketing campaign might have buckets for "Lead Generation", "Content Creation", "Email Campaigns", "Social Media", and "Analytics". This approach ensures that all tasks related to the campaign are properly categorized and managed.

4. IT Projects: In an IT project, you could create buckets such as "Requirements Gathering", "Development", "Testing", "Deployment", and "Support". This structure aligns with the typical phases of an IT project, making it easier to track progress and manage resources.

5. Customer Support: For a customer support team, buckets might include "New Tickets", "In Progress", "Escalated", and "Resolved". This setup helps the team prioritize and manage support tickets based on their status.

Conclusion

Grouping tasks by buckets in Microsoft Planner is a versatile and effective way to organize work, streamline project management, and enhance team collaboration. By strategically setting up and managing buckets, you can create a clear and structured approach to task management that aligns with your project goals and team workflows.

Whether you're managing a small team or overseeing a large project, the ability to group tasks by buckets in Microsoft Planner empowers you to keep everything organized, prioritize work efficiently, and ensure that your projects are completed on time and within scope. By following the steps and best practices outlined in this section, you can harness the full potential of buckets to improve your task management and achieve your project objectives.

2.3.3 Creating Task Checklists

Creating task checklists within Microsoft Planner is a powerful way to break down larger tasks into smaller, manageable steps. This feature enables you to keep track of detailed actions required to complete a task, ensuring nothing is overlooked. Task checklists can enhance productivity, promote accountability, and improve task completion rates, especially in collaborative environments.

Understanding the Importance of Task Checklists

In project management, a task checklist serves as a mini roadmap within a larger project. Whether you're managing a simple to-do list or a complex project, checklists ensure that every necessary step is documented and completed. This approach is particularly beneficial when a task involves multiple steps or when the task must be completed by several team members.

Benefits of Using Task Checklists:

1. Clarity: Checklists provide a clear breakdown of what needs to be done, reducing ambiguity and ensuring that every task component is identified.

2. Focus: They help team members stay focused on the specific steps required to complete a task, preventing them from getting overwhelmed by the overall task's complexity.

3. Accountability: With checklists, it's easier to assign specific steps to team members, promoting ownership and accountability.

4. Progress Tracking: As each step in the checklist is completed, it visually tracks progress, giving team members and managers a sense of accomplishment and keeping everyone informed of the task's status.

Creating Task Checklists in Microsoft Planner

Creating a task checklist in Microsoft Planner is a straightforward process that can be tailored to fit the specific needs of your project. The steps outlined below will guide you through creating and managing checklists effectively.

Step 1: Creating a New Task

Before adding a checklist, you need to create a task within your plan:

- Open Your Plan: Navigate to the plan where you want to create the task.

  - Add Task: Click on the "+ Add Task" button in the relevant bucket or section of your plan.

- Name the Task: Enter a descriptive title for the task, clearly indicating what needs to be done.

- Assign Task (Optional): If necessary, assign the task to one or more team members by clicking on the "Assign" button and selecting the appropriate individuals.

Step 2: Adding a Checklist to the Task

Once your task is created, you can begin adding items to your checklist:

- Open Task Details: Click on the task name to open the task details panel.

- Locate the Checklist Option: In the task details panel, you'll find the option to add a checklist, usually located under the "Description" or "Notes" section.

- Add Checklist Items: Start by entering the first item of your checklist in the provided field and press "Enter" or click "Add item" to add it to the checklist.

- Continue Adding Items: Repeat the process for each subsequent item until all necessary steps are included in the checklist.

Step 3: Customizing the Checklist

Microsoft Planner allows you to customize your checklist to better suit your project's needs:

- Reordering Items: Drag and drop items within the checklist to prioritize or rearrange steps according to their importance or sequence.

- Assigning Specific Checklist Items (Advanced): Although Planner doesn't allow assigning individual checklist items to different users, you can split a task into sub-tasks and then assign these to different team members.

- Marking Items as Complete: As team members work through the checklist, they can click the checkbox next to each item to mark it as complete. This provides a visual indication of progress.

Best Practices for Using Task Checklists

To maximize the effectiveness of your task checklists, consider the following best practices:

1. Be Detailed but Concise:

When creating checklist items, ensure that each item is detailed enough to be actionable but concise enough to be easily understood. Avoid vague descriptions that might confuse team members.

2. Prioritize Checklist Items:

If certain steps need to be completed before others, make sure to list these first. Reordering items in your checklist based on their importance or dependency on other tasks can help ensure a logical workflow.

3. Use Checklists for Repetitive Tasks:

For tasks that are recurring or involve repetitive steps, consider creating a checklist template that can be reused across different tasks. This can save time and ensure consistency in task execution.

4. Regularly Review and Update Checklists:

Checklists should be dynamic, not static. As a project progresses, new steps might need to be added, or existing steps might need to be adjusted. Regularly reviewing and updating checklists ensures they remain relevant and accurate.

5. Encourage Team Collaboration:

Encourage team members to contribute to checklist creation, especially in collaborative projects. Involving the team can lead to more comprehensive checklists and ensure that all necessary steps are considered.

6. Monitor Checklist Progress:

Use the visual progress indication provided by completed checklist items to monitor the status of a task. If items are not being completed as expected, investigate the cause and take corrective action if necessary.

Examples of Effective Task Checklists

To illustrate how task checklists can be effectively utilized in different scenarios, here are a few examples:

Example 1: Marketing Campaign Launch

Task: Prepare for the Product Launch Event

- Checklist:

  1. Design event invitations

  2. Compile guest list

  3. Send invitations

  4. Confirm event venue

  5. Arrange catering

  6. Prepare event materials

  7. Conduct final rehearsal

In this example, the task checklist provides a clear sequence of steps required to successfully prepare for the product launch event. Each item can be ticked off as it's completed, ensuring that nothing is overlooked in the planning process.

Example 2: Software Development

Task: Develop New Feature for Application

- Checklist:

  1. Gather feature requirements

  2. Create wireframes

  3. Develop code for the feature

  4. Conduct code review

  5. Test feature functionality

  6. Debug and fix issues

  7. Deploy feature to production

  8. Document feature details

This checklist breaks down the development of a new software feature into specific tasks, making it easier for the development team to track progress and ensure all necessary steps are completed.

Example 3: Event Planning

Task: Plan Corporate Retreat

- Checklist:

  1. Select retreat location

  2. Book accommodations

  3. Arrange transportation

  4. Schedule team-building activities

  5. Prepare agenda and materials

  6. Confirm attendance

  7. Coordinate catering

  8. Finalize event itinerary

The checklist in this example helps an event planner ensure that all logistical details for the corporate retreat are handled systematically, promoting a well-organized event.

Challenges and Solutions When Using Task Checklists

While task checklists are highly effective, there are some challenges that teams may encounter:

1. Overloading the Checklist:

  Challenge: Too many items in a checklist can overwhelm team members and reduce the effectiveness of the checklist.

  Solution: Break down large tasks into smaller sub-tasks, each with its own checklist. This can make the workload more manageable and help maintain focus.

2. Lack of Specificity:

Challenge: Checklist items that are too vague can lead to confusion and miscommunication.

Solution: Be as specific as possible when creating checklist items. If a step requires clarification, include additional notes or instructions within the task description.

3. Incomplete Checklists:

Challenge: Important steps may be overlooked when creating a checklist, leading to incomplete task execution.

Solution: Collaborate with team members to ensure that all necessary steps are identified and included in the checklist. Regularly review and update checklists as the project evolves.

4. Checklist Fatigue:

Challenge: Repetitive or overly detailed checklists can lead to checklist fatigue, where team members become less engaged with the process.

Solution: Keep checklists focused and relevant. Avoid including unnecessary steps and periodically refresh the checklist to keep it aligned with project goals.

Conclusion

Task checklists in Microsoft Planner are a versatile and powerful tool for breaking down tasks into actionable steps. By effectively creating and managing checklists, you can enhance clarity, focus, and accountability within your team. Whether you are working on a simple task or a complex project, the use of checklists ensures that every detail is attended to, fostering a more organized and efficient workflow.

As you incorporate task checklists into your project management process, remember to continuously review and adapt them to meet the changing needs of your projects. With thoughtful planning and execution, checklists can become an indispensable part of your toolkit for achieving your goals in Microsoft Planner.

CHAPTER III
Collaborating with Your Team

3.1 Sharing Plans and Tasks

Sharing plans and tasks within Microsoft Planner is a fundamental aspect of teamwork and collaboration. It allows teams to stay synchronized, manage workloads effectively, and ensure that everyone is aligned with project goals and timelines. This section will explore how to invite team members to a plan, assign roles and permissions, and collaborate on tasks, all of which are crucial for maximizing the potential of Microsoft Planner in a team environment.

3.1.1 Inviting Team Members to a Plan

Inviting team members to a plan is the first step in fostering collaboration within Microsoft Planner. The process of inviting team members is designed to be straightforward, ensuring that teams can quickly get started on projects and focus on their work without technical hurdles. This section covers the steps involved in inviting team members, considerations for ensuring proper access, and tips for managing invitations.

Step-by-Step Process for Inviting Team Members

1. Access the Plan: Begin by navigating to the specific plan you want to share with your team members. Once in the plan, you will find an option labeled "Members" or "Add Members" typically located at the top or side of the Planner interface.

2. Add Members: Click on the "Members" button to bring up a dialog box where you can enter the names or email addresses of the team members you wish to invite. Microsoft Planner integrates seamlessly with Office 365, which means you can easily add anyone within your organization's directory.

3. Send Invitations: After entering the names or email addresses, click "Add" or "Send" to invite these members to your plan. The invited members will receive a notification via email or within Microsoft Planner, alerting them that they have been added to the plan.

4. Confirm Membership: The new members will appear in the "Members" section of your plan. From here, you can confirm that they have been added successfully and check their roles within the plan.

Best Practices for Inviting Team Members

When inviting team members to a plan, it's important to follow best practices to ensure effective collaboration:

- Clearly Define Roles: Before inviting team members, ensure that each person understands their role within the plan. This clarity helps prevent confusion and ensures that everyone knows what is expected of them.

- Communicate the Purpose: When sending invitations, include a brief message or follow-up communication explaining the purpose of the plan and how each member will contribute. This step sets the context and helps team members understand the plan's objectives.

- Manage Plan Visibility: Depending on the nature of the project, you may need to manage the visibility of the plan. For sensitive projects, restrict access to only those who need it. Microsoft Planner allows you to control who can view and edit the plan, ensuring that information is shared appropriately.

Considerations for Adding External Users

In some cases, you may need to collaborate with external partners or stakeholders who are not part of your organization. Microsoft Planner supports adding external users, provided they have an Office 365 account.

- Adding External Members: To add external users, follow the same process as you would for internal team members. Enter their email addresses, and they will receive an invitation to join the plan.

- Security Considerations: When working with external members, be mindful of the security and confidentiality of your plan's contents. Ensure that external users are only given access to the information they need.

- Communication with External Members: Clearly communicate the expectations and the scope of their involvement. Provide any necessary guidance on how to use Microsoft Planner if they are not familiar with the tool.

Managing Invitations and Membership

Once team members have been invited, you may need to manage the membership of your plan over time. This could involve adding new members, removing those who are no longer involved, or adjusting roles.

- Adding New Members: As your project evolves, you may need to bring additional team members on board. The process is identical to the initial invitation process. Just make sure to onboard new members effectively by bringing them up to speed on the plan's progress and their responsibilities.

- Removing Members: If a team member leaves the project or organization, it's important to remove their access to the plan. You can do this by navigating to the "Members" section, selecting the user, and choosing the option to remove them.

- Adjusting Roles: As the project progresses, you may need to adjust the roles and permissions of team members. Microsoft Planner allows you to change roles from member to owner and vice versa. This flexibility helps ensure that the right people have the right level of access at all times.

Communication Around Invitations

Effective communication around the invitation process is key to successful collaboration. When inviting team members:

- Send a Welcome Message: After sending an invitation, consider sending a separate welcome message to provide context, outline expectations, and offer support for using Microsoft Planner.

- Follow Up: If a team member hasn't responded to the invitation or hasn't engaged with the plan, follow up to ensure they received the invitation and understand how to access and use the plan.

- Clarify Roles and Responsibilities: Use the invitation process as an opportunity to clarify each team member's role and responsibilities within the plan. This ensures everyone is on the same page from the start.

Common Challenges and Solutions

While inviting team members is generally a smooth process, there can be challenges:

- Invitation Not Received: If a team member doesn't receive the invitation, check for typos in the email address, ensure the email didn't go to spam, or resend the invitation.

- Access Issues: Sometimes, team members might face access issues due to permission settings. Review the plan's settings to ensure that all invited members have the appropriate access.

- External User Limitations: External users might face limitations depending on their Office 365 setup. If they encounter issues, work with your IT department or the external user's IT department to resolve them.

Leveraging Office 365 Groups for Invitations

Microsoft Planner is integrated with Office 365 Groups, which can streamline the process of inviting members to a plan:

- Using Existing Groups: If your team is already part of an Office 365 Group, you can invite the entire group to your plan in one step. This saves time and ensures consistent access for all group members.

- Creating a New Group: If you don't have an existing group, consider creating one for your project. This can help manage communication, file sharing, and other collaborative tasks across Office 365 applications.

- Group Permissions: When using Office 365 Groups, the permissions set for the group will apply to the plan. Ensure that the group's settings align with your project's needs.

Summary

Inviting team members to a plan in Microsoft Planner is a critical step in establishing a collaborative environment. By following best practices, managing invitations effectively, and leveraging the integration with Office 365 Groups, you can ensure that your team is set up for success. This process lays the foundation for effective task management, communication, and project execution within Microsoft Planner.

3.1.2 Assigning Roles and Permissions

Assigning roles and permissions within Microsoft Planner is a critical aspect of team collaboration and project management. It ensures that the right people have access to the right information and can carry out their responsibilities effectively. This section delves into the intricacies of assigning roles and permissions in Microsoft Planner, offering detailed guidance on how to manage user roles, set permissions, and maintain the security and integrity of your plans.

Understanding Roles in Microsoft Planner

Microsoft Planner operates within the broader Microsoft 365 ecosystem, meaning that roles and permissions in Planner are closely tied to the Microsoft 365 Group associated with a given plan. Understanding these roles is the first step in effectively managing your team within Planner.

1. Plan Owners:

Plan owners have the highest level of control over a plan. They can create and delete plans, add or remove members, assign tasks, and modify plan settings. Typically, the person who creates a plan is automatically designated as the plan owner. However, ownership can be transferred or shared with other members as needed. Plan owners are responsible for overseeing the project, ensuring that tasks are completed on time, and that the plan is used effectively by the team.

2. Members:

Members are the users who actively participate in the plan. They can add and edit tasks, mark tasks as complete, and comment on tasks. However, they do not have the authority to delete the plan or manage membership. Members collaborate within the framework set by the plan owner, contributing to the completion of assigned tasks and providing input where necessary.

3. Guests:

In some cases, it may be necessary to include individuals outside your organization in a plan, such as contractors, partners, or clients. These external users are designated as guests. Guests have limited access and permissions compared to members. They can view and edit tasks assigned to them, but their capabilities are restricted to maintain the security and confidentiality of your organization's data.

Understanding these roles helps in setting up a plan that aligns with your team structure and project requirements. Proper role assignment ensures that every team member can contribute effectively without compromising the integrity of the plan.

Assigning Roles in Microsoft Planner

Assigning roles in Microsoft Planner is a straightforward process, but it requires careful consideration to ensure that each member has the appropriate level of access. Here's how you can assign roles:

1. Adding Members to a Plan:

To assign roles, you first need to add members to your plan. This can be done by:

- Navigating to your plan and selecting the "Members" tab.

- Clicking on "Add members" and typing the names or email addresses of the individuals you want to add.

- Selecting the correct individuals from the list that appears.

Once members are added, they are automatically assigned the role of "Member." You can then adjust their roles as needed.

2. Assigning the Owner Role:

If you need to designate another user as an owner, this can be done by:

- Navigating to the "Members" tab.

- Finding the member you want to assign as an owner.

- Clicking on the ellipsis (three dots) next to their name and selecting "Make Owner" from the dropdown menu.

This user will now have full control over the plan, including the ability to manage membership and settings.

3. Assigning the Guest Role:

To add a guest:

- Go to the "Members" tab.

- Enter the email address of the external user you wish to invite.

- Select the user when their email appears in the search results.

Guests are automatically assigned the guest role, and their permissions are limited to viewing and editing tasks.

4. Changing Roles:

If you need to change a member's role:

- Navigate to the "Members" tab.

- Find the member whose role you want to change.

- Click on the ellipsis next to their name and select the appropriate role.

It's important to note that only plan owners have the ability to change roles. Members cannot change their own roles or the roles of others.

Setting Permissions in Microsoft Planner

Permissions in Microsoft Planner are primarily managed through the Microsoft 365 Group associated with the plan. Understanding and configuring these permissions is crucial for maintaining control over your plan's data and ensuring that only authorized individuals have access to sensitive information.

1. Plan Visibility:

When creating a plan, you can choose between making it public or private:

- Public Plans: These plans are visible to everyone within your organization. Any employee can join the plan and view its contents. Public plans are suitable for projects that require broad collaboration and input from various departments or teams.

- Private Plans: These plans are restricted to members who are explicitly invited. Private plans are ideal for projects involving sensitive information or a small, focused team.

The visibility setting can be adjusted by the plan owner at any time by navigating to the plan's settings.

2. Task Permissions:

Task permissions are determined by the roles assigned to members:

- Owners can create, edit, and delete tasks, as well as assign tasks to any member.

- Members can create and edit tasks, but they cannot delete tasks created by others.

- Guests can only view and edit tasks assigned to them.

These permissions help ensure that tasks are managed efficiently while preventing unauthorized modifications or deletions.

3. Managing Guest Access:

Since guests have limited permissions, managing their access is crucial for maintaining security. Plan owners can:

- Restrict guest access to specific tasks or information by carefully assigning tasks and controlling what they can view.

- Remove guest access if their involvement in the project is no longer needed by navigating to the "Members" tab and selecting "Remove" next to the guest's name.

It's important to regularly review guest access to ensure that only those who need to participate in the plan have access.

Best Practices for Assigning Roles and Permissions

Effectively assigning roles and permissions in Microsoft Planner is key to successful project management. Here are some best practices to consider:

1. Assign Roles Based on Responsibilities:

Ensure that roles are assigned according to the responsibilities of each team member. Owners should be those who are accountable for the overall success of the project, while members should be those who are directly involved in executing tasks.

2. Limit the Number of Owners:

While it might be tempting to assign the owner role to multiple people, it's generally best to limit the number of owners to avoid confusion and conflicting decisions. A clear hierarchy helps streamline decision-making and maintain control over the plan.

3. Review and Update Roles Regularly:

As projects evolve, the roles of team members may need to be adjusted. Regularly review the roles and permissions within your plan to ensure they still align with the team's needs and responsibilities.

4. Use Guest Access Sparingly:

While guest access is a useful feature, it should be used sparingly and only when necessary. Limit the information that guests can access, and remove their access as soon as their role in the project is complete.

5. Educate Team Members on Their Roles:

Ensure that all team members understand their roles and the permissions that come with them. This helps prevent misunderstandings and ensures that everyone knows their responsibilities and limitations.

6. Monitor Plan Activity:

Keep an eye on plan activity to ensure that permissions are being used appropriately. Microsoft Planner's integration with other tools like Microsoft Teams can help you monitor and manage plan activity more effectively.

Conclusion

Assigning roles and permissions in Microsoft Planner is a fundamental part of managing any project. By understanding the different roles available and how to assign them, you can ensure that your team is organized, responsibilities are clear, and your plan is secure. Proper management of roles and permissions not only facilitates smooth collaboration but also safeguards your project's data, making Microsoft Planner an invaluable tool for achieving your goals.

3.1.3 Collaborating on Tasks

Introduction to Task Collaboration

Collaborating on tasks within Microsoft Planner is central to its effectiveness as a project management tool. When working in a team, the ability to share and collaborate on tasks efficiently ensures that all team members are on the same page, contributing to the progress and success of the project. Task collaboration in Microsoft Planner is designed to be intuitive and flexible, allowing teams to manage workloads, share insights, and track progress in real time.

Understanding the Collaborative Environment

Collaboration in Microsoft Planner is facilitated through various features that allow team members to work together on tasks, exchange ideas, and monitor progress. Each task in a plan can have multiple collaborators who contribute to its completion. This collaborative environment is built on transparency, communication, and shared responsibility.

The key elements of task collaboration in Microsoft Planner include task assignments, comments, attachments, and progress updates. These features create a collaborative workspace where team members can coordinate efforts, provide feedback, and make informed decisions. Understanding how to effectively use these features can significantly enhance team productivity and project outcomes.

Assigning Tasks to Multiple Collaborators

One of the fundamental aspects of collaboration in Microsoft Planner is task assignment. In many projects, tasks require input and effort from multiple team members. Microsoft Planner allows you to assign tasks to one or more collaborators, ensuring that each person involved is aware of their responsibilities and can contribute to the task's completion.

When assigning tasks to multiple collaborators, it's important to clearly define the roles and responsibilities of each team member. This can be done by specifying who is responsible for specific sub-tasks or aspects of the main task. For instance, in a content creation task, one team member might be responsible for writing the content, while another is responsible for editing and proofreading.

Assigning tasks to multiple collaborators also facilitates accountability. Each collaborator can track their progress and update the task status, allowing the entire team to see who is working on what and how close the task is to completion. This transparency is crucial in preventing bottlenecks and ensuring that tasks are completed on time.

Using Comments for Communication

Effective communication is essential for successful collaboration, and Microsoft Planner provides a simple yet powerful way to facilitate this through task comments. Comments allow team members to communicate directly within the context of a specific task, ensuring that all relevant information and discussions are easily accessible.

When collaborating on tasks, team members can use the comments section to ask questions, provide updates, share insights, or give feedback. This ongoing dialogue helps to clarify any uncertainties and ensures that everyone involved in the task is informed of any changes or new developments.

For example, if a task requires additional resources or information, a team member can leave a comment requesting it. Other collaborators can then respond, attach the necessary files, or provide the required information. This real-time communication helps to streamline workflows and reduces the need for back-and-forth emails or meetings.

It's important to use comments effectively by keeping them clear, concise, and relevant to the task at hand. Overloading the comments section with unnecessary information or off-topic discussions can clutter the task and make it difficult for collaborators to find the information they need.

Attaching Files and Resources

Collaboration often involves sharing documents, images, and other resources that are necessary for task completion. Microsoft Planner allows you to attach files directly to tasks, making it easy for collaborators to access and use the resources they need.

Attachments can include documents, spreadsheets, presentations, images, or any other files relevant to the task. For example, if a task involves creating a marketing report, team members can attach drafts, data files, and visual assets to the task, ensuring that everyone has access to the latest version of each file.

By centralizing these resources within the task, Microsoft Planner reduces the need for external file-sharing platforms and minimizes the risk of version control issues. Collaborators can view, download, and edit the attached files directly from the task, ensuring that all changes are tracked and easily accessible to the entire team.

In addition to attaching files, Microsoft Planner also integrates with other Microsoft 365 tools like SharePoint and OneDrive. This integration allows teams to link documents stored in these platforms directly to tasks, further enhancing collaboration by providing seamless access to shared resources.

Tracking Task Progress

Collaboration is not just about working together on tasks; it's also about ensuring that tasks are progressing as planned. Microsoft Planner provides several tools for tracking task progress, allowing collaborators to update and monitor the status of their work.

Each task in Microsoft Planner has a progress indicator that can be set to "Not Started," "In Progress," or "Completed." Collaborators can update this status as they work on the task, providing real-time visibility into how the task is advancing. This feature is particularly useful for managers and team leaders who need to monitor the overall progress of a project.

In addition to the progress status, collaborators can use the checklist feature within tasks to break down the work into smaller, manageable steps. As each step is completed, it can be checked off the list, providing a clear visual representation of what has been done and what still needs to be completed.

Another useful feature for tracking progress is the task due date. Collaborators can set and adjust due dates for tasks, helping to ensure that work is completed on time. Microsoft

Planner also provides notifications and reminders for upcoming deadlines, helping to keep the team on track.

Using Labels and Buckets for Organization

Effective collaboration often requires a well-organized task structure. Microsoft Planner allows you to use labels and buckets to categorize and organize tasks, making it easier for collaborators to find and focus on the tasks that are most relevant to them.

Labels can be used to categorize tasks based on priority, project phase, or any other criteria that are important to your team. For example, you might use labels to indicate high-priority tasks, tasks that require review, or tasks that are part of a specific project phase. Collaborators can then filter tasks by label, allowing them to quickly identify the tasks they need to focus on.

Buckets are another powerful organizational tool in Microsoft Planner. Buckets allow you to group tasks into categories within a plan, providing a clear structure for the work that needs to be done. For example, in a software development project, you might create buckets for "Development," "Testing," and "Deployment," with tasks assigned to the appropriate bucket based on their current status.

By using labels and buckets, you can create a clear, organized task structure that enhances collaboration by making it easy for team members to navigate the plan and focus on the tasks that are most important to them.

Integrating with Other Microsoft Tools

Microsoft Planner is part of the larger Microsoft 365 ecosystem, and it integrates seamlessly with other Microsoft tools to enhance collaboration. One of the most powerful integrations is with Microsoft Teams, which allows you to collaborate on tasks directly within your team's communication platform.

By integrating Microsoft Planner with Microsoft Teams, you can create, view, and update tasks within the Teams interface, making it easier for team members to collaborate without switching between different apps. This integration also allows you to pin specific plans or tasks to a Teams channel, ensuring that they are easily accessible to all team members.

In addition to Teams, Microsoft Planner also integrates with Outlook, SharePoint, and OneNote, among others. These integrations allow you to link emails, documents, and notes to tasks, further enhancing collaboration by centralizing all relevant information within Microsoft Planner.

For example, you can link an email thread from Outlook to a task, providing collaborators with direct access to the communication related to that task. Similarly, you can link a SharePoint document library to a plan, ensuring that all relevant documents are easily accessible to the team.

Monitoring and Managing Task Dependencies

In collaborative projects, tasks are often dependent on the completion of other tasks. Managing these dependencies is crucial to ensuring that the project progresses smoothly. Microsoft Planner allows you to manage task dependencies by linking related tasks and setting dependencies within your plan.

While Microsoft Planner does not have a built-in Gantt chart feature, you can still manage dependencies by clearly defining the order in which tasks need to be completed and by communicating this to the team. For example, you can use the task comments or description to specify that a particular task cannot be started until another task is completed.

Additionally, by regularly reviewing the progress of tasks and updating their status, you can ensure that dependent tasks are started and completed in the correct order. This proactive management of task dependencies helps to prevent delays and ensures that the project stays on track.

Encouraging Collaboration through Best Practices

While Microsoft Planner provides the tools for effective collaboration, it's important to establish best practices that encourage and support collaborative work. Here are a few tips for fostering collaboration within your team:

1. Clearly Define Roles and Responsibilities: Ensure that each collaborator knows their role in the task and what is expected of them. This can be done through task assignments, comments, and regular communication.

2. Promote Open Communication: Encourage team members to use the comments section to ask questions, share updates, and provide feedback. Open communication is key to resolving issues quickly and keeping the project moving forward.

3. Regularly Review and Update Tasks: Regularly review the status of tasks and update them as needed. This ensures that all collaborators are aware of the current state of the task and can adjust their work accordingly.

4. Use Labels and Buckets for Clarity: Organize tasks using labels and buckets to create a clear structure that makes it easy for collaborators to navigate the plan and focus on their tasks.

5. Leverage Integrations: Take advantage of Microsoft Planner's integrations with other Microsoft tools to streamline collaboration and centralize all relevant information.

6. Encourage Feedback and Iteration: Encourage team members to provide feedback on the collaboration process and make adjustments as needed. Continuous improvement is key to enhancing collaboration and achieving better results.

Conclusion

Collaborating on tasks in Microsoft Planner is about more than just working together—it's about creating an environment where team members can efficiently share information, communicate, and track progress. By understanding and utilizing the collaborative features of Microsoft Planner, teams can enhance their productivity, ensure that tasks are completed on time, and ultimately achieve their project goals.

3.2 Communication and Notifications

Effective communication is crucial for team collaboration, and Microsoft Planner offers various tools to facilitate it. One of the primary features in Planner that aids in team communication is the ability to use comments within tasks. This section will explore how to leverage the commenting feature in Microsoft Planner to enhance communication, ensure clarity, and keep everyone on the same page.

3.2.1 Using Comments for Communication

Comments in Microsoft Planner serve as a direct line of communication between team members within the context of specific tasks. By using comments effectively, teams can discuss details, ask questions, provide updates, and share information without leaving the Planner interface. This feature helps maintain a clear and organized record of all communications related to a task, making it easier to track discussions and decisions.

1. Understanding the Role of Comments in Task Management

In Microsoft Planner, each task card has a dedicated comment section where team members can leave messages. These comments are threaded, meaning that responses to a particular comment are grouped together, making it easy to follow the conversation. The role of comments in task management is to provide a centralized place for discussion that is directly tied to the task at hand. This reduces the need for external communication channels such as email or instant messaging, keeping all relevant information in one place.

Comments in Planner can be used for a variety of purposes, including:

- Clarifying Task Requirements: Team members can use comments to ask questions or provide clarifications on task details, ensuring that everyone understands what is required.

- Providing Updates: As progress is made on a task, updates can be communicated through comments, keeping everyone informed.

- Sharing Files and Resources: While Planner itself does not directly allow file attachments in comments, links to documents stored in other Microsoft 365 apps, such as SharePoint or OneDrive, can be shared through comments.

- Decision-Making and Consensus: Comments can be used to discuss options, weigh pros and cons, and reach a consensus on how to proceed with a task.

2. How to Add and Manage Comments

Adding comments to a task in Microsoft Planner is straightforward. To add a comment, follow these steps:

- Open the Task Card: Click on the task to open its details pane.

- Locate the Comment Box: Scroll down to the bottom of the task details pane to find the comment box.

- Type Your Comment: Enter your message in the comment box. If you need to refer to a specific person, you can use the @mention feature by typing the "@" symbol followed by their name.

- Post the Comment: After typing your message, click the "Send" button (represented by a paper plane icon) to post your comment. The comment will appear in the task's comment thread.

Managing comments involves keeping track of conversations and ensuring that all relevant information is recorded. Here are some best practices for managing comments in Planner:

- Be Clear and Concise: Ensure that your comments are clear, concise, and relevant to the task. Avoid off-topic discussions to maintain focus.

- Use @mentions for Direct Communication: If you need a specific team member to address something, use the @mention feature to notify them directly. This helps in getting faster responses and ensures accountability.

- Review Comment History: Regularly review the comment history to stay updated on the latest discussions and decisions. This is especially useful when returning to a task after some time.

- Resolve and Close Conversations: Once an issue has been addressed or a question answered, consider adding a closing comment to mark the end of that particular discussion. This helps in maintaining an organized comment thread.

3. Best Practices for Effective Communication through Comments

To maximize the effectiveness of using comments in Microsoft Planner, consider the following best practices:

- Keep Comments Task-Specific: Ensure that your comments are directly related to the task at hand. If the discussion starts to drift into topics that affect the broader project or multiple tasks, it might be better to take the conversation to another forum, such as Microsoft Teams.

- Use Comments for Asynchronous Communication: Comments are an excellent tool for asynchronous communication, where team members may not be working at the same time. This allows individuals to leave updates or responses that others can read and reply to later.

- Document Key Decisions: Use comments to document important decisions made about the task. This creates a record that can be referred back to if needed, ensuring that everyone is aware of what was decided and why.

- Respond Promptly: Encourage team members to check their notifications and respond to comments promptly. This helps keep the task moving forward and prevents delays in the project timeline.

- Integrate with Microsoft Teams for Broader Discussions: For more extensive discussions that go beyond the scope of a single task, consider integrating Microsoft Planner with Microsoft Teams. This allows you to have in-depth conversations while keeping high-level task comments focused and concise.

4. Using @Mentions to Enhance Communication

The @mention feature in Microsoft Planner is a powerful tool for enhancing communication within tasks. By tagging specific team members in a comment, you can direct their attention to important information or requests, ensuring they don't miss critical updates.

When you @mention someone in a comment, they receive a notification that they have been mentioned, making it easier for them to prioritize their response. This is particularly useful in scenarios where a task requires input or action from multiple team members.

5. Notifications and Comment Alerts

In addition to leaving comments, it's essential to understand how notifications work in Microsoft Planner to ensure that team members stay informed. Notifications in Planner are tied to several actions, including when a task is assigned to a team member, when someone comments on a task you're assigned to, or when a task is nearing its due date.

Here's how notifications enhance communication:

- Real-Time Alerts: Notifications provide real-time alerts when comments are made on tasks, ensuring that team members are immediately aware of updates.

- Email Summaries: Planner can send email summaries of task activities, including new comments. This is helpful for team members who may not be constantly monitoring Planner.

- Customizing Notification Settings: Team members can customize their notification settings to control the frequency and type of alerts they receive. For instance, they can choose to receive notifications for all comments or only when they are mentioned directly.

6. Common Challenges and Solutions in Using Comments

While comments are a valuable communication tool, there are some common challenges that teams might encounter. Here are a few challenges and their solutions:

- Overloaded Comment Threads: As tasks progress, comment threads can become long and unwieldy, making it difficult to find specific information. To mitigate this, encourage team members to start new tasks for major discussion topics or to summarize long threads periodically.

- Missed Notifications: If team members do not receive or act on notifications, they might miss important updates. Ensure that everyone on the team knows how to configure their notification settings and encourage regular checks of Planner and their email.

- Lack of Clarity: Sometimes, comments can be vague or unclear, leading to confusion. To avoid this, team members should strive to be as specific as possible in their comments and use @mentions when they need input from others.

7. The Role of Comments in Remote Work

In the context of remote work, where team members may be spread across different locations and time zones, the role of comments in Microsoft Planner becomes even more critical. Comments facilitate asynchronous communication, allowing teams to stay connected and informed without needing to be online at the same time.

Here's how comments can be particularly beneficial for remote teams:

- Maintaining a Communication Trail: Comments keep a detailed record of all communications related to a task, which is vital for remote teams where face-to-face discussions are not possible.

- Ensuring Accountability: By documenting discussions and decisions in comments, remote teams can ensure that everyone is accountable for their tasks and responsibilities.

- Facilitating Collaboration Across Time Zones: Comments allow team members in different time zones to collaborate effectively by leaving updates and responses that others can address when they come online.

8. Conclusion

In summary, comments in Microsoft Planner are a powerful tool for enhancing communication and collaboration within teams. By using comments effectively, teams can maintain a clear, organized record of discussions, ensure that everyone is on the same page, and keep tasks moving forward efficiently. Understanding how to use comments, leveraging the @mention feature, and managing notifications are all essential components of effective task communication in Planner.

As teams continue to work in increasingly distributed and remote environments, mastering the use of comments in Microsoft Planner will become even more critical for achieving project success and maintaining cohesive team collaboration.

3.2.2 Setting Up Notifications

Notifications in Microsoft Planner are essential for keeping team members informed about updates, task assignments, deadlines, and any changes to the plans. Effective notification management ensures that everyone remains aligned, reducing the risk of missed deadlines or miscommunication. This section will guide you through setting up and optimizing notifications in Microsoft Planner to enhance team collaboration and productivity.

Understanding Notification Types

Before diving into the setup, it's crucial to understand the different types of notifications available in Microsoft Planner:

1. Email Notifications: These are sent directly to your email inbox, providing updates about task assignments, due dates, and comments.

2. Microsoft Teams Notifications: If your Planner is integrated with Microsoft Teams, notifications can appear within Teams, providing real-time updates.

3. Mobile App Notifications: For those using the Microsoft Planner mobile app, push notifications can be enabled to keep you informed on the go.

Configuring Email Notifications

Email notifications are vital for ensuring that critical updates do not go unnoticed. Here's how to configure them:

1. Accessing Notification Settings:

  - Open Microsoft Planner.

  - Click on the gear icon in the upper right corner to access Settings.

  - Select "Notifications" from the dropdown menu.

2. Enabling Task Assignment Notifications:

  - In the Notifications settings, you can choose to receive email notifications when a task is assigned to you. This ensures that you are immediately aware of new responsibilities.

- Check the box next to "Email me when a task is assigned to me."

3. Due Date Reminders:

- To stay on top of deadlines, enable due date reminders. Microsoft Planner can send you an email reminder three days before a task is due.

- Check the box next to "Email me when a task I'm assigned is due in the next 3 days."

4. Comments and Updates:

- Notifications for comments ensure you are kept in the loop on discussions related to your tasks.

- Check the box next to "Email me when someone comments on a task I'm assigned to."

Managing Notifications in Microsoft Teams

Integrating Microsoft Planner with Microsoft Teams allows for seamless notifications within the Teams environment. This is particularly useful for real-time collaboration and instant updates.

1. Adding Planner to a Team:

- Open Microsoft Teams and select the team to which you want to add Planner.

- Click on the "+" icon to add a new tab.

- Select "Planner" from the list of available apps.

- Choose to create a new plan or use an existing one.

2. Configuring Teams Notifications:

- Notifications in Teams are managed through the Teams settings.

- Go to the team channel linked to your Planner.

- Click on the three dots (...) next to the channel name and select "Channel notifications."

- Choose your notification preferences, such as "All activity," "Mentions and replies," or "Off."

3. Task Updates and Mentions:

- When a task is updated in Planner, notifications can appear in the Teams channel, ensuring all team members are aware of changes.

- Use @mentions in comments to notify specific team members about important updates or to request their input.

Optimizing Mobile App Notifications

For team members who are frequently on the go, the Microsoft Planner mobile app provides push notifications to keep them updated.

1. Installing the Mobile App:

   - Download the Microsoft Planner app from the Apple App Store or Google Play Store.

   - Sign in with your Microsoft account.

2. Enabling Push Notifications:

   - Open the Planner app and go to the settings by tapping the gear icon.

   - Select "Notifications."

   - Toggle on "Push Notifications" to receive updates directly on your mobile device.

3. Customizing Notification Preferences:

   - Within the mobile app, you can customize which notifications you receive, such as task assignments, due dates, and comments.

   - Adjust your preferences to ensure you only receive notifications that are most relevant to you.

Best Practices for Notification Management

Effective notification management involves more than just enabling notifications. It requires a thoughtful approach to ensure that notifications enhance productivity without becoming overwhelming.

1. Balancing Notification Frequency:

- Too many notifications can be distracting, while too few can result in missed updates. Find a balance that keeps you informed without causing notification fatigue.

- Periodically review and adjust your notification settings based on your current workload and team dynamics.

2. Utilizing Notification Channels:

- Leverage the strengths of different notification channels. Use email for important updates that require action, Teams for real-time collaboration, and mobile push notifications for on-the-go alerts.

- Ensure that critical notifications are not missed by enabling them across multiple channels when necessary.

3. Encouraging Team Communication:

- Foster a culture of communication within your team, encouraging members to use comments and @mentions effectively.

- Regularly remind team members to check their notifications and keep their settings up to date.

4. Regularly Reviewing and Updating Settings:

- Notification preferences may change as projects evolve. Regularly review and update your settings to ensure they remain aligned with your needs.

- Encourage team members to do the same to maintain optimal communication and collaboration.

Troubleshooting Notification Issues

Occasionally, you may encounter issues with notifications not being received or delayed. Here are some common troubleshooting steps:

1. Check Email Filters:

- Ensure that emails from Microsoft Planner are not being filtered into your spam or junk folder. Add Planner's email address to your safe sender list if necessary.

2. Verify Notification Settings:

- Double-check that the relevant notification settings are enabled both in Planner and any integrated apps like Teams.

  - Confirm that you are using the correct email address for notifications.

3. Update the Mobile App:

  - Ensure that you have the latest version of the Microsoft Planner mobile app installed, as updates often include fixes for notification issues.

4. Restart the App:

  - Sometimes, simply restarting the Planner app or Teams can resolve notification issues.

  - Log out and back into your account to refresh the app's connection.

5. Contact Support:

  - If you continue to experience issues, contact Microsoft Support for assistance. Provide detailed information about the problem to help them diagnose and resolve it quickly.

Conclusion

Effective notification management in Microsoft Planner is crucial for maintaining team alignment, meeting deadlines, and ensuring seamless communication. By understanding the different types of notifications, configuring them appropriately, and following best practices, you can optimize your team's workflow and enhance productivity. Regularly review and adjust your notification settings to ensure they remain effective as your projects and team dynamics evolve.

3.2.3 Integrating with Microsoft Teams

Introduction to Microsoft Teams and Planner Integration

Microsoft Teams is a powerful collaboration tool that integrates seamlessly with various Microsoft 365 applications, including Microsoft Planner. By integrating Planner with Teams, organizations can streamline their workflows, enhance communication, and ensure that project tasks are managed efficiently. The integration allows teams to work together in a centralized platform where they can chat, meet, share files, and track tasks without switching between different applications. This section will explore the benefits of integrating Microsoft Planner with Teams, guide you through the integration process, and provide best practices for maximizing this powerful combination.

Benefits of Integrating Microsoft Planner with Teams

Integrating Microsoft Planner with Teams offers several significant advantages that enhance team collaboration and productivity:

1. Centralized Collaboration Hub: Teams serve as a central hub for team communication and collaboration. By integrating Planner, team members can discuss tasks, share files, and update project statuses all within the same platform, reducing the need to switch between multiple applications.

2. Real-Time Task Updates: The integration ensures that task updates in Planner are immediately reflected in Teams, providing team members with real-time visibility into task progress. This feature helps in maintaining transparency and keeps everyone on the same page.

3. Improved Communication: Teams provides a platform for ongoing communication related to tasks and projects managed in Planner. The ability to chat or have video meetings directly related to Planner tasks enhances understanding and coordination among team members.

4. Increased Accountability: The integration allows for clear assignment of tasks and responsibilities, with visibility on who is accountable for each task. This clarity improves accountability and helps ensure that tasks are completed on time.

5. Simplified Access to Planner: By embedding Planner into Teams, users can easily access their plans directly from the Teams interface, making it more convenient to manage tasks and monitor progress without leaving the collaboration environment.

6. Enhanced File Management: Teams' integration with SharePoint allows for efficient file management. Files shared in Teams are automatically linked to the tasks in Planner, ensuring that all necessary resources are readily available for task completion.

7. Customized Notifications: Teams can be configured to send notifications for specific Planner activities, ensuring that team members are promptly informed of important updates and deadlines. This helps in staying organized and proactive in managing tasks.

Step-by-Step Guide to Integrating Microsoft Planner with Teams

Integrating Microsoft Planner with Microsoft Teams is a straightforward process that can be accomplished in just a few steps. The following guide will walk you through the process:

Step 1: Accessing Microsoft Teams

1.1. Log in to your Microsoft Teams account using your organizational credentials.

1.2. Navigate to the appropriate team or channel where you want to integrate Microsoft Planner.

Step 2: Adding a Planner Tab in Teams

2.1. Once in the desired team or channel, click on the "+" (Add a tab) icon at the top of the channel.

2.2. In the "Add a tab" window, search for Planner and select it from the list of available apps.

2.3. You will be prompted to either create a new plan or use an existing one. Choose the appropriate option:

- Create a new plan: If you want to start a new plan specific to this team or channel.

- Use an existing plan: If you already have a plan in Microsoft Planner that you want to integrate into Teams.

2.4. After selecting or creating the plan, give the tab a name that reflects the purpose of the plan or project.

2.5. Click Save to add the Planner tab to your Teams channel.

Step 3: Managing Tasks Within Teams

3.1. With the Planner tab added, you can now manage tasks directly within Teams. You can create new tasks, assign tasks to team members, set due dates, and update task progress.

3.2. Use the Buckets feature in Planner to organize tasks within the Teams channel. This allows for a clear visual representation of different project phases or categories.

3.3. Leverage the Charts and Board views within the Planner tab to monitor the overall progress of tasks and identify any bottlenecks.

Step 4: Collaborating on Tasks in Teams

4.1. Discuss tasks directly within the Teams channel by using the chat feature. You can tag team members, share updates, or request feedback related to specific tasks.

4.2. To have more in-depth discussions or meetings about tasks, use the Meet Now feature in Teams to start an instant video or audio meeting with relevant team members.

4.3. Share files related to tasks by uploading them directly into the Teams channel. These files will be linked to the Planner tasks, making it easier for team members to access necessary resources.

Step 5: Setting Up Notifications and Alerts

5.1. Customize Teams notifications for Planner activities by clicking on the three dots (ellipsis) next to the Planner tab and selecting Settings.

5.2. Choose the type of notifications you want to receive, such as task assignments, due date reminders, or task completions.

5.3. Teams can also be configured to send notifications to specific channels, ensuring that the entire team is aware of important updates.

Step 6: Using Teams Mobile App for Planner Integration

6.1. Download the Microsoft Teams mobile app to stay connected to your plans on the go.

6.2. Access the Planner tab within the mobile app to view tasks, update progress, and communicate with team members from anywhere.

6.3. Use mobile notifications to stay informed of urgent task updates or deadlines even when you are away from your computer.

Best Practices for Using Planner and Teams Together

To get the most out of the integration between Microsoft Planner and Teams, consider the following best practices:

1. Establish Clear Communication Protocols: Define how your team will use Teams for communication related to Planner tasks. This could include guidelines on when to use chat vs. email, how to structure messages for clarity, and how often to update the team on task progress.

2. Regularly Review and Update Plans: Schedule regular team meetings to review the Planner board within Teams. This will help keep everyone aligned on progress, address any issues early, and make necessary adjustments to the plan.

3. Utilize @Mentions for Task Updates: Use @mentions in Teams to notify specific team members about task updates or to request feedback. This ensures that the right people are informed without cluttering the channel with unnecessary messages.

4. Leverage Teams Channels for Task-Specific Discussions: Create dedicated channels within Teams for different aspects of a project. Integrate specific Planner boards into these channels to focus discussions and task management around particular workstreams or project phases.

5. Automate Routine Tasks: Use Power Automate to set up workflows that automatically create tasks in Planner based on actions in Teams. For example, you can automate task creation when certain keywords are mentioned in a Teams chat or when a file is uploaded to a specific channel.

6. Encourage Transparency and Accountability: Make sure all team members are using the Planner tab in Teams to update their tasks. This transparency helps keep everyone informed and holds individuals accountable for their responsibilities.

7. Monitor Progress Using Teams Insights: Use the reporting and insights features in Teams to monitor overall team activity related to Planner tasks. This can help managers identify areas where additional support may be needed or where productivity can be improved.

Case Study: Effective Use of Planner and Teams Integration

Consider a project team responsible for launching a new marketing campaign. By integrating Microsoft Planner with Teams, the team can manage the entire project lifecycle, from initial brainstorming sessions to final execution, within one platform.

Project Setup: The project manager creates a new marketing plan in Planner and integrates it with the Teams channel dedicated to the campaign. Buckets are created for different phases of the project, such as "Research," "Content Creation," "Design," and "Distribution."

Task Assignment: Tasks are assigned to team members directly within Teams, with clear deadlines and priorities. The team uses the chat feature in Teams to discuss task details and share updates.

File Sharing: All campaign-related files, including content drafts, design assets, and research documents, are uploaded to the Teams channel and linked to their corresponding tasks in Planner.

Progress Monitoring: The team holds weekly meetings via Teams to review the Planner board, discuss progress, and address any challenges. Real-time updates in Planner are visible to everyone, ensuring that the project stays on track.

Outcome: The integration of Planner with Teams enables the marketing team to collaborate efficiently, meet deadlines, and achieve the campaign goals without the need for constant email exchanges or switching between different tools.

Conclusion

Integrating Microsoft Planner with Microsoft Teams is a powerful way to enhance team collaboration and productivity. By bringing task management and communication into one unified platform, teams can work more efficiently, stay aligned on project goals, and ensure that tasks are completed on time. Whether you're managing a small project or overseeing a large team, the Planner-Teams integration provides the tools you need to organize your work and achieve your goals effectively.

As you continue to explore and use Microsoft Planner and Teams together, remember to leverage the full range of features available in both platforms. Regularly review and adjust your workflow to ensure that it meets the evolving needs of your team, and take advantage of the ongoing updates and enhancements that Microsoft provides to further streamline your processes.

3.3 Monitoring Progress and Updates

3.3.1 Tracking Task Completion

Effective task completion tracking is vital to the success of any project or plan. Microsoft Planner provides several tools and features to help teams monitor the progress of tasks and ensure that deadlines are met. This section delves into the mechanisms for tracking task completion within Microsoft Planner, emphasizing the importance of keeping tasks on track, identifying bottlenecks, and ensuring accountability.

Understanding the Importance of Tracking Task Completion

Tracking task completion is more than just marking off completed items on a checklist. It involves a systematic approach to managing tasks, ensuring that each task is completed on time, within scope, and to the required quality standards. By actively monitoring task completion, team leaders can identify potential delays or issues early, adjust workloads, and maintain momentum throughout the project lifecycle.

Microsoft Planner's intuitive interface and integration with other Microsoft tools make it an excellent choice for teams looking to streamline their task management and tracking processes. Whether working on a small team project or a large-scale organizational initiative, Planner's features can be customized to meet the needs of any workflow.

Setting Up Task Completion Criteria

Before diving into the specifics of tracking tasks, it is essential to establish clear criteria for what constitutes task completion. This can vary depending on the project but generally includes the following:

1. Definition of Done: Establish a clear definition of what "done" means for each task. This might include specific deliverables, quality standards, or approval requirements. Defining this upfront ensures that all team members have the same understanding of when a task is truly complete.

2. Assigning Responsibility: Clearly assign each task to a specific team member or group. This helps in tracking who is responsible for the task's completion and holds individuals accountable for their assigned work.

3. Setting Deadlines: Every task should have a deadline associated with it. Deadlines provide a time-bound framework for task completion and help in managing workload and prioritization.

4. Dependencies and Prerequisites: Identify any dependencies between tasks. Some tasks may need to be completed before others can begin. Tracking these dependencies is crucial for maintaining the project's timeline.

Using Microsoft Planner to Track Task Completion

Microsoft Planner offers several built-in features to help teams track the progress of their tasks. These features are designed to provide both a high-level overview and detailed insights into task status.

1. Task Progress Indicators: Each task in Microsoft Planner has a progress indicator, which can be set to "Not Started," "In Progress," or "Completed." This simple yet effective tool allows team members to update the status of their tasks as they work on them. The progress indicator provides an at-a-glance view of where each task stands, making it easy to identify tasks that need attention.

2. Task Details and Checklists: For tasks that involve multiple steps, Planner allows you to create checklists within the task card. These checklists break down the task into smaller, manageable actions. As team members complete each checklist item, they can check it off, showing incremental progress toward the task's overall completion. This is particularly useful for complex tasks that require multiple stages to be completed.

3. Labels and Buckets: Microsoft Planner allows you to categorize tasks using labels and organize them into buckets. This can help in tracking task completion by grouping similar tasks together and color-coding them based on priority, phase, or other criteria. For example, you might use labels to denote tasks that are "High Priority" or "Client-Facing" and buckets to organize tasks by phase, such as "Planning," "Execution," and "Review."

4. Due Dates and Reminders: Assigning due dates to tasks is crucial for keeping projects on schedule. In Microsoft Planner, tasks with due dates are automatically tracked, and reminders can be set up to notify team members as the deadline approaches. This feature

helps ensure that tasks are completed on time and that team members are aware of upcoming deadlines.

Visualizing Task Progress with Charts

One of the standout features of Microsoft Planner is its ability to visualize task progress through built-in charts. These charts provide a graphical representation of your plan's progress and can be accessed directly from the Planner interface.

1. Status Charts: The status chart gives a visual overview of the number of tasks in each progress category (Not Started, In Progress, and Completed). This chart is particularly useful for identifying overall progress and spotting any tasks that are lagging.

2. Priority Charts: Priority charts display tasks based on their assigned priority level (Low, Medium, Important, Urgent). This allows teams to focus on completing high-priority tasks first, ensuring that critical activities are addressed promptly.

3. Bucket Charts: Bucket charts show the distribution of tasks across different buckets, making it easy to see how tasks are organized and whether any specific phase or category requires more attention.

4. Assignment Charts: Assignment charts provide insights into task distribution among team members. This chart helps identify workload imbalances, where some team members may be overburdened while others have fewer tasks. By monitoring this chart, team leaders can reassign tasks as needed to maintain an even distribution of work.

Tracking Task Completion Over Time

In addition to monitoring current task status, it's important to track task completion over time. This can provide valuable insights into your team's productivity and help identify trends that could affect future projects.

1. Weekly and Monthly Reviews: Set up regular reviews to assess task completion rates. This could be done weekly, bi-weekly, or monthly, depending on the project's duration and complexity. During these reviews, analyze the number of tasks completed, the average time taken to complete tasks, and any patterns of delays or bottlenecks.

2. Burn Down and Burn Up Charts: Although not native to Microsoft Planner, burn down and burn up charts can be created by exporting task data to Excel. Burn down charts show

the amount of work remaining in a project, while burn up charts show the progress toward project completion. Both are useful for tracking task completion over time and forecasting project timelines.

3. Task Histories: Microsoft Planner keeps a history of all task activities, including changes in task status, updates to task details, and comments added by team members. Reviewing task histories can help identify any recurring issues, such as tasks that frequently change status or require multiple revisions before completion.

Addressing Delays and Issues

Despite the best planning and tracking efforts, delays and issues can still arise. Addressing these promptly is crucial to maintaining the project's momentum.

1. Identifying Delayed Tasks: Use the Planner's filtering options to quickly identify tasks that are overdue or at risk of missing their deadlines. Focus on resolving these tasks by reassigning resources, adjusting priorities, or extending deadlines as necessary.

2. Root Cause Analysis: For tasks that are consistently delayed, conduct a root cause analysis to identify underlying issues. This could involve reviewing the task's complexity, dependencies, or the availability of resources. Understanding the root cause allows for targeted interventions to prevent similar delays in the future.

3. Communicating Adjustments: When delays occur, it's essential to communicate any adjustments to the team promptly. Use Planner's commenting feature or integrate with Microsoft Teams to keep everyone informed of changes to task timelines, priorities, or assignments.

Ensuring Accountability

Accountability is a key factor in successful task completion. Microsoft Planner helps promote accountability by clearly defining who is responsible for each task and tracking progress transparently.

1. Task Assignments and Accountability: Ensure that every task is assigned to a specific individual. This not only clarifies responsibility but also makes it easier to track who is accountable for task completion. Microsoft Planner's assignment feature allows you to monitor each team member's progress and address any issues directly with the responsible individual.

2. Task Comments and Updates: Encourage team members to use the task comments feature to provide updates on their progress. This creates a record of how the task is progressing and any challenges faced. Regular updates help maintain accountability and keep the entire team informed.

3. Recognition and Feedback: Positive reinforcement can be a powerful motivator for task completion. Use Planner's tracking tools to recognize team members who consistently complete tasks on time and provide constructive feedback to those who may need additional support. This approach fosters a culture of accountability and continuous improvement.

Continuous Improvement Through Reflection

Finally, tracking task completion is not just about ensuring that tasks are done; it's also an opportunity for continuous improvement. After each project or major milestone, take the time to reflect on what worked well and what could be improved.

1. Post-Mortem Analysis: Conduct a post-mortem analysis at the end of each project to review task completion data. Identify any recurring issues or delays and develop strategies to address them in future projects.

2. Feedback Loops: Establish feedback loops where team members can share their experiences and suggest improvements. This could be done through surveys, meetings, or informal discussions. Incorporating feedback into your task management practices ensures that your team continuously evolves and improves.

3. Adjusting Task Tracking Methods: As your team gains experience with Microsoft Planner, you may find that certain tracking methods work better than others. Be open to adjusting your approach, whether it's tweaking how you use labels and buckets, experimenting with different review schedules, or integrating new tools for visualizing progress.

Conclusion

Tracking task completion is a critical component of effective project management. Microsoft Planner provides a robust set of tools and features that make it easy to monitor progress, identify issues, and ensure that tasks are completed on time. By establishing clear criteria for task completion, utilizing Planner's tracking features, and promoting accountability, teams can achieve their project goals efficiently and effectively. As you continue to use Microsoft Planner, remember to reflect on your processes and seek opportunities for continuous improvement, ensuring that your team remains productive and aligned with project objectives.

3.3.2 Reviewing Plan Progress

Reviewing plan progress is a crucial aspect of managing any project in Microsoft Planner. It ensures that tasks are on track, deadlines are met, and team members are aligned with the project's objectives. Regularly reviewing progress allows you to identify potential bottlenecks, make necessary adjustments, and keep stakeholders informed. This section will explore the tools and techniques available in Microsoft Planner to effectively review and manage the progress of your plans.

1. Understanding Plan Views

Microsoft Planner offers several views that help you visualize and review the progress of your plan. Each view provides a different perspective, allowing you to assess various aspects of the project.

a. Board View

The Board View is the default view in Microsoft Planner, where tasks are organized into buckets. This view gives you an at-a-glance overview of all tasks within the plan, categorized by their respective stages or types. You can see which tasks are in progress, completed, or yet to be started. The Board View is ideal for identifying the overall status of tasks and determining where the team's focus currently lies.

b. Charts View

The Charts View offers a more analytical perspective, presenting your plan's progress through visual representations such as pie charts and bar graphs. These visuals help you quickly identify the distribution of tasks across various statuses (e.g., Not Started, In Progress, Completed) and the workload of each team member. The Charts View is particularly useful for identifying trends, such as an overload of tasks on a particular team member or delays in task completion.

c. Schedule View

The Schedule View allows you to see tasks in a calendar format, making it easier to track deadlines and upcoming milestones. This view is helpful for ensuring that all tasks are scheduled appropriately and that there are no overlaps or conflicts. It also allows you to reschedule tasks by dragging them to different dates on the calendar, providing a more intuitive way to manage deadlines.

d. My Tasks View

While the My Tasks View is more individualized, it can still be valuable for plan managers who want to review the progress of specific team members. This view consolidates all the tasks assigned to an individual across all plans, making it easier to monitor their workload and productivity. It's a useful tool for one-on-one reviews or when addressing the progress of specific tasks with team members.

2. Analyzing Task Status

To effectively review plan progress, you must analyze the status of individual tasks. Task status in Microsoft Planner can typically be categorized as Not Started, In Progress, or Completed. Each of these statuses provides insight into the current state of the project.

a. Not Started

Tasks that are marked as Not Started indicate that these tasks have not yet been initiated. During a progress review, it's important to assess why these tasks have not started. Are there dependencies holding them up? Are team members awaiting additional information or resources? Identifying the reasons behind these stalled tasks is crucial for preventing delays in the overall project.

b. In Progress

Tasks marked as In Progress are currently being worked on. Reviewing these tasks involves assessing whether they are on track to meet their deadlines. Microsoft Planner allows you to add progress updates within the task itself, which can provide additional context, such as noting any obstacles that the team is facing. During reviews, it's important to discuss these updates and provide support or resources as needed to ensure tasks continue moving forward.

c. Completed

Completed tasks indicate that work has been finished and objectives have been met. Reviewing completed tasks helps you ensure that they meet the quality standards and expectations set at the beginning of the project. Additionally, analyzing the pace at which tasks are completed can help you predict the likelihood of meeting future deadlines and milestones.

3. Identifying Bottlenecks and Risks

One of the key goals of reviewing plan progress is to identify potential bottlenecks and risks that could impede the success of the project. Microsoft Planner provides several features to help with this.

a. Overloaded Team Members

By using the Charts View, you can quickly see if certain team members are overloaded with tasks. An uneven distribution of work can lead to delays and decreased productivity. If a team member is consistently struggling to complete tasks on time, it may be necessary to redistribute their workload or provide additional support.

b. Delayed Tasks

Tasks that are not completed by their due dates are a clear indicator of potential issues within the plan. The Schedule View can help you identify these delays and adjust deadlines accordingly. During your review, it's important to understand why these delays occurred and what can be done to prevent them in the future.

c. Dependency Conflicts

Some tasks in Microsoft Planner may be dependent on the completion of others. If a task that is a prerequisite for another is delayed, it can create a ripple effect, causing delays throughout the project. Identifying these dependency conflicts early allows you to adjust timelines and resources to keep the project on track.

4. Communicating Progress to Stakeholders

Communicating the progress of your plan to stakeholders is essential for maintaining transparency and ensuring that everyone involved is aligned with the project's goals.

a. Status Meetings

Regular status meetings with your team and stakeholders provide an opportunity to review progress collectively. During these meetings, you can use Microsoft Planner's visual tools, such as the Charts and Schedule Views, to present the current status of the project. These visuals make it easier for stakeholders to understand the progress and any challenges the team is facing.

b. Progress Reports

Microsoft Planner allows you to generate progress reports that can be shared with stakeholders. These reports can include task statuses, workload distribution, and any issues or risks that have been identified. Reports can be generated on a regular basis or as needed, depending on the needs of the project.

c. Real-Time Updates

For projects that require close monitoring, Microsoft Planner's integration with Microsoft Teams can provide real-time updates on task progress. This integration allows stakeholders to stay informed without needing to access Planner directly. Notifications and updates can be set up within Teams to ensure that all relevant parties are kept in the loop.

5. Adjusting Plans Based on Progress Reviews

After reviewing the progress of your plan, it's often necessary to make adjustments to keep the project on track. Microsoft Planner provides several tools to help you adapt to changes and ensure that your plan remains aligned with project goals.

a. Rescheduling Tasks

If certain tasks are delayed or if new tasks are added, you may need to reschedule existing tasks to accommodate these changes. The Schedule View allows you to easily move tasks to new dates by dragging and dropping them on the calendar. This flexibility ensures that your plan can adapt to the evolving needs of the project.

b. Reassigning Tasks

In some cases, it may be necessary to reassign tasks to different team members. This could be due to workload imbalances, changes in team composition, or the need for specific expertise. Microsoft Planner allows you to reassign tasks easily, ensuring that the right people are working on the right tasks at the right time.

c. Updating Plan Goals

As the project progresses, it's important to regularly review and update the goals of your plan. This might involve setting new milestones, adjusting the scope of work, or refining objectives based on the progress that has been made. Microsoft Planner's flexibility allows you to update these goals and communicate them to the team effectively.

6. Best Practices for Reviewing Plan Progress

To ensure that your plan reviews are effective and lead to meaningful improvements, it's important to follow some best practices.

a. Regular Reviews

Establish a regular schedule for reviewing plan progress. This could be weekly, bi-weekly, or monthly, depending on the size and complexity of the project. Regular reviews help to keep the team focused and ensure that any issues are addressed in a timely manner.

b. Collaborative Reviews

Involve the entire team in the progress review process. Collaborative reviews ensure that all perspectives are considered and that team members feel engaged and accountable for their tasks. Use the Planner comments feature to gather feedback and suggestions from the team before and during reviews.

c. Focus on Solutions

When issues are identified during a review, focus on finding solutions rather than placing blame. Encourage a problem-solving mindset within the team, and work together to develop action plans that will keep the project on track.

d. Documenting Progress

Keep detailed records of each progress review, including the decisions made and the actions to be taken. These records can be valuable for future reference and ensure that everyone is clear on what needs to be done.

7. Conclusion

Reviewing plan progress is a vital part of project management in Microsoft Planner. By using the various views and tools available, you can effectively monitor the status of your project, identify potential issues, and make informed decisions to keep your plan on track. Regular and collaborative reviews not only help to ensure the success of your current project but also build a foundation of best practices that can be applied to future projects. By following the guidelines and best practices outlined in this section, you can make the most of Microsoft Planner's capabilities and achieve your project goals efficiently.

3.3.3 Setting Up Progress Reports

Setting up progress reports in Microsoft Planner is a crucial aspect of managing any project. Progress reports provide a clear snapshot of the current status of tasks and plans, helping teams stay on track, identify potential issues early, and communicate effectively with stakeholders. In this section, we will explore the process of setting up progress reports, customizing them to meet your specific needs, and utilizing them to ensure the successful completion of your projects.

Understanding the Importance of Progress Reports

Before diving into the technical aspects of setting up progress reports, it's important to understand why they are essential. Progress reports serve multiple purposes:

1. Visibility: They provide transparency into the current state of a project, allowing team members, managers, and stakeholders to see what has been completed, what is in progress, and what is yet to be started.

2. Accountability: Regular progress reporting holds team members accountable for their assigned tasks. When everyone knows their work will be reviewed, there's a greater emphasis on meeting deadlines and maintaining quality.

3. Communication: Progress reports facilitate communication within the team and with external stakeholders. They ensure that everyone is on the same page and that there are no surprises as the project progresses.

4. Decision-Making: By providing an up-to-date view of project progress, these reports assist in decision-making, helping project managers and team leads allocate resources more effectively, prioritize tasks, and address potential risks.

5. Motivation: Seeing progress can be highly motivating for a team. It helps reinforce the value of their efforts and can drive momentum as they work toward the project's completion.

Setting Up Progress Reports in Microsoft Planner

Microsoft Planner does not have a dedicated progress reporting feature in the traditional sense. However, it offers several tools and integrations that allow you to set up and generate progress reports effectively.

1. Using the Planner Hub

The Planner Hub is your central dashboard in Microsoft Planner, where you can view all your plans at a glance. It provides a visual overview of the progress of each plan, showing how many tasks are completed, in progress, or not started.

- Accessing the Planner Hub: To access the Planner Hub, go to the Planner homepage and select "Planner Hub" from the navigation pane. Here, you'll see a summary of all your active plans, along with progress bars that indicate the overall status.

- Understanding the Progress Indicators: The progress bars in the Planner Hub are color-coded: green for completed tasks, yellow for in-progress tasks, and gray for tasks that haven't started. This gives you a quick visual representation of where each plan stands.

2. Using Buckets and Labels for Reporting

Buckets and labels are key organizational tools in Microsoft Planner that can be leveraged to generate more detailed progress reports.

- Organizing Tasks by Buckets: Buckets allow you to group tasks within a plan. For example, you could create buckets for different phases of a project, such as "Planning," "Execution," and "Review." This makes it easier to track the progress of specific project stages.

- Using Labels for Categorization: Labels provide another layer of categorization, allowing you to tag tasks with specific attributes, such as "High Priority," "Blocked," or "Client Review." These labels can be used to filter tasks and generate reports that focus on particular aspects of the project.

- Generating Reports Based on Buckets and Labels: While Microsoft Planner does not have built-in reporting tools, you can manually create reports by filtering tasks by bucket or label and then exporting this information to a tool like Microsoft Excel for further analysis.

3. Integrating with Microsoft Power BI

For more advanced reporting, integrating Microsoft Planner with Power BI offers powerful capabilities to visualize and analyze your project data.

- Connecting Planner to Power BI: Power BI can connect directly to Microsoft Planner via the Microsoft 365 data connector. This integration allows you to pull data from your Planner tasks and plans into Power BI, where you can create customized dashboards and reports.

- Creating Progress Dashboards: In Power BI, you can create dashboards that display real-time data on task completion, overdue tasks, and other key metrics. These dashboards can be shared with your team or stakeholders, providing a dynamic and interactive way to monitor project progress.

- Customizing Reports: Power BI allows for deep customization of reports. You can create visualizations such as Gantt charts, progress bars, and pie charts that represent different aspects of your plan's progress. You can also set up automated reports that refresh at regular intervals, ensuring that your data is always up to date.

4. Using Microsoft Teams and SharePoint for Reporting

Microsoft Teams and SharePoint are two other tools that can enhance your progress reporting in Microsoft Planner.

- Planner Integration with Teams: If your team uses Microsoft Teams, you can integrate Planner directly into your Teams channels. This integration allows you to view and manage Planner tasks without leaving Teams, and it also supports the creation of progress reports within the Teams environment.

- Creating Planner Tabs in Teams: By adding a Planner tab to your Teams channel, you can create a space where team members can view the progress of tasks and plans. This tab can be customized to show only certain tasks, buckets, or labels, providing a focused view of project progress.

- Using SharePoint for Reporting: SharePoint can be used to store and share progress reports generated from Planner data. For example, you can create a SharePoint site dedicated to a project and embed Planner dashboards or Power BI reports within that site.

This creates a centralized location where all project-related information, including progress reports, can be accessed.

5. Manual Reporting in Excel

If you prefer a more manual approach, exporting Planner data to Excel is a straightforward way to create progress reports.

- Exporting Planner Data: Microsoft Planner allows you to export your plan data to Excel. This includes information about tasks, assignees, due dates, and completion status. To export a plan, select "Export Plan to Excel" from the options menu in Planner.

- Creating Progress Reports in Excel: Once you have your data in Excel, you can use various Excel features to create progress reports. For example, you can create pivot tables to summarize task progress, use conditional formatting to highlight overdue tasks, or create charts that visualize the completion status of different tasks or buckets.

- Automating Report Generation: If you regularly export data from Planner to Excel, you can automate parts of the report generation process using Excel's built-in tools. For example, you can record macros to automate data formatting, or use Power Query to refresh your data automatically.

6. Scheduling and Distributing Progress Reports

Creating progress reports is only part of the process. It's equally important to ensure that these reports are regularly scheduled and distributed to the right people.

- Setting Up Regular Reporting Intervals: Determine how often progress reports need to be generated—daily, weekly, or monthly—depending on the needs of your project. Regular intervals ensure that all stakeholders are kept informed and can take timely action if needed.

- Automating Report Distribution: If you're using Power BI or another automated reporting tool, you can set up automated report distribution. For example, Power BI allows you to schedule email delivery of reports to specific team members or stakeholders at predefined intervals.

- Sharing Reports via Teams or SharePoint: Use Microsoft Teams or SharePoint to distribute reports. For example, you can post progress reports in a Teams channel dedicated to the project, or store them in a SharePoint document library where team members can access them as needed.

- Archiving Progress Reports: It's a good practice to archive progress reports, especially for long-term projects. This allows you to track historical progress and refer back to previous reports if needed. SharePoint is an ideal tool for archiving, as it allows you to organize and store documents securely.

Best Practices for Effective Progress Reporting

To ensure that your progress reports are effective, consider the following best practices:

1. Keep Reports Clear and Concise: Avoid overwhelming your audience with too much data. Focus on the key metrics that matter most to your project and ensure that your reports are easy to understand at a glance.

2. Tailor Reports to Your Audience: Different stakeholders may require different levels of detail. For example, a project sponsor might only need a high-level summary, while team members might need detailed task-level data. Customize your reports to meet the needs of your audience.

3. Ensure Timeliness: Timely reporting is crucial for maintaining project momentum. Make sure that reports are generated and distributed on time, so that any necessary actions can be taken promptly.

4. Incorporate Feedback: Regularly seek feedback from your team and stakeholders on the usefulness of the reports. Are they getting the information they need? Are there areas where the reports could be improved? Use this feedback to refine your reporting process.

5. Use Visuals Wisely: Visuals can enhance the clarity of your reports, but they should be used judiciously. Make sure that charts, graphs, and other visual elements add value and don't clutter the report.

6. Regularly Review and Adjust: As your project evolves, so too should your reporting process. Regularly review the effectiveness of your reports and make adjustments as necessary to ensure that they continue to meet the needs of the project.

Conclusion

Setting up progress reports in Microsoft Planner is an essential task for any project manager or team leader. While Planner provides a variety of tools and integrations to help you generate these reports, the key to success lies in understanding your project's specific needs and tailoring your reports accordingly. Whether you're using the Planner Hub, integrating with Power BI, or manually creating reports in Excel, the goal is always the same: to provide clear, actionable insights that help your team stay on track and achieve its goals. By following the best practices outlined in this section, you can ensure that your progress reports are both effective and impactful, driving your project to successful completion.

CHAPTER IV
Advanced Features of Microsoft Planner

4.1 Using Charts and Visualizations

4.1.1 Understanding the Planner Charts

In Microsoft Planner, visual representations of data, particularly through charts, play a crucial role in helping users manage tasks and projects effectively. These charts provide a bird's-eye view of your plan's progress, enabling you to quickly assess the state of your tasks, identify bottlenecks, and ensure that your team stays on track to meet deadlines. This section delves into the different types of charts available in Microsoft Planner, how to interpret them, and how to use them to your advantage.

Overview of Planner Charts

Microsoft Planner offers several built-in charts that give users a quick snapshot of their plan's status. The most commonly used charts in Planner include:

- Task Status Chart: Displays the current status of tasks, such as Not Started, In Progress, Late, or Completed.

- Task Progress Chart: Visualizes the progress of tasks over time, helping you understand the pace at which work is being completed.

- Assignment Distribution Chart: Shows how tasks are distributed among team members, which can help in identifying workload imbalances.

- Due Date Chart: Provides an overview of upcoming deadlines, highlighting tasks that are due soon or overdue.

These charts are automatically generated based on the data entered in your plans, making it easy to access real-time insights without needing to manually create reports.

Interpreting the Task Status Chart

The Task Status Chart is one of the most important charts in Microsoft Planner. It categorizes tasks into different statuses:

- Not Started: Tasks that have been created but not yet begun.

- In Progress: Tasks that are currently being worked on.

- Late: Tasks that have not been completed by their due date.

- Completed: Tasks that have been finished.

Understanding this chart is vital for monitoring the overall progress of your project. For example, if a significant portion of tasks is categorized as "Late," it could indicate that your project is behind schedule, requiring immediate attention. Conversely, a high number of "Completed" tasks suggests that your team is on track, possibly even ahead of schedule.

Analyzing Task Distribution

The Task Distribution Chart offers insights into how tasks are spread across different team members. This chart is particularly useful for project managers who need to ensure that the workload is evenly distributed. Analyzing this chart involves looking at the number of tasks assigned to each team member and their respective statuses.

If the chart shows that one team member has significantly more tasks than others, it might be necessary to redistribute tasks to avoid overloading any single person. On the other hand, if certain team members have fewer tasks, they could be underutilized, and you might consider assigning them additional responsibilities.

Tracking Progress with Visuals

Visual representations of progress, such as the Task Progress Chart, are crucial for keeping a project on track. This chart typically displays tasks along a timeline, showing how many tasks are completed versus those that are still in progress or late.

To effectively use this chart, you should regularly compare the number of tasks in each category (Not Started, In Progress, Late, Completed) to your project timeline. This comparison helps you determine if your team is meeting deadlines or if adjustments are necessary. For example, if the "In Progress" tasks remain constant while the "Completed" tasks do not increase, it may indicate a slowdown in productivity, which could be a red flag.

Due Date Chart: A Critical Tool for Time Management

The Due Date Chart is designed to help you manage time more effectively. It provides a visual representation of tasks according to their due dates, highlighting which tasks are due soon, which are overdue, and which have flexible deadlines.

This chart is especially useful in prioritizing tasks. By focusing on tasks that are due soon or overdue, you can ensure that the most critical work is completed on time. Moreover, by regularly monitoring this chart, you can prevent the accumulation of overdue tasks, which can become overwhelming if not managed properly.

Using Charts for Team Meetings and Status Updates

Charts in Microsoft Planner are not just for personal use; they can also be powerful tools for team meetings and status updates. During these meetings, you can share your screen and walk through the charts to give everyone a clear picture of the project's status. This practice ensures that all team members are on the same page and that any issues are identified and addressed promptly.

For instance, reviewing the Task Status Chart during a meeting can help the team focus on what needs to be completed next. Similarly, the Task Distribution Chart can foster discussions about workload balance, encouraging collaboration and support among team members.

Customizing Chart Views

While the default charts in Microsoft Planner are incredibly useful, there are times when you may want to customize these views to better suit your needs. Microsoft Planner allows you to filter tasks by different criteria (e.g., due date, label, priority) and adjust the chart views accordingly.

For example, if you're managing a large project with multiple phases, you might want to filter the charts to show tasks only related to the current phase. This filtering makes it easier to focus on relevant tasks without being overwhelmed by the full scope of the project.

Exporting Chart Data for Reports

There might be situations where you need to present your data outside of Microsoft Planner, such as in a formal report or presentation. Microsoft Planner allows you to export chart data to Excel, where you can create custom reports or integrate the data with other project management tools.

When exporting data, you can choose to include all tasks or filter specific data points that are most relevant to your report. This flexibility ensures that your reports are tailored to the audience, whether it's a detailed project review for stakeholders or a quick update for your team.

Leveraging Charts for Continuous Improvement

The insights gained from Planner charts should not only be used for monitoring the current project but also for improving future projects. By analyzing chart data at the end of a project, you can identify patterns and areas for improvement.

For example, if the Task Status Chart consistently shows a high number of late tasks, it may indicate a need for better time management strategies or more realistic deadline setting. Similarly, if the Task Distribution Chart reveals persistent workload imbalances, it could prompt a review of how tasks are assigned to team members in future projects.

Case Study: Using Planner Charts to Improve Team Efficiency

To illustrate the power of Planner charts, consider the case of a marketing team that used Microsoft Planner to manage a product launch. Initially, the Task Distribution Chart revealed that a few team members were overloaded with tasks, leading to delays and missed deadlines.

By analyzing the charts, the project manager was able to redistribute tasks more evenly, ensuring that all team members had a manageable workload. Additionally, the Task Progress Chart helped the team identify areas where they were falling behind, allowing them to take corrective actions early in the process. As a result, the team was able to complete the project on time, with all tasks successfully delivered.

Best Practices for Using Charts in Microsoft Planner

To get the most out of Microsoft Planner charts, consider the following best practices:

1. Regularly Review Charts: Make it a habit to review charts regularly, especially during team meetings or status updates. This practice keeps everyone informed and helps identify issues early.

2. Use Filters to Focus: Customize chart views by filtering tasks to focus on specific aspects of your project, such as high-priority tasks or tasks due in the next week.

3. Balance Workload: Use the Task Distribution Chart to ensure that tasks are evenly distributed among team members. Address any imbalances promptly to maintain productivity.

4. Integrate with Other Tools: Consider exporting chart data to Excel for more detailed analysis or integration with other project management tools. This approach allows for more customized reporting and analysis.

5. Learn from Past Projects: After completing a project, review the charts to identify patterns and areas for improvement. Use these insights to refine your planning and execution strategies for future projects.

Conclusion

Understanding and effectively using the charts in Microsoft Planner can significantly enhance your ability to manage projects and teams. These visual tools provide real-time insights into task status, workload distribution, and overall progress, enabling you to make informed decisions and keep your projects on track. By regularly reviewing and analyzing these charts, you can not only ensure the successful completion of your current projects but also continuously improve your project management practices over time.

4.1.2 Analyzing Task Distribution

Analyzing task distribution is a critical aspect of managing and optimizing workflows in Microsoft Planner. It allows you to understand how tasks are allocated among team members, how workload is distributed across different projects, and where bottlenecks might be occurring. By leveraging the built-in chart and visualization tools in Microsoft Planner, you can gain valuable insights into task distribution, which can help improve efficiency, productivity, and team morale.

Understanding Task Distribution

At its core, task distribution refers to how tasks are spread among team members or across different categories within a project. This analysis helps identify whether tasks are being assigned equitably and whether any team member is overburdened or underutilized. It also provides a clear view of how tasks are progressing, where delays might be happening, and what adjustments might be needed to keep the project on track.

In Microsoft Planner, task distribution can be visualized through a variety of built-in charts and graphs. These visual tools provide a real-time snapshot of task assignments, allowing you to quickly assess the state of your project and make informed decisions about resource allocation.

Using the Planner Dashboard

The Planner dashboard is the central hub for visualizing task distribution. When you open a plan in Microsoft Planner, you'll notice the "Charts" tab, which gives you access to a comprehensive set of visual tools. These charts are automatically generated based on the data entered into the Planner, offering an up-to-date view of your plan's progress.

The main charts available in Microsoft Planner for analyzing task distribution include:

1. Task Status Chart: This chart provides an overview of tasks based on their current status. It categorizes tasks as "Not Started," "In Progress," "Late," or "Completed." By analyzing this

chart, you can quickly determine how many tasks are on track, how many are behind schedule, and how much work remains to be done.

2. Tasks by Bucket: Buckets are a way to organize tasks within a plan. The "Tasks by Bucket" chart shows the distribution of tasks across different buckets, giving you insight into how tasks are grouped and whether any specific bucket (or project phase) is overloaded or underutilized.

3. Tasks by Priority: This chart categorizes tasks based on their assigned priority levels, such as "Urgent," "Important," "Medium," or "Low." This helps in understanding how much high-priority work is pending and whether priority tasks are being addressed promptly.

4. Tasks by Progress: This visualization breaks down tasks by their progress status, showing how many tasks are in each stage of completion. It provides a clear view of how work is advancing and where potential delays might be occurring.

5. Tasks by Assignee: Perhaps the most crucial chart for task distribution analysis, this chart shows how tasks are allocated among team members. It highlights who is handling the most tasks, who might have bandwidth for additional work, and whether the distribution aligns with each team member's capacity.

Analyzing the Task Status Chart

The Task Status chart is particularly useful for project managers and team leads. It gives a high-level overview of where each task stands in the workflow. Here's how you can analyze it effectively:

- Identify Delays: Tasks categorized as "Late" indicate potential issues in the workflow. Analyzing these tasks helps you identify what is causing the delays. It could be due to resource constraints, external dependencies, or unclear task instructions. By addressing these issues promptly, you can prevent further delays and keep the project on track.

- Evaluate Progress: Tasks that are "In Progress" show how work is advancing. By monitoring this category, you can assess whether tasks are moving forward as planned or if they are stalling at certain stages. This can help you identify process improvements or additional support that might be needed.

- Monitor Completion Rates: The "Completed" category is a direct indicator of how much work has been finished. Comparing the number of completed tasks to the total number of tasks gives you an immediate sense of how far along the project is and whether you're on track to meet deadlines.

Analyzing Tasks by Bucket

Buckets are a powerful organizational tool in Microsoft Planner, allowing you to group tasks by phases, categories, or workstreams. The "Tasks by Bucket" chart helps you analyze how tasks are distributed across these different segments.

- Evaluate Workstream Balance: By analyzing tasks within each bucket, you can determine whether certain workstreams are overloaded. For example, if the "Design" bucket has significantly more tasks than the "Development" bucket, it may indicate an imbalance in how work is being allocated. This could lead to delays in later phases if not addressed.

- Identify Overloaded Buckets: An overloaded bucket might suggest that a particular phase or category is consuming more resources than planned. This could require reallocation of tasks to ensure that no single phase becomes a bottleneck in the project timeline.

- Streamline Task Movement: If tasks are moving slowly from one bucket to another, it might indicate issues with handoffs between phases. Analyzing the distribution of tasks by bucket can help you pinpoint where these slowdowns are happening, allowing you to make process adjustments or provide additional resources.

Analyzing Tasks by Priority

Priority levels in Microsoft Planner help teams focus on what's most important. The "Tasks by Priority" chart provides a visual representation of how tasks are prioritized within a plan.

- Balance Workloads Based on Priority: By analyzing this chart, you can ensure that high-priority tasks are not being overlooked. If too many high-priority tasks are assigned to a single team member, it might indicate a need to redistribute some of the workload to prevent burnout and ensure that critical tasks are completed on time.

- Focus on High-Priority Tasks: If there are many high-priority tasks that are not yet started or are still in progress, it could be a sign that the team needs to refocus their efforts. This chart helps you identify where attention should be concentrated to keep the project moving forward.

- Manage Low-Priority Tasks: While low-priority tasks may not need immediate attention, it's important to ensure that they don't accumulate to the point where they become a significant burden. Analyzing their distribution helps you plan when and how these tasks should be tackled, ensuring that they don't impact the completion of higher-priority work.

Analyzing Tasks by Assignee

The "Tasks by Assignee" chart is one of the most crucial tools for managing team workload and ensuring that tasks are distributed equitably.

- Identify Overloaded Team Members: If a team member has significantly more tasks than others, it could indicate that they are overloaded. This might lead to delays in task completion or reduced quality of work. By analyzing this chart, you can reassign tasks to balance the workload more evenly across the team.

- Assess Team Capacity: The chart also helps in identifying team members who may have less on their plate and could take on additional tasks. This ensures that resources are being used effectively and that no team member is underutilized.

- Monitor Task Completion Rates: Analyzing how many tasks each team member has completed can also provide insights into their productivity. If certain team members consistently complete tasks more efficiently, they may be well-suited for taking on more critical tasks or mentoring others.

Using Data to Improve Task Distribution

Analyzing task distribution in Microsoft Planner is not just about understanding the current state of your project but also about using this data to make improvements. Here are some ways to leverage task distribution data to enhance your project management practices:

- Redistribute Workload: If you identify that certain team members are overloaded, use the data to redistribute tasks more equitably. This not only helps in balancing the workload but also improves team morale and productivity.

- Adjust Priorities: If you notice that too many high-priority tasks are still in progress or not started, consider revisiting the project's priority settings. Adjusting priorities based on task distribution data ensures that the team is focusing on what's most important at any given time.

- Improve Resource Allocation: Use the insights from task distribution analysis to allocate resources more effectively. For example, if certain buckets or phases are overloaded, you might need to assign additional resources to those areas or adjust timelines to ensure that the project stays on track.

- Enhance Communication: Task distribution data can also highlight areas where communication may need to be improved. For example, if tasks are stalling in certain phases, it could indicate that team members need clearer instructions or better coordination. Addressing these communication gaps can help improve overall project efficiency.

- Plan for Future Projects: The insights gained from analyzing task distribution can also inform the planning of future projects. By understanding how tasks were distributed and managed in previous projects, you can make better decisions when setting up new plans, leading to more efficient and successful project outcomes.

Best Practices for Task Distribution Analysis

To make the most of the task distribution analysis in Microsoft Planner, consider the following best practices:

- Regularly Review Charts: Make it a habit to regularly review the task distribution charts in Planner. Frequent reviews help you stay on top of the project's progress and allow you to make timely adjustments as needed.

- Collaborate with Team Members: Involve your team in the analysis process. Encourage team members to review their own task distribution charts and provide feedback. This collaborative approach ensures that everyone is on the same page and can help identify potential issues early on.

- Use Data to Foster Continuous Improvement: Use the insights gained from task distribution analysis to foster a culture of continuous improvement within your team. Regularly discuss what's working and what's not, and make adjustments to your processes based on the data.

- *Combine with Other Data Sources*

: While task distribution data is valuable on its own, it becomes even more powerful when combined with other data sources. For example, consider integrating Planner data with time tracking or project management tools to get a more comprehensive view of your project's health.

By effectively analyzing task distribution using Microsoft Planner's visualization tools, you can ensure that your projects are managed efficiently, workloads are balanced, and your team is set up for success. This proactive approach to managing tasks will help you achieve your project goals more consistently and with greater ease.

4.1.3 Tracking Progress with Visuals

Tracking progress in any project management tool is essential for ensuring that tasks are completed on time, resources are used efficiently, and goals are met. Microsoft Planner offers a range of visual tools that make it easier for teams to monitor their progress. In this section, we'll delve into how you can leverage these visual tools in Microsoft Planner to keep track of your projects effectively.

Understanding Visual Progress Tracking

Visual progress tracking involves using graphical representations to monitor the status of tasks, plans, and overall project health. The primary benefit of using visuals is that they provide a quick, at-a-glance view of how your project is progressing. This is particularly useful in collaborative environments where multiple stakeholders need to stay informed.

In Microsoft Planner, progress tracking is facilitated through various visual tools such as charts, task boards, and dashboards. These tools help you to:

- Monitor task completion: Easily see which tasks are completed, in progress, or not yet started.

- Identify bottlenecks: Quickly spot areas where progress is slow or stalled.

- Allocate resources effectively: Ensure that team members are not overloaded and that tasks are evenly distributed.

- Communicate progress: Share visual progress updates with team members and stakeholders to keep everyone aligned.

Using the Planner Dashboard

The Planner Dashboard is the central hub for tracking progress within a plan. It provides an overview of all tasks in the plan, showing their current status and any potential issues. The Dashboard is divided into several sections, each offering a different perspective on your project's progress.

- Progress Bar: The progress bar is a simple, linear visual that shows the overall completion rate of your plan. It is typically divided into segments representing completed, in-progress, and not-started tasks. As tasks are completed, the progress bar fills up, giving you a clear visual indicator of how close you are to finishing the project.

- Task Status Overview: This section breaks down tasks into different statuses, such as "Not Started," "In Progress," and "Completed." Each status is represented by a colored segment or bar, making it easy to see the distribution of tasks across these categories.

- Team Member Contribution: The Planner Dashboard also allows you to see how tasks are distributed among team members. This feature helps in ensuring that no one is overburdened and that tasks are evenly assigned. It also shows which team members are lagging behind or ahead in their task completion.

Leveraging Task Boards for Visual Tracking

The task board is one of the most intuitive and widely used features in Microsoft Planner for visual progress tracking. The task board mimics a physical Kanban board, where tasks are represented as cards that can be moved across different columns, each representing a different stage of progress.

- Customizing Columns: By default, the task board includes columns for "Not Started," "In Progress," and "Completed." However, you can customize these columns to match the specific stages of your workflow. For example, you might add columns for "Review," "Testing," or "Approval" to better track the different phases of a project.

- Using Labels for Additional Insights: Labels in Microsoft Planner can be used to categorize tasks further. For instance, you can assign different colors to labels such as "High Priority," "Urgent," or "Requires Attention." These labels then provide a visual cue on the task board, helping you quickly identify tasks that need immediate focus.

- Drag-and-Drop Functionality: The drag-and-drop feature of the task board makes it easy to update the status of tasks. Simply drag a task card from one column to another to reflect its current status. This action is automatically recorded in Planner, keeping the entire team updated in real-time.

- Visualizing Task Dependencies: While Planner does not have native support for task dependencies like some more complex project management tools, you can use the task board creatively to indicate dependencies. For example, tasks that depend on the completion of others can be placed in the same column and arranged in a specific order. Using labels or comments can further clarify these dependencies.

Utilizing Planner Charts

Planner Charts provide a graphical representation of your plan's progress, offering a more analytical view compared to the task board. These charts are automatically generated based on the data in your Planner and can be accessed from the Planner Hub.

- Task Distribution Chart: This pie chart shows how tasks are distributed across different statuses (e.g., "Not Started," "In Progress," "Completed"). It provides a quick snapshot of how many tasks are yet to be started, how many are currently being worked on, and how many have been completed.

- Task Assignment Chart: This chart displays the distribution of tasks among team members. It helps you identify if tasks are evenly distributed or if certain team members are overloaded. You can use this information to reassign tasks and balance the workload.

- Completion Progress Chart: This chart tracks the progress of task completion over time. It's a valuable tool for understanding whether the project is on track to meet its deadlines. If the progress line is flat, it might indicate that tasks are not being completed as expected, signaling a need for intervention.

- Task Priority Chart: This chart categorizes tasks based on their priority levels. It helps you ensure that high-priority tasks are being addressed promptly and not overshadowed by less critical tasks.

Setting Up Notifications and Alerts

While visuals are great for at-a-glance monitoring, setting up notifications and alerts ensures that you are immediately informed of any critical changes or delays in your plan. Microsoft Planner allows you to configure notifications for various events, such as:

- Task Assignments: Get notified when a task is assigned to you or when a task you assigned is accepted by a team member.

- Due Date Reminders: Receive reminders when a task's due date is approaching or if a task is overdue.

- Task Updates: Stay informed when the status of a task changes, for instance, when a task moves from "In Progress" to "Completed."

Notifications can be received via email or through the Microsoft Teams integration, depending on your preference. These notifications help you stay on top of your tasks and ensure that nothing falls through the cracks.

Exporting Visual Data for Reporting

At times, you may need to present your plan's progress to stakeholders or include it in broader project reports. Microsoft Planner allows you to export visual data for these purposes. You can export your Planner data to Excel, where you can create more customized charts and graphs or include it in a larger project report.

- Exporting Charts: You can take screenshots of the charts directly from Planner or use the Excel export feature to create more detailed reports. Excel allows you to manipulate the data further, create pivot tables, or apply advanced filters to gain deeper insights.

- Integrating with Power BI: For more advanced reporting, consider integrating Microsoft Planner with Power BI. This allows you to create interactive dashboards that can be shared with stakeholders. Power BI's advanced data visualization capabilities enable you to combine Planner data with other data sources, providing a comprehensive view of project progress.

Best Practices for Visual Progress Tracking

To make the most of the visual tracking tools in Microsoft Planner, consider the following best practices:

- Regularly Update Task Status: Ensure that all team members regularly update the status of their tasks. This keeps the visual data in Planner accurate and reflective of the current state of the project.

- Use Consistent Labeling: Establish a consistent labeling system across all tasks and plans. This consistency makes it easier to interpret visual data and ensures that everyone is on the same page.

- Review Visuals in Team Meetings: Incorporate visual progress reviews into your regular team meetings. Use the Planner Dashboard, task boards, and charts to discuss progress, identify issues, and make necessary adjustments.

- Leverage Automation: Use Microsoft Power Automate to set up automated alerts and updates. For example, you can create flows that automatically notify you when a task is overdue or when the overall progress of a plan falls below a certain threshold.

- Customize Views for Different Stakeholders: Different stakeholders may require different levels of detail. Customize your Planner views and exported reports to meet the needs of each stakeholder group, ensuring that everyone receives the information they need in a format that is easy to understand.

Conclusion

Visual tools in Microsoft Planner are a powerful way to track progress, identify issues early, and keep your team aligned with project goals. By effectively using the Planner Dashboard, task boards, and charts, you can ensure that your projects stay on track and that your team remains productive. Remember to regularly update your tasks, use consistent labeling, and review visual data in team meetings to maximize the effectiveness of these tools. Whether you're managing a small team or a complex project, visual progress tracking in Microsoft Planner will help you achieve your goals more efficiently.

4.2 Integrating with Other Tools

Integration is one of the most powerful aspects of Microsoft Planner, enabling users to enhance productivity by connecting Planner with other essential tools within the Microsoft ecosystem and beyond. This seamless integration allows teams to manage tasks, schedules, and projects more effectively, leveraging the strengths of different applications. In this section, we will delve into the specifics of integrating Microsoft Planner with Microsoft Outlook, exploring how these two tools can work together to streamline workflows, improve communication, and ensure that nothing falls through the cracks.

4.2.1 Linking Planner with Microsoft Outlook

Microsoft Outlook is a cornerstone of productivity in many organizations, serving as the primary platform for email communication, calendar management, and task tracking. Integrating Microsoft Planner with Outlook offers a powerful way to centralize task management and ensure that deadlines are met without the need to switch constantly between applications. This integration enables users to view and manage their Planner tasks directly from Outlook, providing a more cohesive workflow and helping to keep all essential tasks in one place.

Understanding the Integration

The integration between Microsoft Planner and Outlook is designed to bridge the gap between task management and email communication, two activities that often go hand in hand. When you link Planner with Outlook, you can perform several key functions, such as:

- Viewing Planner tasks within your Outlook calendar.

- Receiving email notifications for task updates.

- Converting Outlook emails into Planner tasks.

- Synchronizing tasks across both platforms to ensure consistency.

This integration is particularly useful for teams who rely heavily on email for communication and task assignment, as it brings the two tools together, making it easier to manage tasks that arise from email conversations.

Setting Up the Integration

To begin integrating Microsoft Planner with Outlook, you need to follow a few simple steps. The process is straightforward, and once set up, it greatly enhances the way you manage tasks across both platforms.

1. Accessing Planner from Outlook:

   - Open Outlook and navigate to the "Calendar" view.

   - In the ribbon, select "Add Calendar" and choose "From Planner."

   - A list of available Planner plans will appear. Select the plan you want to integrate.

   - The tasks from the selected plan will now appear in your Outlook calendar, allowing you to view deadlines and upcoming tasks alongside your other calendar events.

2. Syncing Tasks with Outlook:

   - When tasks are created or updated in Planner, these changes are automatically reflected in the Outlook calendar.

   - This synchronization ensures that all team members are on the same page and can see deadlines and task details without needing to switch between different tools.

3. Customizing Task Notifications:

   - To receive email notifications for task updates, go to Planner, select the plan you want to customize, and click on "Plan Settings."

   - Under "Notifications," choose the types of updates you want to receive via email, such as when a task is assigned to you or when a deadline is approaching.

   - These notifications will appear in your Outlook inbox, keeping you informed about important task changes without needing to check Planner constantly.

4. Creating Planner Tasks from Outlook Emails:

- Often, tasks originate from email conversations. To streamline this process, you can create Planner tasks directly from an Outlook email.

- Open the email that you want to convert into a task.

- Click on "More Actions" (usually represented by three dots) and select "Create Task in Planner."

- A new task will be created in Planner with the email content included in the task description. You can then assign the task, set a due date, and add it to the appropriate plan.

Benefits of Linking Planner with Outlook

Integrating Microsoft Planner with Outlook offers numerous benefits, making it easier to manage tasks, deadlines, and communication in one cohesive environment.

1. Centralized Task Management:

- By linking Planner tasks with Outlook, you centralize all your task management activities within a single platform. This integration allows you to view all tasks and deadlines directly from your Outlook calendar, reducing the need to switch between multiple applications and ensuring that important tasks are not overlooked.

2. Enhanced Productivity:

- The integration streamlines workflows by allowing you to create Planner tasks directly from emails. This feature is particularly useful for teams that frequently receive task-related requests via email, as it reduces the steps required to create and manage tasks.

3. Improved Communication:

- With email notifications enabled, team members are kept in the loop about task updates and changes, fostering better communication and collaboration. This feature is particularly beneficial for remote teams or large organizations where keeping everyone informed can be challenging.

4. Consistent Task Tracking:

- The synchronization between Planner and Outlook ensures that all tasks and deadlines are consistently tracked across both platforms. This consistency is crucial for meeting project deadlines and ensuring that all team members are aligned on what needs to be done.

5. Increased Flexibility:

- The integration provides increased flexibility in how you manage your tasks. Whether you prefer to work primarily from Planner or Outlook, the integration allows you to choose the platform that best suits your workflow without sacrificing access to essential task information.

Use Cases for Planner-Outlook Integration

The integration between Microsoft Planner and Outlook is particularly useful in several scenarios:

1. Project Management:

- Project managers can use the integration to view all project-related tasks within their Outlook calendar. This centralized view helps in scheduling meetings, setting deadlines, and ensuring that all project milestones are visible to the team.

2. Sales Teams:

- Sales teams can benefit from creating Planner tasks directly from client emails in Outlook. This feature ensures that no customer request or follow-up is missed, and tasks are assigned to the appropriate team member promptly.

3. Marketing Campaigns:

- Marketing teams can use the integration to track campaign-related tasks alongside other calendar events, such as launch dates and promotional activities. This integration ensures that all marketing tasks are aligned with key campaign milestones.

4. Event Planning:

- Event planners can link their Planner tasks with Outlook to manage event logistics, schedules, and vendor communication more effectively. This integration provides a comprehensive view of all tasks and deadlines in relation to the event timeline.

5. Personal Task Management:

- Individuals can use the integration to manage personal and professional tasks within the same calendar. This feature is particularly useful for those who prefer to keep all their tasks in one place, ensuring that nothing is overlooked.

Best Practices for Using Planner-Outlook Integration

To get the most out of the integration between Microsoft Planner and Outlook, consider the following best practices:

1. Regularly Review Your Tasks:

- Set aside time at the beginning or end of each day to review your Planner tasks in Outlook. This practice helps you stay on top of upcoming deadlines and ensures that no tasks are missed.

2. Utilize Labels and Priorities:

- Use labels and priorities in Planner to categorize tasks and ensure that the most important tasks are easily identifiable in your Outlook calendar. This practice helps you focus on high-priority tasks first.

3. Customize Notifications Wisely:

- Be selective about the types of notifications you receive via email. Too many notifications can become overwhelming, so choose to receive updates only for critical tasks or milestones.

4. Keep Tasks and Emails Organized:

- If you frequently create Planner tasks from emails, ensure that your Outlook inbox is well-organized. Use folders, categories, or flags to manage emails that require follow-up, making it easier to create tasks later.

5. Leverage Calendar Views:

- Take advantage of different calendar views in Outlook, such as the daily, weekly, or monthly view, to get a broader perspective of your tasks. This practice helps you plan your time more effectively and ensures that you are not over-committing yourself.

Potential Challenges and How to Overcome Them

While integrating Microsoft Planner with Outlook offers numerous benefits, there are also potential challenges that users may encounter. Understanding these challenges and how to address them can help ensure a smooth integration experience.

1. Task Overload:

- With the integration, it can be easy to become overwhelmed by the number of tasks displayed in your Outlook calendar. To manage this, consider filtering tasks by priority or using a separate calendar view for specific plans.

2. Email Notification Overload:

- Receiving too many email notifications can become disruptive. To mitigate this, customize your notification settings to only receive updates for tasks that require immediate attention or are of high importance.

3. Synchronization Delays:

- In some cases, there may be a delay in task updates reflecting in Outlook. If this happens, try refreshing your calendar or checking the Planner app directly for the latest updates.

4. Limited Integration Scope:

- Currently, the integration primarily focuses on task visibility and notifications. If you require deeper integration, such as automating complex workflows, consider using additional tools like Microsoft Power Automate to extend the functionality.

5. Training and Adoption:

- For teams unfamiliar with Microsoft Planner or Outlook, there may be a learning curve. Providing training sessions or creating user guides can help ease the transition and ensure that all team members are comfortable with the integration.

In summary, integrating Microsoft Planner with Microsoft Outlook is a powerful way to enhance productivity, improve task management, and streamline communication. By following the setup steps and best practices outlined in this section, users can fully leverage the benefits of this integration, ensuring that tasks are managed effectively across both platforms. Whether you're managing projects, collaborating with a team, or organizing personal tasks, the Planner-Outlook integration offers a cohesive solution to keep everything on track and ensure that goals are met efficiently.

4.2.2 Syncing Planner with SharePoint

Introduction

Integrating Microsoft Planner with SharePoint provides organizations with a powerful combination of task management and document management capabilities. SharePoint, being a robust platform for document storage, collaboration, and content management, complements Planner's task tracking and project management functionalities. When these two tools are synced, teams can manage tasks in Planner while simultaneously accessing, storing, and collaborating on related documents within SharePoint. This integration ensures that all project-related resources are centrally located and easily accessible, thereby enhancing efficiency, collaboration, and transparency across the organization.

This section will explore the benefits, steps, and best practices for syncing Microsoft Planner with SharePoint, ensuring that your organization can fully leverage the strengths of both platforms.

Benefits of Syncing Planner with SharePoint

1. Centralized Information Hub: By syncing Planner with SharePoint, teams can create a central repository where all project-related tasks, documents, and resources are stored. This ensures that everyone involved in the project can access the information they need without having to search through multiple systems.

2. Enhanced Collaboration: SharePoint's collaborative features, such as co-authoring and version control, complement Planner's task management capabilities. Team members can work together on documents in real-time, while Planner keeps everyone on track with task assignments and deadlines.

3. Streamlined Workflow: Integration simplifies workflow processes by allowing tasks to be directly linked to documents stored in SharePoint. This reduces the time spent switching between different tools and ensures that all relevant documents are easily accessible within the context of the task.

4. Improved Transparency: With tasks and documents in one place, it's easier for project managers and stakeholders to track progress and ensure that everyone is aligned. This transparency can help to identify potential issues early and make more informed decisions.

5. Compliance and Security: SharePoint provides robust security and compliance features, ensuring that sensitive documents are protected and that the organization's compliance requirements are met. Syncing with Planner ensures that tasks related to these documents are managed with the same level of security.

Setting Up Sync Between Planner and SharePoint

To sync Microsoft Planner with SharePoint, it is important to understand how both platforms interact within the Microsoft 365 ecosystem. The integration primarily happens at the Group level since both Planner and SharePoint are components of Microsoft 365 Groups. Here are the steps to effectively set up the sync:

1. Create or Identify the Microsoft 365 Group:

  - If you already have a Microsoft 365 Group that your team is using, it will already have a connected SharePoint site and Planner. If not, you can create a new Group in Outlook or Microsoft Teams. Creating a Group automatically generates a corresponding SharePoint site and Planner.

2. Accessing the SharePoint Site from Planner:

  - Within the Planner interface, navigate to the associated Microsoft 365 Group. From here, you can access the linked SharePoint site by selecting the Group name and then clicking on "Files" in the Planner's interface, which will direct you to the document library in SharePoint.

3. Adding Planner to a SharePoint Site:

  - To integrate a specific Planner with a SharePoint site, you can add it as a web part on a SharePoint page. Edit the SharePoint page where you want to display the Planner board, click on the "+" icon to add a new web part, and select the "Planner" web part. Choose the appropriate Plan to display on this page.

4. Linking Tasks to SharePoint Documents:

  - Within Planner, you can directly link tasks to documents stored in SharePoint. While creating or editing a task, use the "Add Attachment" option, and then select "SharePoint" to browse and attach relevant files directly from the linked SharePoint site.

5. Syncing Task Information:

  - While there isn't a direct sync option that automatically reflects task details in SharePoint, you can manually sync essential task information by creating lists or libraries in SharePoint that correspond with tasks in Planner. Power Automate can be used to automate certain processes, like copying task details into SharePoint lists.

Best Practices for Syncing Planner with SharePoint

1. Maintain Consistency in Naming Conventions:

- To avoid confusion, ensure that the names of your Plans in Planner and the corresponding document libraries or lists in SharePoint are consistent. This will make it easier for team members to locate the right documents and tasks.

2. Utilize SharePoint Metadata and Tags:

- Leverage SharePoint's metadata features to categorize and tag documents related to specific Planner tasks or projects. This helps in organizing the files effectively and enables powerful search capabilities within SharePoint.

3. Automate Workflows with Power Automate:

- Use Power Automate (formerly Microsoft Flow) to create automated workflows between Planner and SharePoint. For example, you can set up a flow that automatically creates a SharePoint document or folder when a new task is created in Planner, ensuring that all related documents are organized from the outset.

4. Regularly Review and Archive:

- Establish a process for regularly reviewing and archiving completed tasks and associated documents. This not only keeps your Planner and SharePoint environments clutter-free but also ensures that important documents are stored securely for future reference.

5. Enable Co-Authoring and Collaboration:

- Make sure that your team members are aware of SharePoint's co-authoring capabilities. Encourage them to collaborate on documents directly within SharePoint while keeping track of task progress in Planner. This reduces the need for multiple versions of documents and enhances real-time collaboration.

6. Security and Permissions Management:

- Carefully manage permissions in SharePoint to ensure that sensitive documents are only accessible to authorized personnel. While syncing with Planner, ensure that these permissions are reflected in the tasks to avoid unintentional data breaches.

Real-World Applications and Examples

Example 1: Marketing Campaign Management

A marketing team can create a Plan in Microsoft Planner to manage an upcoming campaign. Each task in Planner could correspond to different campaign elements, such as content creation, ad placement, and social media scheduling. By syncing with SharePoint, all the related documents (e.g., ad creatives, content drafts, campaign briefs) can be stored in a dedicated SharePoint document library. Team members can collaborate on these documents, make real-time updates, and track progress in Planner. This ensures that all campaign materials are centrally located, and tasks are completed on schedule.

Example 2: Product Development Project

In a product development scenario, a company might use Planner to track the different stages of a product launch. Each stage, from design to testing to final rollout, can be represented as a task in Planner. By syncing Planner with SharePoint, the design team can store CAD files, testing reports, and other critical documents in SharePoint. The development team can then link these documents to specific tasks in Planner, ensuring that everyone involved in the project has easy access to the latest files, and progress is tracked systematically.

Example 3: Event Planning and Execution

For event planning, teams can use Planner to manage the various aspects of the event, such as venue selection, vendor coordination, and marketing efforts. By integrating with SharePoint, all contracts, venue details, and promotional materials can be stored in a SharePoint document library. Tasks in Planner can be linked to these documents, ensuring that team members have access to all necessary information and can update task statuses as they complete different planning phases.

Challenges and How to Overcome Them

1. Complexity of Setup:

   - Integrating Planner with SharePoint may require initial setup and configuration, particularly if you plan to use advanced features like Power Automate. To mitigate this, provide team members with training and resources to help them understand the integration process and maximize its benefits.

2. Managing Permissions:

- Ensuring that the correct permissions are applied across Planner and SharePoint can be challenging, especially in larger organizations. It's essential to work closely with your IT department to establish clear guidelines and processes for managing permissions.

3. Data Duplication:

- There is a risk of data duplication when syncing tasks and documents between Planner and SharePoint, particularly if the integration is not set up properly. To avoid this, regularly audit your Planner and SharePoint environments to identify and eliminate duplicate entries.

4. Keeping Information Up-to-Date:

- Ensuring that task details and documents are regularly updated across both platforms can be difficult. Encourage team members to maintain up-to-date information and consider setting up automated reminders or workflows to assist with this.

Conclusion

Syncing Microsoft Planner with SharePoint can greatly enhance your organization's ability to manage tasks and documents in a cohesive, streamlined manner. By following best practices and understanding the potential challenges, you can ensure a successful integration that leverages the strengths of both platforms. This integration not only improves collaboration and efficiency but also helps in maintaining transparency and control over projects, making it a valuable addition to any organization's toolkit.

As teams become more familiar with the capabilities of both Planner and SharePoint, the potential for innovative and efficient workflows grows. Whether managing complex projects or everyday tasks, syncing Planner with SharePoint empowers teams to work more effectively and achieve their goals with greater confidence and ease.

4.2.3 Automating Tasks with Power Automate

Automation is a critical component of modern workflow management. In today's fast-paced business environment, efficiency and speed are essential. Automating repetitive tasks not only saves time but also reduces the potential for human error, ensures consistency in task execution, and frees up valuable resources for more strategic activities. Microsoft Planner, while powerful in its own right, becomes even more effective when combined with Microsoft Power Automate (formerly known as Microsoft Flow). Power Automate allows you to create automated workflows between your favorite apps and services, synchronize files, get notifications, collect data, and much more—all with minimal effort.

What is Power Automate?

Power Automate is a cloud-based service that enables users to create workflows that automate tasks and processes across multiple applications and services. It is a part of the Microsoft Power Platform, which also includes Power BI, Power Apps, and Power Virtual Agents. Power Automate offers a user-friendly, drag-and-drop interface that allows you to create automated workflows, known as "flows," without requiring any programming knowledge. These flows can be as simple or as complex as needed, depending on your requirements.

Power Automate connects Microsoft Planner with other Microsoft services like Outlook, SharePoint, Teams, and third-party applications such as Twitter, Dropbox, and Google Drive. By integrating Microsoft Planner with Power Automate, you can automate tasks such as creating tasks in Planner based on specific triggers, sending notifications when tasks are completed, or synchronizing tasks with your calendar.

Benefits of Automating Tasks with Power Automate

Automating tasks in Microsoft Planner using Power Automate offers numerous benefits:

1. Time Savings: Automation can drastically reduce the time spent on repetitive tasks, allowing you to focus on more important activities.

2. Consistency: Automated workflows ensure that tasks are performed the same way every time, reducing the likelihood of errors and inconsistencies.

3. Improved Productivity: By automating routine tasks, teams can work more efficiently, leading to improved productivity.

4. Better Collaboration: Automation can enhance collaboration by automatically updating team members on task progress, sending reminders, and synchronizing tasks across different platforms.

5. Real-Time Updates: Automated workflows provide real-time updates, ensuring that everyone involved in a project is on the same page.

6. Scalability: As your business grows, automation allows you to scale your processes without a proportional increase in workload.

Getting Started with Power Automate

To begin automating tasks with Power Automate, follow these steps:

1. Access Power Automate:

- Power Automate can be accessed through the web at flow.microsoft.com. If you are already using Microsoft 365, you can find Power Automate in the app launcher.

2. Create a New Flow:

- Once you are in Power Automate, you can start by creating a new flow. There are several types of flows you can create, but for integrating with Microsoft Planner, the most commonly used are:

- Automated Flow: Triggers when a specific event occurs, such as the creation of a new task in Planner.

- Instant Flow: Manually triggered flows that run with the push of a button.

- Scheduled Flow: Flows that run on a schedule, such as daily or weekly.

3. Choose a Trigger:

- A flow begins with a trigger, which is an event that starts the flow. For example, you might choose the trigger "When a new task is created in Microsoft Planner" to start the automation whenever a new task is added to a specific plan.

4. Add Actions:

- After selecting a trigger, you can add one or more actions that will occur as a result of the trigger. Actions might include sending an email, updating another task, or creating a new item in a different application.

- For instance, if you want to create a new task in Microsoft Planner whenever you receive an email from a specific sender in Outlook, you would set the trigger as receiving an email from that sender and the action as creating a task in Planner.

5. Customize Your Flow:

- You can add conditions, loops, and variables to make your flow more dynamic. For example, you can set a condition that only creates a Planner task if the email contains certain keywords.

6. Test and Monitor Your Flow:

- Before using your flow in a live environment, it's important to test it to ensure that it works as expected. Power Automate provides testing tools and a run history that allows you to monitor the flow and troubleshoot any issues.

Examples of Task Automation with Power Automate

To give you a better idea of how Power Automate can be used with Microsoft Planner, here are some practical examples:

Example 1: Automated Task Creation from Emails

Let's say you receive multiple project-related emails daily, and it's important to track these tasks in Microsoft Planner. Instead of manually creating tasks, you can set up a flow in Power Automate that automatically creates a new task in a specific Planner bucket whenever an email with a particular subject line or from a specific sender arrives in your inbox.

Steps:

1. Trigger: "When a new email arrives" in Outlook.

2. Condition: Check if the email subject contains "Project Update".

3. Action: Create a new task in Planner under a specific plan and bucket, using the email subject as the task title and the email body as the task description.

Example 2: Sync Planner Tasks with Outlook Calendar

If you need to track Planner tasks alongside other calendar appointments, you can set up a flow that automatically adds Planner tasks to your Outlook calendar when they are created.

Steps:

1. Trigger: "When a task is created" in Microsoft Planner.

2. Action: "Create an event" in Outlook Calendar with the task title and due date.

Example 3: Notify Team Members of Task Assignments

Communication is key in team collaboration. You can automate notifications to team members when they are assigned a new task in Planner, ensuring they are immediately aware of their responsibilities.

Steps:

1. Trigger: "When a task is assigned" in Microsoft Planner.

2. Action: "Send a Teams notification" or "Send an email" to the assigned team member with task details.

Example 4: Archiving Completed Tasks

Once tasks are completed, it might be necessary to archive them or move them to a different location for record-keeping. You can automate this process to ensure that your Planner remains organized.

Steps:

1. Trigger: "When a task is completed" in Microsoft Planner.

2. Action: "Create a new item" in a SharePoint list or "Move task" to a different bucket for archiving.

Example 5: Generating Weekly Reports

If your team relies on regular reports to track progress, you can set up a flow to generate and send a summary of completed tasks every week.

Steps:

1. Trigger: "On a schedule" (e.g., every Monday at 8 AM).

2. Action: "Get tasks" from Planner that were completed last week.

3. Action: "Send an email" with the list of completed tasks to stakeholders.

Advanced Power Automate Features for Planner

While the above examples provide a solid foundation, Power Automate offers advanced features that can further enhance your Planner experience:

1. Conditional Logic:

  - Use conditional statements to create more sophisticated workflows. For example, you can set conditions to create tasks only if certain criteria are met, such as a specific priority level or deadline.

2. Loops and Variables:

  - Automate repetitive tasks by looping through multiple items and applying actions to each. Variables allow you to store and manipulate data within the flow.

3. Error Handling:

  - Implement error handling to manage exceptions gracefully. For example, if a flow fails due to a connection issue, you can set it to retry the operation or notify you of the failure.

4. Parallel Branching:

  - Execute multiple actions simultaneously using parallel branches. This is useful when you need to perform different tasks concurrently, such as sending notifications and updating records in different systems.

Best Practices for Using Power Automate with Planner

To maximize the effectiveness of Power Automate with Microsoft Planner, consider the following best practices:

1. Start Simple:

   - Begin with simple flows to get comfortable with the platform. As you gain experience, you can create more complex workflows.

2. Test Thoroughly:

   - Always test your flows in a controlled environment before deploying them in a live setting. This helps identify any issues and ensures the flow behaves as expected.

3. Monitor and Optimize:

   - Regularly review the performance of your flows. Power Automate provides analytics and run histories that help you monitor execution times, errors, and overall efficiency. Use this data to optimize your flows.

4. Document Your Flows:

   - Keep a record of the flows you create, including the purpose, trigger, actions, and any conditions. Documentation helps in managing flows, especially when collaborating with others or revisiting them in the future.

5. Keep It Secure:

   - Ensure that your flows are secure by managing permissions carefully. Be mindful of the data you are automating, especially when dealing with sensitive information.

6. Stay Updated:

   - Microsoft frequently updates Power Automate with new features and capabilities. Stay informed about these updates to take advantage of new functionalities that can further enhance your workflows.

Conclusion

Automating tasks in Microsoft Planner using Power Automate unlocks a new level of productivity and efficiency. By connecting Planner with other tools and services, you can create powerful, automated workflows that streamline your processes and ensure consistency across your projects. Whether you are managing a small team or a large organization, Power Automate provides the flexibility and scalability to meet your automation needs. By following the best practices outlined in this section, you can harness the full potential of Power Automate to enhance your use of Microsoft Planner and achieve your goals more efficiently.

4.3 Managing Multiple Plans

Managing multiple plans efficiently in Microsoft Planner is crucial for teams and individuals juggling several projects simultaneously. With the right strategies, Microsoft Planner's tools can help keep everything organized, ensuring that nothing falls through the cracks. This section will cover how to effectively organize, manage, and streamline your plans within the Planner Hub, allowing you to stay on top of multiple projects.

4.3.1 Organizing Plans in Microsoft Planner Hub

The Planner Hub is the central interface where all your plans are visible, providing a bird's-eye view of your tasks and projects. This section will guide you through best practices for organizing your plans in the Planner Hub, enabling you to manage them effectively.

Understanding the Planner Hub Interface

When you first access the Planner Hub, you'll notice that it serves as a dashboard, displaying all the plans you're involved with, either as a member or an owner. The interface is divided into several sections, each serving a specific function:

- Pinned Plans: This section allows you to keep your most important plans at the top for easy access. Pinned plans are visible as cards with quick access to task details and the progress chart.

- All Plans: Below the pinned section, you'll find a list of all your plans. This list includes every plan you've created or been added to, allowing you to browse through them without leaving the Planner Hub.

- Recent Plans: Recent plans show the last few plans you've accessed, providing a convenient way to return to ongoing tasks or recently viewed projects.

The Planner Hub is designed to give you a comprehensive view of your workload, allowing you to switch between plans effortlessly and keep track of progress across multiple projects.

Pinning and Prioritizing Plans

One of the most useful features in the Planner Hub is the ability to pin plans. Pinning is simple but powerful: it allows you to prioritize your most critical projects by keeping them at the top of your Planner Hub. Here's how to make the most of this feature:

1. Pinning a Plan: To pin a plan, simply hover over the plan card in the "All Plans" section and click on the pin icon. The plan will immediately move to the top of your Planner Hub under the "Pinned Plans" section.

2. Prioritizing Plans: Use the pinned section to prioritize your workload. Plans that require immediate attention or have approaching deadlines should be pinned. This ensures that your most urgent tasks are always at your fingertips.

3. Reordering Pinned Plans: You can drag and drop pinned plans to rearrange their order. This flexibility allows you to prioritize tasks dynamically, adjusting as new priorities arise.

4. Unpinning a Plan: If a plan is no longer a top priority, you can unpin it by clicking the pin icon again. This will move the plan back to the "All Plans" section.

By carefully curating your pinned plans, you can focus your attention on what matters most without getting overwhelmed by less urgent projects.

Categorizing Plans for Better Organization

As the number of plans you manage increases, it becomes essential to categorize them effectively. Categorization helps you quickly identify the nature of each plan, making it easier to navigate the Planner Hub. Here are some strategies for categorizing your plans:

1. Using Labels: Microsoft Planner allows you to assign labels to tasks within a plan. While this feature is designed for tasks, you can use a similar method for plans by grouping them according to labels in your mind. For instance, you might mentally categorize plans as "High Priority," "Ongoing," or "Completed."

2. Creating Naming Conventions: Establishing consistent naming conventions for your plans can help you quickly identify the purpose and status of each plan. For example, you could prefix your plan names with categories like "Marketing - Q3 Campaign" or "HR - Recruitment Drive." This makes it easier to scan through your list of plans and locate the one you need.

3. Grouping by Teams or Departments: If you are managing plans across multiple teams or departments, consider grouping your plans by the team responsible. This can be done either through naming conventions or by mentally associating certain plans with specific departments.

4. Sorting by Deadlines: While the Planner Hub doesn't automatically sort plans by deadlines, you can use the deadline dates within each plan to inform how you prioritize and categorize your plans. Plans with imminent deadlines should be more accessible, perhaps by being pinned or placed at the top of your list.

Using Filters and Views to Focus on Specific Plans

The Planner Hub includes various filters and views that help you focus on specific plans or tasks within those plans. Understanding how to use these tools effectively can significantly enhance your ability to manage multiple plans:

1. Filtering by Progress: You can filter tasks within a plan by their progress status (Not Started, In Progress, or Completed). While this filter is available within individual plans, using it in the Planner Hub can help you quickly gauge the overall status of multiple projects.

2. Filtering by Due Date: Use the due date filter to see which tasks across all your plans are due soon. This is particularly useful for ensuring that no deadlines are missed, even when managing multiple plans.

3. Switching Between Plan Views: The Planner Hub allows you to switch between different views, such as Board, Charts, and Schedule. Each view provides a different perspective on your plans:

   - Board View: Shows tasks grouped by buckets, providing a clear picture of task distribution within each plan.

   - Charts View: Visualizes the overall progress of tasks, helping you quickly identify bottlenecks or areas that need attention.

   - Schedule View: Displays tasks on a calendar, making it easy to see upcoming deadlines and plan your work accordingly.

By mastering these filters and views, you can better navigate the complexities of managing multiple plans, ensuring that you stay organized and efficient.

Archiving and Closing Completed Plans

As you complete projects, it's important to keep your Planner Hub organized by archiving or closing plans that are no longer active. While Microsoft Planner doesn't currently offer a direct archiving feature, there are several ways to manage completed plans:

1. Marking Plans as Completed: Once all tasks within a plan are finished, mark the plan as completed. This can be done by ensuring all tasks are marked as complete and noting the plan's completion in its title or description.

2. Moving Completed Plans to the Bottom: You can manually move completed plans to the bottom of your list in the Planner Hub by unpinning them and leaving them in the "All Plans" section. This keeps your active plans at the top while still retaining access to completed ones for reference.

3. Exporting Data for Archival: If you need to keep a record of a completed plan, consider exporting the data before removing it from your Planner Hub. You can manually export tasks and their details to Excel or another tool for long-term storage.

4. Deleting Old Plans: If a plan is no longer needed and you have no reason to keep its data, consider deleting it to reduce clutter in your Planner Hub. Be cautious with this option, as deleting a plan is permanent.

By regularly archiving or closing completed plans, you maintain a clean and focused Planner Hub, making it easier to manage your ongoing projects.

Best Practices for Managing Multiple Plans

Managing multiple plans requires discipline and a strategic approach. Here are some best practices to help you stay organized and efficient:

1. Regular Review and Updates: Set aside time each week to review and update your plans. This practice ensures that all tasks are current, priorities are aligned, and any issues are addressed promptly.

2. Clear Communication with Team Members: When managing multiple plans, communication becomes crucial. Ensure that all team members are aware of their

responsibilities and deadlines. Use comments and notifications within Planner to keep everyone informed.

3. Staying Flexible: Plans can change, and it's important to remain flexible. Be prepared to adjust your plans as new information arises or priorities shift. The Planner Hub's tools for reordering and updating plans make it easier to stay agile.

4. Using Integrations Wisely: Take advantage of Planner's integrations with other Microsoft tools like Outlook, Teams, and SharePoint to streamline your workflow. For example, syncing tasks with Outlook can help you manage deadlines across multiple plans more effectively.

5. Avoiding Overcommitment: Managing multiple plans can lead to overcommitment if not done carefully. Be realistic about what you can achieve and don't hesitate to delegate tasks when necessary.

By following these best practices, you can effectively manage multiple plans in Microsoft Planner, ensuring that all your projects are completed on time and to the highest standard.

Conclusion

Organizing plans in the Microsoft Planner Hub is a crucial skill for anyone managing multiple projects. By leveraging the features discussed in this section—such as pinning and prioritizing plans, categorizing them effectively, using filters and views, and archiving completed projects—you can maintain an organized and efficient workflow. These strategies will help you navigate the complexities of managing multiple plans, allowing you to achieve your goals with Microsoft Planner.

4.3.2 Cross-Plan Task Management

Managing tasks across multiple plans is one of the most critical aspects of effectively using Microsoft Planner, especially in complex projects or when managing multiple teams. Cross-plan task management involves coordinating and overseeing tasks spread across different plans to ensure that all activities align with the broader objectives of an organization or project. This section delves into strategies, tools, and best practices for managing tasks across multiple plans within Microsoft Planner, enabling users to achieve seamless integration and execution of their work.

Understanding the Need for Cross-Plan Task Management

In many organizations, tasks are often distributed across various plans that correspond to different teams, departments, or projects. This approach, while useful for breaking down work into manageable units, can lead to challenges in ensuring that all tasks across these plans are synchronized and aligned with overall business goals. Without proper cross-plan task management, there is a risk of duplicating work, missing deadlines, or failing to address interdependencies between tasks in different plans.

Cross-plan task management is particularly important in scenarios such as:

- Large Projects: Where different teams or departments work on different aspects of the project but must align their tasks to meet the overall project deadlines and objectives.

- Resource Management: When resources (like personnel, equipment, or budget) are shared across multiple plans, and careful coordination is needed to avoid over-allocation or underutilization.

- Multi-departmental Initiatives: Where tasks across different departments need to be coordinated to ensure the success of company-wide initiatives.

- Agile Workflows: In environments where teams use Agile methodologies, cross-plan task management can help in tracking progress across multiple sprints or projects.

Key Features of Microsoft Planner for Cross-Plan Task Management

Microsoft Planner provides several features that facilitate cross-plan task management, enabling users to efficiently coordinate tasks across different plans.

1. Planner Hub: The Planner Hub serves as a central dashboard where users can view all the plans they are a part of. This feature allows users to get a holistic view of all tasks across different plans, making it easier to identify which tasks are pending, in progress, or completed. The Planner Hub is the starting point for managing tasks across multiple plans as it aggregates information and provides insights at a glance.

2. Task Filtering and Sorting: Within the Planner Hub or any individual plan, tasks can be filtered and sorted based on criteria such as due date, priority, or assignee. This functionality is crucial when managing tasks across multiple plans because it allows users

to focus on tasks that are most critical at any given time, regardless of which plan they belong to.

3. Labeling and Tagging: Labels and tags in Microsoft Planner are useful tools for categorizing tasks across plans. By assigning consistent labels to related tasks in different plans, users can quickly identify and group these tasks, making it easier to manage them collectively.

4. Assigned to Me: The "Assigned to Me" view is another powerful feature that aggregates all tasks assigned to a particular user across all their plans. This view helps users prioritize their work, ensuring that they do not miss any critical tasks, even if they are spread across multiple plans.

5. Export to Excel: Microsoft Planner allows users to export their tasks to Excel, where they can create custom reports or dashboards to track and manage tasks across multiple plans. This feature is especially useful for generating high-level reports for management or for conducting in-depth analysis of task progress.

6. Integration with Microsoft Teams: For organizations using Microsoft Teams, the integration with Planner allows for the seamless management of tasks across plans directly within Teams channels. Users can add multiple Planner tabs within Teams, each corresponding to a different plan, and manage tasks across these plans in a single workspace.

Strategies for Effective Cross-Plan Task Management

To effectively manage tasks across multiple plans in Microsoft Planner, users should consider the following strategies:

1. Establish Clear Task Dependencies: In any project, understanding the dependencies between tasks is crucial for managing them effectively. When tasks span multiple plans, it's important to identify and document these dependencies clearly. This ensures that tasks are completed in the correct sequence, and that any delays in one plan do not adversely affect the overall project timeline.

2. Use Consistent Labels Across Plans: Consistent labeling across plans helps in organizing and tracking related tasks. For example, if you have marketing, sales, and product development plans, using a common label like "Q3 Launch" across all plans will allow you to quickly filter and view all tasks related to that initiative, regardless of which plan they belong to.

3. Regularly Review and Update Tasks: Cross-plan task management requires regular reviews to ensure that all tasks are progressing as planned. Schedule periodic reviews where team leaders or project managers can update the status of tasks, reassign resources if necessary, and address any bottlenecks that may have arisen.

4. Leverage Integration Tools: Integrating Microsoft Planner with other tools in the Microsoft ecosystem, such as Power BI, Outlook, or SharePoint, can greatly enhance your ability to manage tasks across plans. For example, using Power BI, you can create dashboards that visualize task progress across multiple plans, providing insights that can inform decision-making.

5. Assign a Cross-Plan Coordinator: In large projects or complex environments, it may be beneficial to designate a team member as a cross-plan coordinator. This person's role would be to oversee the tasks across all plans, ensuring that they are aligned with the project's overall objectives, and that communication between different teams or departments is maintained.

6. Set Up Notifications and Alerts: Microsoft Planner allows users to set up notifications for task assignments, due dates, and status changes. When managing tasks across multiple plans, it's important to ensure that key stakeholders receive timely notifications so they can act on tasks that require immediate attention.

Best Practices for Cross-Plan Task Management

Implementing best practices in cross-plan task management can significantly improve the efficiency and success of your projects. Below are some recommended practices:

1. Centralize Task Management: Whenever possible, centralize the management of tasks across plans. This can be done by using the Planner Hub as the primary interface for monitoring and updating tasks, or by creating a master plan that aggregates tasks from multiple plans for high-level oversight.

2. Create and Share a Task Management Protocol: Establish a protocol for how tasks should be managed across plans. This protocol should include guidelines on how tasks are created, assigned, labeled, and reviewed. Sharing this protocol with all team members ensures consistency in task management practices across the organization.

3. Monitor Task Progress Using Dashboards: Utilize dashboards to monitor task progress across multiple plans. Dashboards can provide real-time updates on task status,

highlighting areas that may need attention. This visual representation makes it easier to track progress and address issues before they become critical.

4. Regularly Communicate with Stakeholders: Communication is key when managing tasks across plans. Ensure that there are regular check-ins or meetings where stakeholders from different plans can discuss progress, share updates, and address any challenges that may arise.

5. Document Learnings and Improvements: After the completion of a project, take the time to document what worked well and what could be improved in your cross-plan task management approach. These learnings can be invaluable for refining your process and improving efficiency in future projects.

Challenges in Cross-Plan Task Management

While cross-plan task management offers many benefits, it also comes with its own set of challenges. Understanding these challenges can help you prepare and develop strategies to mitigate them.

1. Overlapping Tasks and Resources: One of the most common challenges is dealing with overlapping tasks and resources across multiple plans. This can lead to confusion, duplicated efforts, or resource constraints. To address this, it's essential to have clear visibility into all tasks and resources, and to use tools like the Planner Hub to manage overlaps.

2. Maintaining Consistency Across Plans: Ensuring consistency in task management practices across different plans can be difficult, especially when different teams have their own ways of working. Developing and enforcing a standard protocol for task management can help in maintaining consistency.

3. Coordination Between Teams: Coordinating between teams that are working on different plans but contributing to the same project can be challenging. Regular communication, clearly defined roles, and a cross-plan coordinator can help in maintaining coordination.

4. Scalability Issues: As the number of plans and tasks grows, managing them effectively can become increasingly complex. To address scalability issues, it may be necessary to use additional tools or integrations that can handle larger volumes of tasks and data.

5. Integration Limitations: While Microsoft Planner integrates well with other Microsoft tools, there may be limitations when trying to integrate it with third-party tools or when managing very complex projects. Being aware of these limitations and planning around them is crucial.

Conclusion

Cross-plan task management is a powerful capability of Microsoft Planner that can greatly enhance your ability to manage complex projects or initiatives involving multiple teams or departments. By leveraging Planner's features, implementing effective strategies, and following best practices, you can ensure that tasks across all plans are well-coordinated, aligned with your objectives, and completed on time.

As organizations continue to embrace more collaborative and decentralized ways of working, the ability to manage tasks across multiple plans will become increasingly important. By mastering cross-plan task management in Microsoft Planner, you can improve your team's productivity, ensure better alignment with business goals, and ultimately achieve greater success in your projects.

4.3.3 Creating Templates for Reusable Plans

Creating templates for reusable plans in Microsoft Planner is a powerful feature that allows you to streamline your planning process, save time, and maintain consistency across multiple projects. By leveraging templates, you can establish a standard framework that can be quickly adapted to various projects or tasks, ensuring that all necessary steps and components are included without starting from scratch each time.

Understanding the Benefits of Templates

Templates in Microsoft Planner offer several key benefits:

1. Efficiency and Time-Saving: By creating a template, you eliminate the need to recreate similar plans repeatedly. This is particularly useful for recurring projects or tasks that follow a similar structure.

2. Consistency and Standardization: Templates ensure that all team members follow the same process and standards, reducing the risk of missing crucial steps or information.

3. Simplified Onboarding: New team members can quickly understand and follow established processes by using templates, facilitating faster onboarding and integration into the team.

4. Improved Collaboration: Templates provide a clear framework for collaboration, making it easier for team members to understand their roles and responsibilities.

Creating a Template in Microsoft Planner

Creating a template involves designing a plan that can be reused for future projects. Here's a step-by-step guide:

Step 1: Identify Common Elements

Before creating a template, identify the common elements that are consistent across your projects. These elements might include:

- Tasks: Recurring tasks that are present in multiple projects.

- Buckets: Categories or stages that tasks go through.

- Labels: Tags or labels used for categorizing tasks.

- Assignments: Roles or team members typically responsible for certain tasks.

- Deadlines: Standard timelines or due dates for tasks.

Step 2: Create a Plan

Start by creating a new plan in Microsoft Planner. Name it something indicative of its purpose as a template, such as "Project Template" or "Standard Workflow Template."

Step 3: Add Buckets

Organize your plan by adding buckets that represent different phases or categories of your project. For example, if you're creating a template for a marketing campaign, your buckets might be "Planning," "Content Creation," "Approval," and "Launch."

Step 4: Add Tasks

Populate each bucket with tasks that are commonly part of your projects. For instance, under the "Planning" bucket, you might add tasks like "Define Goals," "Identify Target Audience," and "Set Budget."

Step 5: Assign Roles and Due Dates

Assign tasks to roles rather than specific individuals if the template is intended for different teams. For example, assign the task "Create Content" to the role "Content Creator." Set standard due dates relative to the project start date, such as "2 days after project start."

Step 6: Add Labels

Use labels to categorize tasks further. Labels can indicate priority, type of work, or any other relevant categorization. For instance, you might use labels like "High Priority," "Design Task," or "Client Review."

Step 7: Save as a Template

Once your plan is set up with all the necessary buckets, tasks, assignments, and labels, it's ready to be saved as a template. Although Microsoft Planner doesn't have a dedicated "Save as Template" feature, you can achieve this by copying the plan.

Using Your Template

To use your template for a new project:

1. Copy the Plan: Open the template plan and select the option to copy the plan. This action creates a new plan with the same structure, tasks, and details.

2. Rename the Plan: Give the copied plan a new name relevant to the specific project you're starting.

3. Customize as Needed: Adjust the tasks, assignments, and due dates as necessary to fit the new project's requirements.

Best Practices for Creating and Using Templates

Regularly Update Templates

As processes evolve and improve, ensure that your templates reflect these changes. Regularly review and update templates to incorporate new best practices, tools, or steps.

Gather Feedback from Team Members

Involve your team in the creation and refinement of templates. Their feedback can provide valuable insights into improving the templates and ensuring they meet everyone's needs.

Keep Templates Simple and Clear

While it's essential to include all necessary steps, avoid making templates overly complex. Simple and clear templates are easier to follow and adapt to different projects.

Document Template Usage

Provide documentation or guidelines on how to use the templates effectively. This can include instructions on customizing the template, assigning tasks, and managing timelines.

Ensure Templates Are Accessible

Make templates easily accessible to all team members. Store them in a shared location, such as a team SharePoint site or within a dedicated Planner group, so everyone can find and use them.

Examples of Templates for Different Scenarios

Marketing Campaign Template

A marketing campaign typically involves several recurring tasks and stages. A template for this might include:

- Buckets: Research, Content Creation, Review, Launch, Post-Launch Analysis

- Tasks: Define Campaign Goals, Research Target Audience, Create Content Calendar, Design Marketing Materials, Approve Content, Schedule Posts, Monitor Campaign Performance, Analyze Results

- Labels: High Priority, Social Media, Email Marketing, Design, Approval Required

Event Planning Template

Event planning often follows a predictable pattern. A template for event planning could include:

- Buckets: Pre-Event Planning, Marketing and Promotion, Logistics, On-Site Management, Post-Event Follow-Up

- Tasks: Book Venue, Confirm Speakers, Create Event Website, Design Invitations, Send Invitations, Coordinate Catering, Arrange Transportation, On-Site Registration, Post-Event Surveys, Analyze Feedback

- Labels: Urgent, External Vendor, Internal Coordination, Follow-Up Required

Product Development Template

Product development projects benefit from a structured approach. A template might feature:

- Buckets: Ideation, Development, Testing, Launch, Post-Launch Review

- Tasks: Brainstorm Ideas, Conduct Market Research, Develop Prototype, Test Prototype, Gather User Feedback, Refine Product, Prepare Marketing Materials, Launch Product, Monitor Sales, Collect Post-Launch Feedback

- Labels: Critical Path, Development Task, Testing Phase, User Feedback

Conclusion

Creating and utilizing templates in Microsoft Planner can greatly enhance the efficiency, consistency, and effectiveness of your project management efforts. By establishing reusable templates, you ensure that all necessary steps are included in your projects, save time on repetitive tasks, and provide a clear and standardized framework for your team to follow. As you refine and improve your templates over time, they become valuable tools that contribute to the overall success of your projects and organization.

CHAPTER V
Best Practices for Using Microsoft Planner

5.1 Enhancing Productivity with Planner

Microsoft Planner is an essential tool for individuals and teams looking to enhance their productivity. It allows users to organize tasks, set deadlines, and collaborate effectively. The tool's flexibility and integration with other Microsoft 365 applications make it a powerful resource for managing time and achieving goals. In this section, we will explore various time management techniques that can be applied within Microsoft Planner to maximize productivity.

5.1.1 Time Management Techniques

Effective time management is crucial in today's fast-paced work environment. Microsoft Planner provides several features that can help users manage their time efficiently. By understanding and applying these techniques, individuals and teams can ensure that they meet their deadlines and complete their tasks efficiently.

1. Setting Clear Priorities

One of the most important aspects of time management is setting clear priorities. In Microsoft Planner, tasks can be categorized and prioritized based on their importance and urgency. By creating buckets or labels such as "High Priority," "Medium Priority," and "Low Priority," users can easily visualize which tasks need immediate attention. This allows team members to focus on high-impact tasks and ensure that critical deadlines are met.

When setting priorities, it's also essential to consider the dependencies between tasks. For instance, some tasks may need to be completed before others can start. Microsoft Planner allows users to set dependencies by indicating task order or linking related tasks. This ensures that team members understand the sequence of tasks and can plan their time accordingly.

2. Breaking Down Tasks into Manageable Steps

Large tasks can often seem overwhelming, leading to procrastination or inefficient use of time. Microsoft Planner addresses this issue by allowing users to break down tasks into smaller, more manageable steps. These subtasks can be added directly within a task card, providing a clear roadmap for completing the task.

Breaking down tasks has several benefits. First, it allows users to focus on completing one small part of the task at a time, which can increase motivation and reduce stress. Second, it makes it easier to track progress, as each subtask can be checked off as it is completed. Finally, breaking down tasks into smaller steps helps identify potential bottlenecks or challenges early in the process, allowing teams to address them before they impact the overall timeline.

3. Utilizing Deadlines and Reminders

Deadlines are an integral part of time management, and Microsoft Planner makes it easy to set and track deadlines for individual tasks. Each task card in Planner includes a field for setting a due date. This date can be used to trigger reminders and notifications, ensuring that tasks are completed on time.

To make the most of deadlines, it's important to set realistic due dates that take into account the complexity of the task and the availability of resources. Microsoft Planner's calendar view can be a valuable tool for visualizing deadlines and planning tasks accordingly. By mapping out tasks on the calendar, users can avoid overloading themselves or their teams and ensure that deadlines are staggered appropriately.

In addition to setting deadlines, Microsoft Planner allows users to set reminders. These reminders can be configured to notify team members of upcoming deadlines, ensuring that tasks remain on track. Regular reminders can be particularly useful for long-term projects where deadlines may be weeks or months away.

4. Time Blocking and Scheduling

Time blocking is a time management technique that involves dedicating specific blocks of time to particular tasks or activities. This technique can be effectively implemented using Microsoft Planner by scheduling tasks within a calendar or planner view. By assigning specific time slots to tasks, users can ensure that they allocate sufficient time to complete each task without interruptions.

Microsoft Planner integrates seamlessly with Outlook, allowing users to sync their tasks with their Outlook calendar. This integration enables users to schedule tasks directly in their calendar, making it easier to manage their time and avoid over-committing. Time blocking also helps reduce context switching, where users jump between tasks without completing them, which can lead to inefficiencies and increased stress.

5. Focus on One Task at a Time

Multitasking is often seen as a way to increase productivity, but in reality, it can lead to decreased efficiency and quality of work. Microsoft Planner encourages users to focus on one task at a time by providing a clear and organized view of tasks. By using Planner's filters and sorting options, users can narrow down their task list to focus only on what needs to be done at the moment.

One effective way to implement single-tasking is by using the "My Tasks" view in Microsoft Planner. This view consolidates all tasks assigned to the user across different plans, allowing them to focus on one task without being distracted by others. By working on tasks one at a time, users can complete them more efficiently and with greater attention to detail.

6. Prioritize Based on the Eisenhower Matrix

The Eisenhower Matrix is a time management tool that categorizes tasks based on their urgency and importance. It divides tasks into four quadrants:

- Urgent and Important: Tasks that need immediate attention and have significant consequences.

- Important but Not Urgent: Tasks that are important but can be scheduled for later.

- Urgent but Not Important: Tasks that are urgent but can be delegated or minimized.

- Neither Urgent nor Important: Tasks that are low priority and can be deferred or eliminated.

Microsoft Planner can be used to implement the Eisenhower Matrix by creating buckets or labels corresponding to each quadrant. By organizing tasks in this way, users can focus on the most critical tasks first, ensuring that they spend their time on activities that will have the greatest impact.

7. Delegating Tasks Effectively

Delegation is a key aspect of time management, especially in team settings. Microsoft Planner makes it easy to delegate tasks by assigning them to specific team members. When delegating tasks, it's important to consider each team member's strengths, availability, and workload. By assigning tasks to the most suitable team member, teams can ensure that tasks are completed efficiently and to a high standard.

In addition to assigning tasks, Microsoft Planner allows users to monitor the progress of delegated tasks. This visibility ensures that the team leader or project manager can provide support and guidance as needed, and it helps prevent tasks from falling behind schedule.

8. Regularly Reviewing and Adjusting Plans

Time management is not a static process; it requires regular review and adjustment. Microsoft Planner supports this by providing various views and reports that allow users to monitor progress and make adjustments as needed. Regular reviews can help identify tasks that are falling behind, resources that are over-allocated, or deadlines that may need to be adjusted.

To conduct effective reviews, it's important to schedule regular check-ins, either individually or as a team. During these check-ins, users can review the status of their tasks, adjust priorities, and reassign tasks if necessary. Microsoft Planner's reporting features, such as task charts and progress indicators, can provide valuable insights during these reviews.

9. Using the Pomodoro Technique

The Pomodoro Technique is a time management method that involves working in short, focused bursts (usually 25 minutes) followed by a short break. Microsoft Planner can be used to implement this technique by breaking down tasks into "Pomodoros" or work sessions. Users can create subtasks or checklists within a task card to represent each Pomodoro session, allowing them to track their progress.

This technique is particularly effective for tasks that require sustained concentration. By working in short bursts, users can maintain their focus and avoid burnout. The breaks between sessions also provide an opportunity to rest and recharge, leading to increased productivity over the long term.

10. Implementing the GTD (Getting Things Done) Methodology

The GTD methodology, created by David Allen, is a popular time management approach that emphasizes capturing, clarifying, organizing, reflecting, and engaging with tasks. Microsoft Planner can be an excellent tool for implementing the GTD methodology:

- Capture: Use Microsoft Planner to capture all tasks, ideas, and projects as soon as they arise. Create a plan or bucket specifically for capturing these tasks.

- Clarify: Review the captured tasks and clarify what needs to be done for each. Break down larger tasks into actionable steps and move them to the appropriate plan or bucket.

- Organize: Organize tasks by priority, due date, or project. Use labels, buckets, and task details in Microsoft Planner to categorize and organize tasks effectively.

- Reflect: Regularly review your tasks and plans to ensure they align with your goals. Use Planner's reporting features to track progress and adjust your plans as needed.

- Engage: Focus on the tasks that require immediate attention, using Planner's prioritization and scheduling features to guide your work.

By following the GTD methodology, users can maintain control over their tasks and projects, ensuring that nothing falls through the cracks.

11. Leveraging the "2-Minute Rule"

The 2-Minute Rule, another concept from the GTD methodology, suggests that if a task can be completed in two minutes or less, it should be done immediately. This rule helps prevent small tasks from piling up and becoming overwhelming. Microsoft Planner users can apply the 2-Minute Rule by quickly addressing minor tasks and checking them off in their task list. This approach frees up time for more significant tasks and keeps the task list manageable.

12. Scheduling Time for Deep Work

Deep Work, a concept popularized by Cal Newport, refers to the ability to focus without distraction on a cognitively demanding task. Microsoft Planner can help users schedule and protect time for deep work by blocking off dedicated periods in the day for focused tasks. During these deep work sessions, users should avoid checking emails, attending meetings, or engaging in any non-essential activities.

By using Microsoft Planner to schedule deep work sessions, users can ensure they have uninterrupted time to focus on complex tasks that require concentration. This technique can lead to higher quality work and faster completion of important projects.

13. Setting Buffer Times Between Tasks

Another effective time management strategy is setting buffer times between tasks. Buffer times are short breaks or intervals that allow users to transition from one task

 to another. Microsoft Planner can help users schedule buffer times by allocating extra time around each task in the calendar view.

Buffer times are particularly useful for reducing stress and maintaining productivity throughout the day. They provide a cushion for unexpected delays or interruptions and help prevent the feeling of being rushed from one task to the next.

14. Tracking Time Spent on Tasks

Tracking the time spent on tasks is an important aspect of time management, as it provides insights into productivity and helps identify areas for improvement. While Microsoft Planner does not have built-in time-tracking features, it can be integrated with third-party time-tracking tools like Microsoft Teams or Trello. These tools allow users to monitor how much time they spend on each task and analyze their work patterns.

By tracking time, users can gain a better understanding of how long tasks take to complete and identify any inefficiencies. This information can be used to refine time management strategies and improve overall productivity.

15. Implementing Agile Practices

Agile practices, commonly used in software development, can also be applied to general time management and task planning. Microsoft Planner supports Agile methodologies by allowing users to create sprints, backlogs, and Kanban boards. Teams can use Planner to organize tasks into sprints (short, time-boxed periods) and track progress using the board view.

Agile practices promote flexibility and continuous improvement, making them ideal for dynamic work environments. By adopting Agile techniques in Microsoft Planner, teams can respond more effectively to changes, prioritize tasks more efficiently, and deliver high-quality work in shorter time frames.

Conclusion

By leveraging the time management techniques outlined above, users can significantly enhance their productivity with Microsoft Planner. Whether you're an individual looking to manage your personal tasks more effectively or a team leader seeking to optimize your team's workflow, Microsoft Planner offers a wide range of features and tools to help you achieve your goals. From setting clear priorities and breaking down tasks to scheduling deep work sessions and implementing Agile practices, these strategies will empower you to manage your time more effectively and get the most out of Microsoft Planner.

5.1.2 Prioritizing Work Effectively

Prioritizing work effectively is crucial in any project management tool, and Microsoft Planner offers several features to help you achieve this. Proper prioritization ensures that your team focuses on the most important tasks first, thereby enhancing productivity and meeting deadlines efficiently. This section will delve into various strategies and techniques for prioritizing work using Microsoft Planner.

Understanding Task Prioritization

Before diving into the specifics of Microsoft Planner, it's important to understand what task prioritization entails. Task prioritization is the process of ordering tasks based on their importance and urgency. This ensures that high-priority tasks receive the attention they need to keep the project on track.

In the context of Microsoft Planner, tasks can be prioritized using a variety of features such as labels, due dates, and buckets. Utilizing these features effectively can significantly improve your workflow and productivity.

Using Buckets to Organize Tasks

Buckets in Microsoft Planner are a great way to categorize and prioritize tasks. Buckets can be used to separate tasks based on phases, departments, or priority levels.

1. Creating Priority Buckets: One approach is to create buckets specifically for different priority levels, such as "High Priority," "Medium Priority," and "Low Priority." This visual separation makes it easy to see at a glance which tasks need immediate attention.

2. Phase-Based Buckets: Another method is to create buckets based on project phases, such as "Planning," "Execution," and "Review." Within each phase, tasks can be further prioritized based on their criticality to the project's success.

3. Department-Based Buckets: For larger teams, creating buckets based on departments or teams can help in managing tasks specific to each group. Prioritization within these buckets can then be managed by team leads.

Assigning Priority Levels to Tasks

Microsoft Planner allows you to set priority levels for tasks, making it easy to identify which tasks are most critical.

1. Priority Labels: Use labels such as "Urgent," "High," "Medium," and "Low" to categorize tasks. This simple yet effective method ensures that everyone on the team understands the importance of each task.

2. Due Dates and Deadlines: Setting due dates helps in prioritizing tasks based on their deadlines. Tasks with nearer deadlines should be prioritized over those with more time. Microsoft Planner allows you to set and adjust due dates easily.

3. Task Descriptions and Checklists: Detailed task descriptions and checklists within tasks can help in identifying subtasks and their priorities. Breaking down a large task into smaller subtasks and prioritizing them can make complex projects more manageable.

Leveraging Microsoft Planner's Visual Tools

The visual tools in Microsoft Planner are instrumental in prioritizing tasks effectively.

1. Task Board View: The Task Board view in Planner offers a visual representation of all tasks and their statuses. This kanban-style board makes it easy to see which tasks are in progress, completed, or yet to be started, and helps in quickly identifying high-priority tasks.

2. Charts View: The Charts view provides an overview of task distribution and progress. It includes pie charts and bar graphs that show task statuses and priorities, allowing you to identify bottlenecks and areas that need immediate attention.

3. Calendar View: Integrating Planner with Outlook Calendar can help visualize task deadlines and schedule your work accordingly. This integration ensures that high-priority tasks are visible alongside your other commitments.

Collaborative Prioritization Techniques

Effective prioritization often requires collaboration, especially in team settings. Microsoft Planner supports various collaborative features to ensure that prioritization is a team effort.

1. Team Meetings and Discussions: Regular team meetings can be used to discuss and agree on task priorities. Use Microsoft Teams in conjunction with Planner to facilitate these discussions.

2. Comments and Notes: Utilize the comments section within tasks to discuss priority levels with team members. This ensures that everyone is on the same page regarding which tasks are most critical.

3. Real-Time Updates: Microsoft Planner allows real-time updates, so any changes in task priority can be immediately reflected. This is crucial for dynamic project environments where priorities may shift frequently.

Prioritizing Work Based on Impact and Effort

One effective strategy for prioritizing tasks is to evaluate them based on their impact and effort required.

1. Impact-Effort Matrix: Create an impact-effort matrix to categorize tasks into four quadrants: Quick Wins (high impact, low effort), Major Projects (high impact, high effort), Fill-Ins (low impact, low effort), and Thankless Tasks (low impact, high effort). This helps in focusing on tasks that provide the most value.

2. Value-Based Prioritization: Focus on tasks that offer the highest value to the project or organization. Tasks that align with strategic goals or have significant client impact should be prioritized.

3. Risk Assessment: Consider the risks associated with delaying certain tasks. Tasks that pose high risks if not completed on time should be given higher priority.

Automating Prioritization with Microsoft Power Automate

For advanced users, Microsoft Power Automate (formerly Flow) can be used to automate task prioritization in Planner.

1. Automated Reminders: Set up automated reminders for high-priority tasks. This ensures that important tasks are not overlooked and are completed on time.

2. Conditional Task Creation: Use Power Automate to create tasks based on specific conditions. For example, if a task is marked as high priority in another system, a corresponding high-priority task can be automatically created in Planner.

3. Priority-Based Notifications: Set up notifications based on task priority. Team members can receive alerts for high-priority tasks, ensuring prompt attention.

Continuous Review and Adjustment

Prioritization is not a one-time activity but a continuous process. Regular reviews and adjustments are necessary to keep the project on track.

1. Weekly Reviews: Conduct weekly reviews of all tasks and their priorities. Adjust priorities based on progress, new information, and changes in project scope.

2. Feedback Loops: Establish feedback loops where team members can suggest changes in task priorities. This collaborative approach ensures that all perspectives are considered.

3. Adaptability: Be prepared to adapt priorities as project dynamics change. Flexibility is key to effective task management and ensuring that high-priority tasks are always at the forefront.

Conclusion

Prioritizing work effectively in Microsoft Planner involves a combination of strategic planning, effective use of Planner's features, and continuous collaboration and review. By using buckets, priority labels, visual tools, collaborative techniques, and automation, you can ensure that your team focuses on the most important tasks first, enhancing overall productivity and achieving project goals efficiently.

5.1.3 Using Planner for Goal Setting

Setting and achieving goals is a fundamental aspect of both personal and professional success. Microsoft Planner offers a versatile platform that enables users to set, track, and achieve goals effectively. This section explores how to utilize Microsoft Planner for goal setting, ensuring that your goals are well-organized, actionable, and attainable.

1. Understanding the Importance of Goal Setting

Goal setting is more than just defining what you want to achieve; it's about creating a clear roadmap that guides your efforts and ensures that your actions are aligned with your desired outcomes. Proper goal setting involves identifying specific, measurable, achievable, relevant, and time-bound (SMART) objectives. When done correctly, goal setting can:

- Provide clarity and focus on what needs to be accomplished.

- Enhance motivation and commitment to achieving the set objectives.

- Offer a framework for measuring progress and success.

- Facilitate effective time management and resource allocation.

Microsoft Planner can serve as a powerful tool to translate your goals into actionable tasks, ensuring that each step of the way is documented, tracked, and adjusted as necessary.

2. Setting SMART Goals in Microsoft Planner

The SMART framework is a widely recognized method for setting goals that are clear and reachable. Here's how you can set SMART goals using Microsoft Planner:

- Specific: Define your goal in clear, specific terms. Instead of setting a vague goal like "Improve team communication," make it specific, such as "Implement weekly team meetings and use Planner to track action items."

- Measurable: Determine how you will measure success. For instance, you could set a goal to "Complete 90% of assigned tasks within the deadlines set in Planner over the next quarter."

- Achievable: Ensure that your goal is realistic given the resources and time available. Using Planner, you can break down larger goals into smaller, manageable tasks that are easier to accomplish.

- Relevant: Align your goals with broader objectives. For example, if your organization is focused on enhancing customer satisfaction, your goal in Planner might be "Resolve all customer service tickets within 24 hours by tracking tasks in Planner."

- Time-bound: Set a clear deadline for your goal. Planner's scheduling features allow you to set due dates and reminders, ensuring that your goals are time-sensitive and deadlines are met.

3. Creating Goals in Microsoft Planner

To set a goal in Microsoft Planner, you can start by creating a new plan dedicated to that specific goal or adding it to an existing plan. Here's a step-by-step guide:

- Step 1: Define Your Goal: Write down your goal in clear terms and create a plan in Microsoft Planner with a title that reflects the objective. For example, if your goal is to "Launch a new marketing campaign," you can name your plan "Q4 Marketing Campaign Launch."

- Step 2: Break Down the Goal into Tasks: Divide your goal into smaller, actionable tasks. Each task should represent a step towards achieving the goal. For example, tasks for the marketing campaign goal might include "Develop campaign concept," "Create marketing materials," "Plan social media strategy," and "Launch campaign."

- Step 3: Assign Tasks and Set Deadlines: Assign each task to the relevant team member or yourself, and set deadlines for each task. This will help ensure that the work is distributed evenly and that the goal remains on track.

- Step 4: Add Labels and Prioritize Tasks: Use labels in Planner to categorize tasks by priority, phase, or department. Prioritizing tasks allows you to focus on the most critical steps first, ensuring that the goal progresses smoothly.

- Step 5: Monitor Progress: Use the progress tracking features in Planner, such as the "Charts" view, to monitor the completion of tasks. Regularly update task statuses to reflect progress and adjust deadlines as needed.

4. Tracking and Adjusting Goals

Once your goals are set in Microsoft Planner, tracking progress becomes crucial. The ability to monitor how close you are to achieving your goals provides insight into whether you're on track or need to make adjustments.

- Regular Check-ins: Schedule regular check-ins within Planner to review the progress of your goals. You can do this by setting recurring tasks or meetings to assess the completion of tasks and overall goal progress.

- Adjusting Tasks and Deadlines: If you find that certain tasks are taking longer than anticipated, use Planner's flexible task management features to adjust deadlines and reassign tasks as necessary. This ensures that your goals remain realistic and achievable.

- Using Planner's Visual Tools: Microsoft Planner's visual tools, such as charts and dashboards, offer a quick overview of how much progress has been made towards your goal. The charts display the number of tasks completed, in progress, or not started, allowing you to quickly identify any bottlenecks.

- Tracking Milestones: Milestones are significant points in the process of achieving a goal. In Planner, you can set certain tasks as milestones by labeling them or marking them as high priority. Tracking milestones helps ensure that the project stays on course and that significant achievements are recognized and celebrated.

5. Collaboration and Team Goal Setting

Microsoft Planner is designed to be a collaborative tool, making it ideal for setting and achieving team goals. When working towards a collective goal, it's important to ensure that every team member is aligned and understands their role in the process.

- Collaborative Planning Sessions: Use Microsoft Planner during team meetings to collaboratively set goals. This can involve brainstorming sessions where tasks are created and assigned in real-time, ensuring that everyone is on the same page.

- Assigning Roles and Responsibilities: Clearly define roles within Planner by assigning tasks to specific team members. This not only helps distribute the workload evenly but also holds individuals accountable for their contributions to the goal.

- Communication and Feedback: Use the comment section within each task in Planner to facilitate ongoing communication. Team members can provide updates, ask questions, or offer suggestions, ensuring that the goal-setting process remains dynamic and inclusive.

- Tracking Team Progress: Just as you would track personal goals, monitor team progress regularly. Use Planner's tools to see which tasks are completed, which are pending, and what may require additional attention. Regular updates help the team stay motivated and focused.

6. Examples of Using Planner for Different Types of Goals

The versatility of Microsoft Planner allows it to be used for a wide range of goals, whether they are related to project management, personal development, or organizational objectives. Here are some examples:

- Project-Based Goals: For a goal such as "Launch a new product," Planner can be used to create a comprehensive project plan that includes research, development, marketing, and launch phases. Each phase can be broken down into tasks with specific deadlines, ensuring that the project stays on track.

- Personal Development Goals: If your goal is to "Improve professional skills," you can use Planner to track progress towards completing courses, attending workshops, or achieving certifications. Tasks can include researching training options, enrolling in courses, and completing assignments.

- Organizational Goals: For a company-wide objective like "Increase customer satisfaction by 20%," Planner can help track initiatives across different departments, such as customer service, product development, and marketing. Each department can have its own plan, with tasks that contribute to the overall goal.

7. Reviewing and Reflecting on Goals

Achieving a goal is not the end of the process; it's important to review and reflect on what was accomplished, what challenges were faced, and what can be improved in the future.

- Post-Goal Review: Once a goal is achieved, use Planner to conduct a review session. This can involve going through each task to see what worked well and what didn't. Gathering feedback from team members is also valuable for future goal-setting.

- Documenting Lessons Learned: Use Planner to document any lessons learned during the process. This might include best practices, effective strategies, or areas that need improvement. Having a record of these insights will be beneficial for future projects.

- Setting New Goals: Reflecting on completed goals often leads to the identification of new objectives. Use Planner to set these new goals, building on the momentum of your recent success.

8. Conclusion: Achieving Success with Planner

Using Microsoft Planner for goal setting is a powerful way to ensure that your objectives are clear, actionable, and achievable. By leveraging Planner's features, you can break down complex goals into manageable tasks, track progress in real-time, collaborate effectively with your team, and ultimately achieve your desired outcomes.

Whether you're working towards personal milestones or driving organizational success, Microsoft Planner provides the tools and framework needed to keep you on track and moving forward. The key to success lies in setting clear goals, consistently monitoring progress, making adjustments when necessary, and reflecting on what has been achieved to continuously improve your approach to goal setting and attainment.

5.2 Tips for Team Collaboration

Collaboration is a crucial element for the success of any project, especially when multiple team members are involved in planning and executing tasks. Microsoft Planner, as part of the Microsoft 365 suite, is designed to enhance team collaboration by offering tools that streamline communication, task assignment, and progress tracking. This section focuses on best practices and tips for improving team collaboration using Microsoft Planner, beginning with ways to encourage team engagement.

5.2.1 Encouraging Team Engagement

Engagement within a team is essential for productivity and project success. When team members are engaged, they are more likely to contribute ideas, complete tasks on time, and collaborate effectively. Microsoft Planner can serve as a central hub for promoting engagement by providing visibility, accountability, and communication tools. Here are several strategies to encourage team engagement using Microsoft Planner:

1. Establish Clear Roles and Responsibilities

One of the first steps in fostering engagement is to ensure that each team member understands their role within the project. Microsoft Planner allows you to assign tasks to specific individuals, making it clear who is responsible for what. When team members know their responsibilities, they are more likely to take ownership of their tasks.

- Assign Tasks Thoughtfully: When creating tasks in Planner, assign them to the most appropriate team members based on their skills and workload. This helps prevent burnout and ensures that tasks are handled by those best suited to complete them.

- Set Clear Expectations: Use the task description and checklist features in Planner to outline the specific requirements for each task. By setting clear expectations, you reduce ambiguity and increase the likelihood that tasks will be completed accurately and on time.

2. Foster Open Communication

Effective communication is the backbone of any successful team. Microsoft Planner offers several features that facilitate communication and ensure that everyone is on the same page.

- Utilize Comments: The comments section in each task allows team members to communicate directly within the context of the task. Encourage team members to use this feature to ask questions, provide updates, and offer feedback. This keeps all communication related to a task in one place, making it easier to track.

- Integrate with Microsoft Teams: For more dynamic communication, integrate Microsoft Planner with Microsoft Teams. This integration allows you to discuss tasks in real-time, hold virtual meetings, and collaborate on documents without leaving the Planner environment. Teams also provides notifications about task updates, helping to keep everyone informed.

3. Provide Regular Feedback

Feedback is essential for maintaining engagement and helping team members improve their performance. Microsoft Planner can be used as a tool for providing both formal and informal feedback.

- Use Task Comments for Immediate Feedback: Provide real-time feedback on tasks as they progress by adding comments. This can be particularly useful for correcting course mid-task or acknowledging good work.

- Conduct Regular Check-Ins: Schedule regular team check-ins using the Planner or Teams integration. These can be used to review progress, discuss any challenges, and provide feedback on completed tasks. Regular check-ins help keep everyone aligned and provide opportunities for continuous improvement.

4. Encourage Accountability

When team members are accountable for their work, they are more likely to stay engaged and committed to the project's success. Microsoft Planner can be leveraged to create a sense of accountability across the team.

- Monitor Task Progress: Microsoft Planner's dashboard provides a visual overview of task progress. Use this feature to monitor which tasks are on track, which are overdue, and which are completed. Publicly tracking progress can motivate team members to stay on top of their responsibilities.

- Set Due Dates: Assigning due dates to tasks is another way to encourage accountability. Ensure that due dates are realistic and that team members are aware of them. Planner sends notifications when due dates are approaching or have passed, which helps keep everyone on schedule.

5. Recognize and Reward Contributions

Recognition is a powerful motivator that can significantly boost engagement. When team members feel that their contributions are valued, they are more likely to stay engaged and continue performing at a high level.

- Celebrate Milestones: Use Microsoft Planner to track project milestones and celebrate when they are achieved. This could be as simple as sending a congratulatory message through the comments section or as involved as organizing a virtual celebration through Teams.

- Highlight Individual Achievements: Recognize individual contributions by calling out team members who have gone above and beyond. This could be done during team meetings or through Planner's communication features.

6. Encourage Collaboration on Tasks

Tasks that require collaboration can benefit from having multiple team members working together. Microsoft Planner's task management features make it easy to involve multiple people in a task.

- Assign Multiple Owners to a Task: In Planner, you can assign more than one team member to a task. This is particularly useful for tasks that require input from different skill sets. By assigning multiple owners, you encourage collaboration and ensure that the task is completed comprehensively.

- Share Task Checklists: For tasks that involve multiple steps, use the checklist feature to divide the work. Each team member can be responsible for different checklist items, making it clear who is doing what. This also provides visibility into the progress of each step.

7. Make Use of Visuals and Charts

Visual representations of progress can be motivating and help keep the team engaged. Microsoft Planner offers various visual tools that can enhance engagement.

- Utilize Planner's Charts: The Charts view in Planner provides a visual overview of task progress, including completed, in-progress, and not-started tasks. Share these charts during team meetings to highlight progress and identify any areas that need attention.

- Use Kanban Boards for Task Management: The Kanban-style board in Microsoft Planner allows you to organize tasks by buckets. This visual representation can help team members see how their work fits into the broader project and can encourage them to stay engaged by providing a clear overview of progress.

8. Promote a Positive Team Culture

A positive team culture is vital for maintaining long-term engagement. Microsoft Planner can support a positive culture by facilitating transparent communication and collaboration.

- Encourage Transparency: Use Planner to keep all project-related information in one place, accessible to all team members. This transparency can help build trust within the team and reduce misunderstandings.

- Support Team Bonding: Use Planner to organize team-building activities or social events. These events can be planned just like any other task, and having them within the Planner keeps them visible and emphasizes their importance to the team.

9. Encourage Continuous Learning

Learning and development are key to keeping team members engaged. Encourage your team to use Microsoft Planner as a tool for tracking their learning goals.

- Create Learning Plans: Use Planner to create plans dedicated to learning and development. Team members can set personal goals, track progress, and share resources with the team.

- Promote Knowledge Sharing: Encourage team members to share what they've learned with the rest of the team. This could be done by creating tasks related to training sessions, workshops, or articles they've found helpful.

10. Facilitate Remote Collaboration

With the increase in remote work, it's essential to have tools that support collaboration regardless of location. Microsoft Planner is well-suited to facilitate remote teamwork.

- Use Planner as a Virtual Workspace: Treat Planner as the central hub for your remote team. All tasks, updates, and communication can be managed within the platform, ensuring that remote team members stay connected and engaged.

- Leverage Time Zone Features: When working with a global team, it's important to be mindful of different time zones. Planner allows you to set deadlines and task assignments while taking time zones into consideration, ensuring that work is evenly distributed and expectations are clear.

11. Encourage Team Autonomy

Empowering your team to make decisions and take ownership of their work can lead to higher engagement. Microsoft Planner can be used to promote autonomy within your team.

- Allow Teams to Self-Organize: Encourage teams to create their own plans within Planner for specific projects or initiatives. This gives them control over how they manage their work and can lead to more creative and effective solutions.

- Promote Decision-Making: Use Planner's task assignment and commenting features to delegate decision-making authority to team members. By involving them in the decision-making process, you increase their investment in the project's success.

12. Address and Resolve Conflicts

Conflicts are a natural part of any team dynamic, but they must be addressed promptly to maintain engagement. Microsoft Planner can help manage and resolve conflicts effectively.

- Document Issues in Planner: If conflicts arise related to specific tasks, use Planner to document the issues and outline the steps needed to resolve them. This keeps the process transparent and ensures that everyone involved is aware of the situation.

- Facilitate Mediation: If needed, use Planner's integration with Teams to facilitate a mediation session where the involved parties can discuss the issue and work towards a resolution. Having a neutral platform like Planner to document the resolution can help prevent future conflicts.

By implementing these strategies, you can create a more engaged, collaborative, and productive team environment. Microsoft Planner's features are designed to support team collaboration at every stage, from planning and execution to feedback and conflict resolution. Encouraging team engagement through thoughtful use of Planner not only improves project outcomes but also enhances team morale and cohesion.

5.2.2 Managing Remote Teams with Planner

In today's increasingly digital and globalized work environment, managing remote teams has become an essential skill for leaders and project managers. Microsoft Planner offers a powerful platform to coordinate tasks, communicate effectively, and ensure that remote teams remain productive and engaged, regardless of their physical location. This section will explore best practices and strategies for managing remote teams using Microsoft Planner, focusing on how to optimize collaboration, maintain accountability, and foster a positive team culture in a virtual setting.

Understanding the Challenges of Remote Team Management

Managing a remote team presents unique challenges that differ significantly from those encountered in traditional, co-located work environments. These challenges include:

- Communication Barriers: Without face-to-face interaction, team members may struggle with miscommunication or delays in receiving important information. Time zone differences can further complicate communication, making it difficult to find overlapping hours for synchronous discussions.

- Lack of Visibility: In a remote setting, it can be challenging for managers to keep track of what each team member is working on, potentially leading to misunderstandings about workload and progress.

- Team Engagement and Morale: Remote workers can feel isolated or disconnected from the team, leading to lower morale and engagement. This disconnection can impact productivity and the quality of work.

- Accountability Issues: Without the physical presence of a manager, there may be concerns about accountability, with some team members potentially not meeting deadlines or contributing less than expected.

Microsoft Planner can address these challenges by providing a structured environment where tasks, communication, and progress tracking are centralized and accessible to all team members.

Setting Up Your Planner for Remote Teams

When managing remote teams, it's crucial to set up Microsoft Planner in a way that supports clear communication, visibility, and accountability. Here's how to configure your Planner to optimize remote team management:

- Create a Dedicated Plan for Remote Work: Start by setting up a specific plan dedicated to managing your remote team's tasks and projects. This plan should be accessible to all team members and serve as the central hub for all work-related activities. Include all relevant projects, tasks, and deadlines to ensure that everyone knows what is expected of them.

- Organize Tasks by Project or Department: Depending on the structure of your team, you may want to organize tasks by project or department within your plan. Use buckets to group tasks according to different projects, milestones, or team members' areas of responsibility. This organization helps clarify roles and responsibilities and makes it easier to track progress on specific aspects of the work.

- Utilize Task Labels and Categories: Use labels and categories to further organize tasks. For example, you can label tasks based on priority, project phase, or specific team members. This practice allows team members to quickly identify their tasks and prioritize their workload accordingly.

- Assign Tasks Clearly: Assign tasks to specific team members and include detailed descriptions of what needs to be done. This step ensures that everyone knows their responsibilities and reduces the risk of tasks being overlooked or misunderstood.

- Set Clear Deadlines: Assign due dates to each task and communicate these deadlines clearly to the team. This practice helps keep everyone on track and ensures that projects progress smoothly, even when team members are working asynchronously.

Promoting Effective Communication

Effective communication is the backbone of successful remote team management. Microsoft Planner, when integrated with other Microsoft tools such as Teams and Outlook, can facilitate clear and timely communication across the team.

- Use Comments for Task-Related Communication: Encourage team members to use the comments section within each task to discuss details, ask questions, and provide updates. This feature keeps all communication related to a specific task in one place, making it easy to track discussions and decisions.

- Leverage Microsoft Teams Integration: Integrate Planner with Microsoft Teams to facilitate real-time communication and collaboration. You can create channels within Teams dedicated to specific projects or departments and link Planner tasks to these channels. This integration allows team members to discuss tasks in real-time and provides an easy way to access and update their Planner assignments from within Teams.

- Set Up Regular Check-Ins and Updates: Schedule regular check-ins with your team, using Planner to track these meetings and their agendas. These check-ins can be conducted via video calls or chat in Microsoft Teams and provide an opportunity for team members to discuss progress, address challenges, and stay aligned on goals. Use Planner to track action items from these meetings and ensure follow-up on any decisions made.

- Automate Notifications and Reminders: Utilize Planner's integration with Outlook to send automated notifications and reminders to team members about upcoming deadlines and task updates. This automation helps ensure that everyone stays informed and on schedule, even when working across different time zones.

Maintaining Accountability and Transparency

In a remote work environment, maintaining accountability is crucial to ensuring that all team members contribute effectively to the project's success. Microsoft Planner offers several features that can help managers track progress and hold team members accountable for their work.

- Track Task Progress: Use Planner's progress tracking feature to monitor the status of each task. Tasks can be marked as "Not Started," "In Progress," or "Completed," giving you a clear overview of how the project is progressing. Encourage team members to update their task status regularly to maintain transparency.

- Monitor Task Assignments: Keep an eye on task assignments to ensure that work is distributed evenly across the team. Planner allows you to see which tasks are assigned to each team member, making it easy to identify if someone is overloaded or if tasks need to be reassigned.

- Review Completed Work: Use the completed tasks view in Planner to review work that has been finished. This review process allows you to ensure that all tasks have been completed to the required standard and provides an opportunity to recognize and reward team members for their contributions.

- Set Up Progress Reports: Generate regular progress reports using Planner's reporting features or by integrating with tools like Power BI. These reports can provide insights into team performance, task completion rates, and any areas where the team may be falling behind. Share these reports with the team to keep everyone informed and accountable.

Fostering Team Engagement and Culture

Remote work can sometimes lead to feelings of isolation among team members, making it essential to foster a sense of community and engagement. Microsoft Planner, when used effectively, can help build a positive team culture even when members are not physically together.

- Celebrate Achievements: Use Planner to track and celebrate team achievements. Mark milestones within the plan and take time to recognize when these milestones are reached. Acknowledging accomplishments can boost morale and motivate the team to continue performing at a high level.

- Encourage Collaboration on Tasks: Assign tasks that require collaboration among team members to foster a sense of teamwork. Use Planner to coordinate these collaborative efforts, ensuring that everyone knows their role in the task and how they can contribute.

- Create a Social Space: While Planner is primarily a tool for work-related tasks, consider integrating it with Teams to create a social channel where team members can interact on a more personal level. This space can be used to share non-work-related news, celebrate birthdays or achievements, and maintain the social aspects of team dynamics.

- Solicit Feedback: Regularly seek feedback from your team on how the remote work setup is functioning and how Planner is supporting their work. Use Planner to track suggestions and implement changes where feasible. Involving the team in decision-making processes helps them feel more connected and valued.

Optimizing Planner for Remote Teams: Advanced Tips

For teams looking to get the most out of Microsoft Planner in a remote work environment, there are several advanced strategies and features that can be leveraged:

- Use Power Automate for Task Automation: Power Automate can be used to automate repetitive tasks within Planner, such as sending notifications, updating task statuses, or generating reports. Automating these tasks can save time and reduce the risk of human error, allowing the team to focus on more critical activities.

- Integrate Planner with Time Tracking Tools: If your team needs to track the time spent on tasks, consider integrating Planner with time tracking tools like Toggl or Harvest. This integration allows team members to log their hours directly against tasks in Planner, providing valuable data for resource planning and project costing.

- Customize Planner with PowerApps: For teams with specific needs that go beyond Planner's standard features, PowerApps can be used to create custom apps that integrate with Planner. These apps can be designed to meet unique workflow requirements, such as custom forms for task submission or advanced reporting dashboards.

- Leverage Planner Analytics with Power BI: Integrating Planner with Power BI allows you to create detailed analytics dashboards that visualize task progress, team performance, and project timelines. These dashboards can provide deeper insights into how the team is functioning and help identify areas for improvement.

Case Studies: Successful Remote Team Management with Planner

To illustrate the effectiveness of Microsoft Planner in managing remote teams, consider the following case studies:

- Case Study 1: Global Marketing Team Coordination

A global marketing team with members in the US, Europe, and Asia used Microsoft Planner to coordinate a major product launch. By organizing tasks into buckets for each region and using labels to categorize tasks by priority, the team was able to ensure that all marketing activities were synchronized across time zones. Regular check-ins via Teams, combined with task comments in Planner, kept everyone informed and on track, leading to a successful and timely product launch.

- Case Study 2: Remote Software Development Team

A software development team working remotely across three continents used Microsoft Planner to manage their development sprints. Each sprint was represented by a plan in Planner, with tasks organized by feature and assigned to specific developers. By integrating Planner with GitHub, the team was able to automatically update task statuses based on code commits, streamlining the development process and improving transparency. The team also used Power BI to generate sprint performance reports, which helped them continuously refine their workflow.

- Case Study 3: Managing a Remote Customer Support Team

A customer support team that transitioned to remote work used Microsoft

Planner to manage their ticketing process. By creating a plan for each major client and organizing tickets by priority and type, the team was able to handle customer issues more efficiently. The integration of Planner with Teams allowed for quick communication and resolution of escalated tickets, ensuring that customer satisfaction remained high even in a remote setting.

Conclusion

Managing remote teams effectively requires a combination of clear communication, accountability, and fostering a positive team culture. Microsoft Planner, with its robust task management features and seamless integration with other Microsoft tools, provides an ideal platform for achieving these goals. By setting up your Planner for success, promoting effective communication, maintaining accountability, and engaging your team, you can ensure that your remote team remains productive, motivated, and aligned with organizational objectives. As remote work continues to grow in prevalence, mastering tools like Microsoft Planner will be essential for any team leader or project manager looking to thrive in a virtual environment.

5.2.3 Resolving Task Conflicts

In any collaborative environment, task conflicts are inevitable. They can arise from various sources, including miscommunication, overlapping responsibilities, or differing priorities. Effective conflict resolution is crucial to maintaining productivity and ensuring team cohesion. In this section, we'll explore strategies for resolving task conflicts within Microsoft Planner, focusing on practical approaches and tools to manage and resolve these conflicts efficiently.

Understanding Task Conflicts

Task conflicts typically manifest in the following ways:

1. Overlapping Responsibilities: When multiple team members are assigned similar or identical tasks, it can lead to confusion and duplicated efforts.

2. Priority Discrepancies: Differing opinions on task priorities can result in disagreements about which tasks should be completed first.

3. Resource Constraints: Limited resources may lead to conflicts over who gets access to tools, time, or support.

4. Deadline Disputes: Conflicts can occur when deadlines for tasks are not clearly defined or when team members disagree on the feasibility of meeting them.

Strategies for Resolving Task Conflicts

1. Clear Task Assignment

Define Roles and Responsibilities: Ensure that each team member understands their specific role and responsibilities. Use Microsoft Planner's features to clearly assign tasks to individuals, specifying who is responsible for what. This helps prevent overlapping assignments and clarifies accountability.

Set Clear Deadlines: Assign realistic deadlines for each task and communicate these deadlines clearly to all team members. Microsoft Planner allows you to set due dates, which can be visible to everyone involved in the plan, reducing misunderstandings about timelines.

2. Effective Communication

Regular Team Meetings: Schedule regular check-ins to discuss task progress, address any issues, and adjust priorities as needed. Use these meetings to facilitate open communication and resolve any conflicts that may arise.

Use Comments and @Mentions: Utilize the comment feature within Microsoft Planner to discuss specific tasks. Tag team members using @mentions to ensure that the right people are notified and involved in the discussion.

3. Prioritization and Re-Evaluation

Establish Priorities: Collaboratively set task priorities based on project goals and deadlines. Microsoft Planner's priority settings (Urgent, Important, Medium, Low) can help categorize tasks and make it easier to determine which tasks should take precedence.

Re-Evaluate and Adjust: Periodically review and adjust task priorities as the project evolves. This may involve reassigning tasks or adjusting deadlines based on new information or changing circumstances.

4. Resource Management

Track Resource Allocation: Use Microsoft Planner to monitor resource allocation and ensure that no team member is overburdened. By keeping an eye on the workload of each team member, you can identify and address potential conflicts early.

Allocate Resources Wisely: Make adjustments to task assignments or deadlines if resources are constrained. This might involve redistributing tasks or bringing in additional support to meet deadlines and reduce conflicts.

5. Conflict Resolution Techniques

Identify the Root Cause: When a conflict arises, identify its root cause. Is it due to miscommunication, competing priorities, or unclear responsibilities? Understanding the underlying issue is essential for finding an effective resolution.

Facilitate Open Discussions: Encourage team members to discuss conflicts openly and constructively. Use Microsoft Planner's collaborative tools to facilitate these discussions and find mutually agreeable solutions.

Seek Compromises: In cases where team members have conflicting views, seek compromises that address the concerns of all parties involved. This might involve adjusting task assignments, deadlines, or priorities to find a balanced solution.

6. Utilizing Planner Features

Task Dependencies: Use task dependencies in Microsoft Planner to manage relationships between tasks. Setting dependencies ensures that tasks are completed in the correct order and can help prevent conflicts related to task sequencing.

Progress Tracking: Leverage Planner's visual tools, such as charts and progress indicators, to track the status of tasks. This can help identify potential issues early and provide insights into how conflicts might be resolved.

Task Labels and Tags: Apply labels and tags to tasks to categorize and prioritize them. This helps clarify which tasks are related and can assist in resolving conflicts by providing a clearer view of task relationships and priorities.

7. Documenting Resolutions

Keep Records: Document the outcomes of conflict resolution discussions and any changes made to task assignments, deadlines, or priorities. Microsoft Planner's task comments and history can be useful for tracking these changes.

Review and Reflect: After resolving a conflict, review the process and reflect on what worked well and what could be improved. Use this feedback to enhance future conflict resolution strategies and improve overall team collaboration.

Best Practices for Preventing Task Conflicts

1. Clear Communication Channels: Establish clear communication channels for discussing tasks and project updates. Ensure that all team members are informed about any changes or updates to tasks.

2. Transparent Task Management: Make task assignments and priorities transparent to the entire team. Microsoft Planner's shared plan feature ensures that everyone has access to the same information, reducing the likelihood of conflicts.

3. Regular Plan Updates: Keep the plan updated regularly to reflect the current status of tasks and any changes in priorities or deadlines. This helps prevent conflicts arising from outdated or inaccurate information.

4. Encourage Collaboration and Feedback: Foster a collaborative environment where team members feel comfortable providing feedback and discussing concerns. Encouraging open communication can help address potential conflicts before they escalate.

5. Training and Support: Provide training and support to team members on using Microsoft Planner effectively. This ensures that everyone is familiar with the tool's features and can use them to manage tasks and resolve conflicts efficiently.

Case Study: Resolving Task Conflicts in a Marketing Team

Scenario: A marketing team is working on a campaign with overlapping tasks and conflicting priorities. Team members are unsure about their specific responsibilities and deadlines, leading to confusion and duplicated efforts.

Resolution Steps:

1. Clarify Responsibilities: The team leader uses Microsoft Planner to clearly define and assign specific tasks to each team member. Tasks are categorized by priority and due date.

2. Hold a Team Meeting: A meeting is scheduled to discuss the tasks, address any concerns, and adjust priorities. The team uses Planner's comment feature to collaborate and resolve any issues.

3. Set Clear Deadlines: Deadlines are adjusted based on team feedback and resource availability. Task dependencies are set to ensure that tasks are completed in the correct order.

4. Monitor Progress: The team leader monitors progress using Planner's visual tools and provides regular updates. Any emerging conflicts are addressed promptly through open communication and adjustments to task assignments.

5. Document Changes: All changes and resolutions are documented in Planner's task comments. The team reviews the process and identifies areas for improvement.

Outcome: By clearly defining responsibilities, setting priorities, and using Microsoft Planner's features, the team successfully resolves task conflicts and completes the campaign on time.

Effective conflict resolution in Microsoft Planner requires clear communication, efficient use of Planner's features, and a collaborative approach. By following these strategies and best practices, teams can manage and resolve task conflicts effectively, leading to improved productivity and a more cohesive working environment.

5.3 Maintaining an Organized Workflow

5.3.1 Keeping Plans Updated

Keeping your Microsoft Planner plans updated is crucial for maintaining an organized workflow and ensuring that your projects remain on track. This section will delve into best practices and strategies for keeping your plans current, which will help you manage tasks effectively, improve team productivity, and ensure successful project completion.

1. The Importance of Keeping Plans Updated

Keeping plans updated is not just about changing dates or moving tasks around; it's about ensuring that the plan reflects the current state of the project. An updated plan helps:

- Accurate Tracking: Provides a real-time view of project progress and helps track whether tasks are on schedule.

- Improved Communication: Ensures all team members are on the same page regarding project status, deadlines, and responsibilities.

- Effective Resource Allocation: Helps in adjusting resources and deadlines based on the latest project requirements and challenges.

- Better Decision Making: Provides up-to-date information for informed decision-making and proactive problem-solving.

2. Regularly Review and Update Task Status

Regularly reviewing and updating task status is one of the most effective ways to keep your plans current. Here's how to do it effectively:

- Daily or Weekly Check-ins: Depending on the size and complexity of the project, schedule daily or weekly check-ins to review task statuses. For high-priority or fast-paced projects, daily reviews may be necessary, while weekly reviews might suffice for less urgent tasks.

- Update Task Progress: As tasks are completed or their status changes, make sure to update their progress in Microsoft Planner. Use the built-in progress indicators (Not Started, In Progress, Completed) to reflect the current status accurately.

- Adjust Deadlines: If tasks are falling behind or ahead of schedule, adjust deadlines accordingly. This helps in realigning the project timeline and setting realistic expectations.

- Communicate Changes: Ensure that any changes made to the plan are communicated to all relevant team members. This helps in avoiding confusion and ensures that everyone is aware of the latest updates.

3. Use Labels and Tags for Better Organization

Microsoft Planner allows the use of labels and tags to categorize tasks and provide additional context. Proper use of these features can help in keeping your plans organized:

- Categorize Tasks: Use labels to categorize tasks based on their type, priority, or any other relevant criteria. This helps in quickly identifying tasks that belong to a particular category or phase of the project.

- Filter Tasks: Utilize the filtering options to view tasks based on their labels or tags. This allows you to focus on specific types of tasks or areas that require immediate attention.

- Consistent Labeling: Establish a consistent labeling system that all team members follow. This consistency helps in maintaining organization and ensuring that labels provide meaningful and actionable insights.

4. Track and Manage Dependencies

Tracking dependencies is essential for understanding how tasks are interrelated and ensuring that work progresses smoothly:

- Identify Dependencies: Determine which tasks are dependent on others and map these dependencies in your Planner. This helps in identifying potential bottlenecks and managing task sequencing.

- Update Dependencies: As tasks progress or their statuses change, update dependencies to reflect the current state. This ensures that the plan remains accurate and that any delays or issues are promptly addressed.

- Communicate Impact: Inform team members about any changes in task dependencies that may affect their work. This helps in coordinating efforts and minimizing disruptions.

5. Adjusting Plans Based on Project Changes

Projects are dynamic and may require adjustments to plans based on new information or changes in scope:

- Reassess Project Scope: Periodically reassess the project scope and make adjustments to the plan as needed. This includes updating tasks, deadlines, and resource allocations based on changes in project requirements or objectives.

- Handle Scope Creep: Address any scope creep by evaluating its impact on the project and making necessary adjustments to the plan. Communicate changes to the team and adjust deadlines and resources accordingly.

- Adapt to Feedback: Incorporate feedback from stakeholders and team members into the plan. This may involve revising tasks, updating priorities, or adjusting deadlines to align with evolving project needs.

6. Leverage Microsoft Planner's Integration Features

Microsoft Planner integrates with various other Microsoft tools and third-party applications. Leveraging these integrations can enhance plan updates and overall project management:

- Integration with Microsoft Teams: Use the Planner tab in Microsoft Teams to manage tasks and update plans directly within the Teams interface. This facilitates real-time collaboration and ensures that plans are accessible to all team members.

- Sync with Outlook: Sync Planner tasks with Microsoft Outlook to keep track of deadlines and receive reminders. This helps in ensuring that tasks and deadlines are integrated into your daily schedule.

- Automate Updates with Power Automate: Utilize Microsoft Power Automate to create workflows that automatically update tasks and notify team members based on predefined triggers. This automation can save time and reduce manual effort.

7. Implement a Review and Update Schedule

Establishing a regular review and update schedule helps in maintaining an organized workflow:

- Define Review Intervals: Determine how often plans should be reviewed and updated. This could be daily, weekly, or monthly, depending on the project's complexity and timeline.

- Assign Review Responsibilities: Designate team members responsible for reviewing and updating plans. This ensures that updates are made consistently and that all aspects of the plan are covered.

- Document Changes: Keep a record of changes made to the plan, including reasons for adjustments and impacts on the project. This documentation can be useful for future reference and analysis.

8. Address and Resolve Issues Promptly

Issues and challenges are inevitable in any project. Addressing them promptly helps in keeping the plan updated and minimizing disruptions:

- Identify Issues Early: Monitor the project for potential issues and identify them as soon as they arise. This proactive approach helps in addressing problems before they escalate.

- Communicate Issues: Inform relevant stakeholders and team members about the issues and their potential impact on the project. Open communication helps in finding solutions and making necessary adjustments to the plan.

- Implement Solutions: Develop and implement solutions to address the issues and update the plan accordingly. Ensure that any changes are communicated to the team and that the plan reflects the latest resolution.

9. Ensure Plan Accessibility and Visibility

Making sure that the plan is accessible and visible to all team members is crucial for effective project management:

- Share Plans with the Team: Ensure that all team members have access to the plan and can view or edit tasks as needed. This promotes transparency and collaboration.

- Use Permissions Wisely: Set appropriate permissions for different team members based on their roles and responsibilities. This ensures that sensitive information is protected while allowing team members to contribute effectively.

- Regularly Review Access: Periodically review and update access permissions to ensure that they align with current team structure and project needs.

10. Continually Improve Your Planning Process

Continuous improvement is key to maintaining an effective planning process:

- Seek Feedback: Regularly seek feedback from team members and stakeholders about the planning process and its effectiveness. Use this feedback to identify areas for improvement.

- Analyze Performance: Review project performance and outcomes to assess the effectiveness of the planning process. Identify trends and patterns that can inform future planning efforts.

- Adapt Best Practices: Stay updated on best practices and new features in Microsoft Planner. Implement improvements and adjustments to enhance your planning process and overall project management.

Conclusion

Keeping plans updated is a critical aspect of maintaining an organized workflow in Microsoft Planner. By regularly reviewing and updating task statuses, using labels and tags effectively, tracking dependencies, and addressing project changes promptly, you can ensure that your plans remain current and relevant. Leveraging integrations, establishing a review schedule, and continually improving your planning process will further enhance your project management capabilities and contribute to successful project outcomes.

5.3.2 Regular Plan Reviews

Regular plan reviews are a crucial aspect of maintaining an organized workflow in Microsoft Planner. They ensure that your projects stay on track, help identify and address potential issues early, and enable continuous improvement of your planning processes. This section will explore the importance of regular plan reviews, the best practices for conducting them, and how to effectively implement them in Microsoft Planner.

Importance of Regular Plan Reviews

1. Ensuring Alignment with Goals: Regular reviews help ensure that your plans and tasks align with the overall goals and objectives of your project or organization. They allow you to assess whether the tasks are contributing effectively to the desired outcomes and adjust the plan if necessary.

2. Identifying Issues Early: By reviewing your plans regularly, you can identify any potential issues or bottlenecks before they become significant problems. Early detection allows for timely intervention, which can prevent project delays and minimize disruptions.

3. Improving Task Management: Regular reviews help keep track of task progress, ensuring that deadlines are met and responsibilities are clear. This proactive approach to task management helps maintain accountability and ensures that work is distributed evenly among team members.

4. Enhancing Communication: Plan reviews provide an opportunity to discuss progress and challenges with your team. This fosters better communication, clarifies expectations, and encourages collaborative problem-solving.

5. Facilitating Continuous Improvement: Regular reviews are a chance to reflect on what's working well and what could be improved. This reflection can lead to adjustments in planning practices, task management, and team coordination, ultimately enhancing overall efficiency and effectiveness.

Best Practices for Conducting Regular Plan Reviews

1. Set a Review Schedule: Establish a regular schedule for plan reviews, such as weekly, bi-weekly, or monthly, depending on the complexity and duration of the project. Consistent scheduling ensures that reviews are conducted regularly and are not overlooked.

2. Prepare for the Review: Prior to the review meeting, gather all relevant information, such as task statuses, upcoming deadlines, and recent changes. Ensure that you have up-to-date data from Microsoft Planner and any other tools used in your workflow.

3. Review Plan Progress: During the review, assess the progress of each plan and task. Check whether tasks are on track, delayed, or completed. Evaluate the progress against the set milestones and objectives to determine if the plan is still aligned with the overall goals.

4. Discuss and Address Issues: Identify any issues or challenges that have arisen since the last review. Discuss these with your team to understand the root causes and explore potential solutions. Addressing issues promptly helps prevent them from escalating and affecting the overall project.

5. Update Plans as Needed: Based on the review findings, update the plans in Microsoft Planner. This may involve adjusting deadlines, reassigning tasks, or modifying priorities. Ensure that all changes are communicated to the relevant team members to keep everyone informed.

6. Document Changes and Actions: Keep a record of the decisions made during the review and any actions that need to be taken. Documenting these changes helps track progress and ensures accountability for implementing the agreed-upon actions.

7. Solicit Feedback: Encourage feedback from team members about the review process and any areas for improvement. This feedback can provide valuable insights into how the review process can be enhanced and how planning practices can be improved.

8. Monitor Action Items: Follow up on the action items identified during the review. Ensure that assigned tasks are completed as planned and that any adjustments made to the plan are implemented effectively. Monitoring action items helps ensure that the review outcomes are realized and contribute to project success.

Implementing Plan Reviews in Microsoft Planner

1. Utilize Planner Views and Filters: Microsoft Planner offers various views, such as Board, Charts, and Schedule, that can be used to review plan progress. Use these views to get a comprehensive understanding of task statuses, workload distribution, and upcoming deadlines. Filters can help focus on specific tasks or team members during the review.

2. Leverage Planner's Reporting Features: Use Planner's built-in reporting features to generate progress reports and analyze task data. Reports can provide insights into task completion rates, overdue tasks, and overall project health. Share these reports during the review to facilitate data-driven discussions.

3. Integrate with Microsoft Teams: If you're using Microsoft Teams, integrate Planner with your Teams channels. You can use Teams to schedule and conduct review meetings, share Planner updates, and collaborate with your team in real time. Teams' chat and file-sharing features can enhance the review process.

4. Set Up Notifications and Reminders: Use Planner's notification and reminder features to keep track of upcoming review meetings and important deadlines. Notifications can alert you to tasks that need attention or upcoming reviews, ensuring that nothing is missed.

5. Create Review Templates: Develop templates for your review meetings to streamline the process. Templates can include sections for progress updates, issue identification, and action items. Standardizing the review process helps ensure consistency and efficiency.

6. Use Task Comments for Updates: Encourage team members to use comments on tasks in Microsoft Planner to provide updates and communicate any issues. Comments can serve as a record of progress and discussions, which can be reviewed during plan reviews.

7. Track Review Outcomes with Planner: After each review, use Planner to track the outcomes and action items. Create tasks for follow-up actions, set due dates, and assign responsibilities. Tracking review outcomes in Planner helps ensure that changes are implemented and monitored effectively.

Conclusion

Regular plan reviews are essential for maintaining an organized and efficient workflow in Microsoft Planner. By setting up a consistent review schedule, preparing thoroughly, and leveraging Planner's features, you can ensure that your projects remain on track and that any issues are addressed promptly. Regular reviews foster better communication, improve task management, and facilitate continuous improvement, ultimately contributing to the success of your projects and achieving your goals.

5.3.3 Archiving and Deleting Completed Plans

As organizations and teams use Microsoft Planner for project management, maintaining an organized workspace becomes essential. Archiving and deleting completed plans are crucial practices to ensure that your Planner environment remains clutter-free, efficient, and focused. This section provides a comprehensive guide on how to effectively archive and delete completed plans in Microsoft Planner.

Why Archiving and Deleting Are Important

Managing the lifecycle of plans in Microsoft Planner involves not only creating and updating tasks but also handling completed plans. Properly archiving and deleting plans can enhance productivity, streamline workflows, and improve team collaboration. Here's why these practices are important:

1. *Clutter Reduction:* Over time, completed plans can accumulate, leading to a cluttered workspace. Archiving or deleting these plans helps maintain a clean and navigable interface.

2. *Improved Performance:* A large number of plans can slow down the application's performance. Removing or archiving old plans can help maintain optimal performance.

3. *Focused Planning:* Keeping only active and relevant plans visible helps team members focus on current projects and tasks, reducing the distraction of outdated or irrelevant information.

4. *Compliance and Security:* In some industries, retaining completed project data for a certain period may be required. Archiving ensures that data is stored securely and in compliance with regulations, while deletion ensures that sensitive information is handled appropriately.

Archiving Completed Plans

Archiving is the process of moving completed plans to a storage state where they are no longer active but still accessible if needed. This approach is useful for maintaining historical records while keeping the active workspace uncluttered.

Steps to Archive Completed Plans:

1. Identify Completed Plans: Review your Planner hub to identify plans that have reached their completion. You can sort or filter plans based on their status or completion date to make this task easier.

2. Evaluate the Need for Archiving: Determine if the plan needs to be archived based on its historical value, potential future reference, or compliance requirements. Consider creating an archiving policy for your organization to streamline this decision-making process.

3. Create an Archive Plan:

   - *Label and Categorize:* Use labels or tags to categorize the archived plan. This will help in future retrieval and management.

   - *Set Access Permissions:* Restrict access to archived plans to ensure they are only accessible to authorized users. This can be done by adjusting permissions or moving plans to a separate group or folder.

4. Move to Archive: Microsoft Planner does not have a built-in archiving feature, so you will need to use alternative methods, such as:

   - *Exporting Data:* Export the plan data to Excel or other formats for offline storage. This preserves the plan details for future reference.

   - *Using Microsoft Groups:* If you are using Microsoft 365 Groups, consider moving the completed plan to a dedicated group or a SharePoint site designed for archived projects.

5. Document the Archive Process: Maintain documentation on the archiving process, including how and where the plans are stored, and any relevant metadata such as archiving dates and reasons.

6. Regular Review: Periodically review archived plans to ensure that they are still relevant and properly stored. Update your archiving strategy as needed based on changes in organizational needs or compliance requirements.

Deleting Completed Plans

Deleting plans is a more permanent action compared to archiving. It involves removing the plan and all associated data from Microsoft Planner. This approach is suitable for plans that are no longer needed and do not require historical reference.

Steps to Delete Completed Plans:

1. Confirm Completion: Before deleting a plan, ensure that all tasks are completed, and there are no outstanding issues or dependencies. Verify with team members or stakeholders if necessary.

2. Backup Data: If there is any chance that the plan might be needed in the future, back up the data by exporting it to Excel or another format. This step ensures that you have a copy of the information before it is permanently deleted.

3. Delete the Plan:

   - *Navigate to the Plan:* Go to the Microsoft Planner hub and select the completed plan you wish to delete.

   - *Access Plan Settings:* Click on the three dots (More options) next to the plan name to access plan settings.

   - *Select Delete:* Choose the delete option from the menu. Confirm the deletion when prompted. This action will permanently remove the plan and all its associated data from Planner.

4. Verify Deletion: After deleting the plan, verify that it has been removed from all relevant areas, including Planner hub, Microsoft Groups, and any integrated tools.

5. Update Records: If your organization keeps records of deleted plans for auditing or compliance purposes, update these records accordingly. Document the plan deletion, including the date and reason for removal.

6. Review and Adjust Deletion Policy: Regularly review your deletion policies to ensure they align with organizational needs and compliance requirements. Adjust the policy as necessary to accommodate changes in workflow or data management practices.

Best Practices for Archiving and Deleting Plans

To ensure effective archiving and deletion of plans, follow these best practices:

1. Develop an Archiving and Deletion Policy: Establish clear guidelines for when and how plans should be archived or deleted. This policy should be communicated to all team members and stakeholders.

2. Use Descriptive Labels and Categories: Apply descriptive labels or categories to plans to facilitate easy identification and retrieval during archiving or deletion processes.

3. Regular Maintenance: Schedule regular reviews of your Planner environment to manage completed plans. This proactive approach helps prevent clutter and ensures that your workspace remains organized.

4. Ensure Data Security: When archiving or deleting plans, ensure that sensitive or confidential information is handled securely. Follow best practices for data protection and compliance.

5. Engage Team Members: Involve team members in the archiving and deletion process to ensure that all relevant information is captured and that no critical data is lost.

6. Leverage Automation: Use tools and scripts to automate archiving or deletion tasks where possible. This can save time and reduce the risk of errors.

Archiving and deleting completed plans are essential practices for maintaining an organized and efficient Microsoft Planner environment. By following the steps and best practices outlined in this section, you can ensure that your Planner workspace remains clutter-free, productive, and aligned with organizational goals.

CHAPTER VI
Troubleshooting and Support

6.1 Common Issues and Solutions

6.1.1 Handling Syncing Problems

One of the most common issues users face with Microsoft Planner is syncing problems. Syncing ensures that the most up-to-date information is available across all devices and users, making it a critical component for effective collaboration and task management. In this section, we'll explore common syncing problems, their causes, and step-by-step solutions to resolve them.

Understanding Syncing in Microsoft Planner

Microsoft Planner operates within the Microsoft 365 ecosystem, which means it relies on cloud services to keep data synchronized across different platforms and devices. Syncing involves the continuous update and retrieval of data from the cloud to ensure consistency. Any disruption in this process can lead to outdated information, missing tasks, or discrepancies between different users' views.

Common Syncing Problems and Their Causes

1. Delayed Syncing: Sometimes, changes made in Planner are not immediately reflected on other devices or by other users. This delay can be caused by network latency, server issues, or heavy data load.

2. Incomplete Data Sync: Users may encounter situations where only a portion of their data is synchronized. This can be due to partial network connectivity, corrupted data packets, or interruptions in the sync process.

3. Sync Errors: Sync errors are typically indicated by error messages or symbols within Planner. These errors can arise from authentication issues, permissions problems, or conflicts between local and cloud data.

4. Offline Syncing Problems: When working offline, changes made in Planner may not sync properly once the device reconnects to the internet. This issue can result from improper handling of offline data by the Planner app.

Step-by-Step Solutions to Syncing Problems

1. Check Internet Connectivity

The first step in troubleshooting syncing problems is to ensure a stable internet connection. A weak or intermittent connection can cause syncing delays and errors. Follow these steps to check and improve your internet connectivity:

- Test Your Connection: Use a web browser to visit a few websites to ensure your internet connection is active.

- Switch Networks: If possible, switch to a different Wi-Fi network or use a wired connection to see if the issue persists.

- Restart Router: Restart your Wi-Fi router to resolve any network issues.

2. Verify Microsoft 365 Service Status

Sometimes, syncing problems may be due to service outages or issues on Microsoft's end. You can check the status of Microsoft 365 services to ensure there are no widespread issues:

- Visit the Service Status Page: Go to the [Microsoft 365 Service Status](https://status.office.com/) page to see if there are any ongoing issues or outages.

- Subscribe to Alerts: Consider subscribing to service alerts to stay informed about any potential disruptions.

3. Ensure Up-to-Date Applications

Using outdated versions of Microsoft Planner or related applications can lead to syncing issues. Make sure all your apps are up-to-date:

- Update Planner App: Check for updates to the Microsoft Planner app on your device's app store (Google Play Store, Apple App Store, or Microsoft Store).

- Update Office Applications: Ensure that other Microsoft Office applications, especially Outlook and Teams, are also updated to the latest versions.

4. Check Account Authentication

Authentication issues can prevent Planner from syncing correctly. Verify that your account is properly authenticated:

- Re-authenticate Your Account: Sign out of your Microsoft account in Planner and sign back in.

- Clear Cache and Cookies: Clear your browser's cache and cookies, as they may contain outdated authentication data.

- Check Multi-Factor Authentication (MFA): If your organization uses MFA, ensure that it is correctly set up and that you have completed the authentication process.

5. Resolve Permission Issues

Syncing problems can occur if there are permission conflicts within Planner. Ensure that you have the necessary permissions to access and modify the plan:

- Check Plan Permissions: Verify that you have the correct permissions for the plan you are trying to sync. You may need to request additional permissions from the plan owner.

- Adjust Sharing Settings: Ensure that the plan is shared with the appropriate users and that they have the necessary access rights.

6. Address Data Conflicts

Data conflicts can arise when multiple users make changes to the same task or plan simultaneously. To resolve these conflicts:

- Identify Conflicted Items: Look for tasks or plans that show conflict indicators, such as warning icons or error messages.

- Resolve Conflicts Manually: Compare the conflicting versions and manually merge the changes. Ensure that all users involved are aware of the resolution.

- Avoid Simultaneous Edits: Encourage team members to communicate and avoid making simultaneous changes to the same items.

7. Sync Offline Changes

If you have made changes to Planner while offline, ensure that these changes sync correctly once you reconnect to the internet:

- Refresh Planner: After reconnecting, refresh the Planner app or browser page to initiate the sync process.

- Monitor Sync Status: Check the sync status indicators to ensure that all offline changes are successfully synced to the cloud.

8. Reinstall Microsoft Planner

If the above steps do not resolve the syncing issues, consider reinstalling the Planner app:

- Uninstall the App: Remove the Microsoft Planner app from your device.

- Reinstall the App: Download and install the latest version of the app from the appropriate app store.

- Sign In and Sync: Sign back into your Microsoft account and allow the app to sync your data.

9. Contact Microsoft Support

If syncing problems persist despite following these troubleshooting steps, it may be necessary to contact Microsoft Support for further assistance:

- Submit a Support Ticket: Visit the Microsoft Support website and submit a ticket detailing your issue.

- Provide Detailed Information: Include as much detail as possible, such as error messages, screenshots, and steps you have already taken to troubleshoot the problem.

- Follow Up: Stay in touch with Microsoft Support to ensure your issue is resolved in a timely manner.

Preventative Measures for Avoiding Syncing Problems

To minimize the risk of encountering syncing problems in the future, consider implementing these preventative measures:

1. Regularly Update Applications: Keep all Microsoft applications up-to-date to ensure compatibility and access to the latest features and fixes.

2. Maintain Stable Internet Connections: Use reliable internet connections and avoid working on critical tasks during known periods of network instability.

3. Communicate with Team Members: Establish clear communication protocols to avoid simultaneous edits and conflicts within Planner.

4. Back Up Important Data: Regularly back up important Planner data to avoid data loss in case of sync failures.

5. Monitor Service Status: Stay informed about the status of Microsoft 365 services and plan your work around any known outages or maintenance periods.

By following these steps and implementing best practices, you can effectively handle and prevent syncing problems in Microsoft Planner, ensuring a seamless and productive experience for you and your team.

6.1.2 Resolving Assignment Conflicts

In a collaborative environment, assignment conflicts in Microsoft Planner can disrupt workflows, create misunderstandings, and lead to delays in task completion. Resolving these conflicts efficiently is crucial to maintaining a smooth and productive work environment. This section will explore the common causes of assignment conflicts, strategies to prevent them, and step-by-step solutions to resolve them when they occur.

Understanding Assignment Conflicts

Assignment conflicts typically occur when tasks are misallocated, overlap in responsibility, or when there are competing priorities between team members. Common scenarios include:

- Double Assignment: A task is assigned to multiple people who may not realize they share the responsibility, leading to duplicated efforts or confusion over who is accountable.

- Overlapping Deadlines: When tasks assigned to a team member overlap or have competing deadlines, it can lead to stress and lower productivity.

- Miscommunication: Sometimes, tasks are assigned without clear instructions, leading to misunderstandings about who should do what and when.

- Resource Constraints: A team member might be assigned more tasks than they can handle, leading to bottlenecks and delays.

Identifying these issues early and implementing strategies to prevent them can save time and improve team efficiency.

Preventing Assignment Conflicts

The best way to deal with assignment conflicts is to prevent them from occurring in the first place. Here are some proactive strategies:

1. Clear Communication:

   - Before assigning tasks, ensure that team members understand their roles and responsibilities. Use Microsoft Planner's comment feature to clarify details and expectations.

   - Regularly update the team on task progress and changes to assignments to avoid misunderstandings.

2. Balanced Workloads:

- Monitor the distribution of tasks across the team to ensure that no one is overloaded. Microsoft Planner's dashboard can help you visualize who is assigned to what and adjust workloads accordingly.

- Consider the deadlines and prioritize tasks that are critical, spreading out less urgent tasks to maintain balance.

3. Avoiding Double Assignments:

- Assign tasks to a specific individual rather than multiple people unless collaboration is required. When collaboration is necessary, clearly define each person's role.

- Regularly review assignments to ensure that each task has a clear owner.

4. Set Clear Deadlines:

- Use Planner's scheduling tools to set realistic deadlines for each task. Align deadlines with overall project timelines to prevent conflicts.

- Avoid setting overlapping deadlines for the same team members unless the tasks are manageable simultaneously.

5. Use Labels and Buckets Effectively:

- Organize tasks into buckets and use labels to categorize them by priority, urgency, or type of work. This visual organization helps prevent conflicts by making it easier to see at a glance where potential overlaps or conflicts might occur.

Resolving Assignment Conflicts

Despite best efforts, assignment conflicts may still arise. When they do, it's essential to address them quickly to minimize disruption. Here's how to resolve these conflicts effectively:

1. Identify the Conflict:

- Use Microsoft Planner's visual tools, such as the Board view, to identify where the conflict is occurring. Look for tasks that are assigned to multiple people, have overlapping deadlines, or appear to be misaligned with the overall project goals.

2. Assess the Impact:

- Determine how the conflict is affecting the project timeline and the individuals involved. Assess whether the conflict is causing delays, duplicating efforts, or leading to missed deadlines.

3. Communicate with Team Members:

- Once the conflict is identified, communicate directly with the involved team members to understand their perspectives. Open a dialogue to discuss the conflict, clarify misunderstandings, and gather input on potential solutions.

- Use Planner's comment section or schedule a quick meeting to facilitate this discussion.

4. Reassign or Adjust Tasks:

- If the conflict is due to a double assignment, decide which team member is best suited to take full ownership of the task. You can reassign the task directly in Planner by selecting the task and changing the assignee.

- For overlapping tasks, consider adjusting deadlines or redistributing tasks to other team members who have available capacity. Ensure that these changes are communicated clearly to all involved.

5. Prioritize Tasks:

- If the conflict is due to competing priorities, work with the team to prioritize tasks based on urgency, importance, and resource availability. Use Planner's priority setting feature to rank tasks and adjust deadlines accordingly.

- This may involve negotiating with stakeholders to shift deadlines or reprioritize tasks to align with available resources.

6. Document Changes:

- After resolving the conflict, document any changes made to assignments or deadlines. Update the task notes in Planner to reflect these changes and notify all relevant team members.

- This documentation helps prevent similar conflicts in the future and ensures that everyone is on the same page moving forward.

7. Monitor Progress:

- After resolving the conflict, monitor the progress of the reassigned or adjusted tasks to ensure that the solution is effective. Use Planner's progress tracking tools to stay updated on task completion and any potential issues that may arise.

Case Studies of Assignment Conflict Resolution

To illustrate these strategies in action, consider the following case studies:

Case Study 1: Double Assignment in a Marketing Campaign

A marketing team using Microsoft Planner to manage a campaign realized that two team members were both working on the same task of creating a social media content calendar. This double assignment led to duplicated efforts and confusion over the final product.

Solution:

- The team identified the conflict by reviewing the task assignments in Planner. They communicated with both team members to clarify roles and responsibilities.

- One team member was reassigned to focus on creating content, while the other managed the calendar's structure and scheduling.

- The team documented the change in Planner and updated the project timeline to reflect the new assignments.

Case Study 2: Overlapping Deadlines in a Software Development Project

In a software development project, a developer was assigned to two high-priority tasks with overlapping deadlines. This created a bottleneck, as the developer struggled to meet both deadlines simultaneously.

Solution:

- The project manager used Planner's Board view to visualize the conflict and assess the impact on the project timeline.

- After discussing with the developer, the manager decided to extend the deadline for one task and reassigned some responsibilities to another developer with more availability.

- The manager updated the Planner tasks to reflect these changes and communicated the new deadlines to the team.

Case Study 3: Miscommunication in a Remote Team

A remote team was working on a product launch, and a key task was mistakenly assumed to be handled by multiple team members. Due to unclear communication, the task was delayed, affecting the launch timeline.

Solution:

- The team lead identified the miscommunication by reviewing task comments and realizing that no one had taken ownership of the task.

- A clear discussion was held with the team, and a single owner was assigned to the task. The task notes were updated in Planner to clarify the expectations and the timeline.

- Moving forward, the team agreed to improve communication by using Planner's comment feature more effectively and holding regular check-ins.

Leveraging Microsoft Planner Features to Avoid Future Conflicts

Microsoft Planner offers several features that can help teams avoid assignment conflicts in the future:

1. Task Ownership Visibility:

   - Ensure that each task in Planner is assigned to a specific individual, which helps prevent double assignments and ensures clear ownership.

   - Use Planner's Group By feature to sort tasks by assignee, making it easier to see who is responsible for what.

2. Progress Updates:

   - Encourage team members to update their tasks regularly in Planner, marking tasks as "In Progress" or "Completed" as appropriate. This keeps the team informed about the status of each task and helps identify potential conflicts early.

3. Use of Labels and Priorities:

   - Assign labels to tasks to indicate their priority or category. This can help in visually organizing tasks and ensuring that high-priority tasks are not overlooked.

   - Set task priorities to help team members understand which tasks require immediate attention.

4. Planner Notifications:

 - Enable notifications in Microsoft Planner to keep team members informed about task assignments, changes, and deadlines. Notifications can help prevent misunderstandings and ensure that everyone is aware of their responsibilities.

5. Regular Team Reviews:

 - Schedule regular team reviews to discuss task progress and identify any potential conflicts before they escalate. Use these meetings to realign tasks, adjust deadlines, and ensure that the team is on track to meet project goals.

Conclusion

Assignment conflicts in Microsoft Planner can be disruptive, but with clear communication, proactive planning, and effective use of Planner's features, these conflicts can be minimized and resolved quickly when they do occur. By following the strategies outlined in this section, teams can maintain a smooth workflow, reduce misunderstandings, and achieve their project goals efficiently. Regularly revisiting and refining your team's use of Planner will ensure that it remains a valuable tool for collaboration and task management.

6.1.3 Fixing Display Issues

Microsoft Planner, like any other digital tool, is not immune to display issues that can disrupt the user experience. Display problems in Planner can arise due to a variety of reasons, including browser compatibility issues, incorrect browser settings, outdated software, or even network problems. In this section, we'll delve into common display issues users might encounter in Microsoft Planner, and provide detailed solutions to fix them, ensuring a smooth and efficient workflow.

Understanding Display Issues in Microsoft Planner

Display issues in Microsoft Planner can manifest in several ways, such as:

- Incomplete or Incorrect Rendering of the Planner Interface: Elements like buttons, task lists, or the Planner hub might not display correctly, appear distorted, or fail to load altogether.

- Missing Tasks or Plans: Sometimes, tasks or entire plans may not appear on the screen, even though they exist and can be accessed from other devices or accounts.

- Navigation Problems: Users might find it difficult to navigate between different buckets, tasks, or plans due to unresponsive or misaligned UI elements.

- Slow Loading Times: The Planner might take an unusually long time to load, or specific parts of the interface might lag behind.

These issues can severely hinder productivity, making it crucial to identify and resolve them as quickly as possible.

1. Browser Compatibility and Settings

One of the most common causes of display issues in Microsoft Planner is browser incompatibility or incorrect browser settings. Since Planner is a web-based application, it relies heavily on the browser's capabilities to render its interface.

Solution: Update or Change Your Browser

- Ensure You Are Using a Supported Browser: Microsoft Planner is optimized for modern browsers like Microsoft Edge, Google Chrome, and Mozilla Firefox. If you are using an outdated browser or one that is not fully supported (like Internet Explorer), this could cause display problems. Switching to one of the recommended browsers can often resolve these issues.

- Clear Browser Cache and Cookies: Over time, your browser's cache and cookies can become cluttered, leading to various display issues. Clearing your cache and cookies can often resolve problems where the Planner interface does not load correctly or fails to update.

  - How to Clear Cache and Cookies:

    - For Google Chrome: Go to `Settings` > `Privacy and Security` > `Clear browsing data`.

    - For Microsoft Edge: Go to `Settings` > `Privacy, Search, and Services` > `Clear browsing data`.

- For Mozilla Firefox: Go to `Options` > `Privacy & Security` > `Cookies and Site Data` > `Clear Data`.

- Disable Browser Extensions: Some browser extensions, especially those related to ad-blocking or script-blocking, can interfere with the rendering of Microsoft Planner. Try disabling your extensions one by one to identify if any are causing the issue.

- Reset Browser Settings: If the above steps do not resolve the issue, consider resetting your browser settings to default. This action will disable all extensions and reset your browser settings, which can often resolve more complex display issues.

2. Update and Compatibility of Microsoft Planner

Outdated software is another common culprit behind display issues. Microsoft regularly updates Planner to improve its performance and compatibility with different systems.

Solution: Ensure Your Software is Up to Date

- Update Your Browser: Keeping your browser up to date ensures it has the latest security patches and compatibility improvements needed to run Microsoft Planner smoothly.

- Check for Updates in Microsoft Planner: If you are using Planner as part of the Microsoft 365 suite, ensure that your Office suite is up to date. Microsoft frequently releases updates that can resolve bugs and improve performance.

- Check for Operating System Updates: Sometimes, the issue might not be with Planner or your browser, but with your operating system. Ensure your OS is up to date to avoid any compatibility issues that might affect how Planner is displayed.

3. Network-Related Issues

Sometimes, display issues are not caused by the browser or software but by network-related problems. A slow or unstable internet connection can cause parts of the Planner interface to load incorrectly or not at all.

Solution: Optimize Your Network Connection

- Check Your Internet Connection: Ensure that you have a stable internet connection. You can test this by running a speed test or trying to load other websites. If your internet connection is slow or unstable, this could be the root cause of the display issues.

- Try a Different Network: If possible, switch to a different network to see if the issue persists. Sometimes, network-related display issues can be caused by firewalls, proxies, or other network configurations that might block certain elements of the Planner interface from loading.

- Disable VPNs or Proxies: If you are using a VPN or proxy service, try disabling it temporarily to see if it resolves the issue. Sometimes, these services can interfere with the way Planner loads its content.

4. Device-Related Issues

Display issues can also be device-specific, particularly if you are using older hardware or running multiple resource-intensive applications simultaneously.

Solution: Optimize Your Device's Performance

- Close Unnecessary Applications: If you are running several applications simultaneously, it might strain your system resources, leading to display issues in Planner. Try closing any unnecessary applications and refresh Planner to see if it resolves the issue.

- Restart Your Device: Sometimes, a simple restart can resolve display issues, particularly if your device has been running for an extended period without a reboot.

- Check for Hardware Issues: Ensure that your device meets the minimum system requirements for running modern web applications. If you are using outdated or underpowered hardware, it might struggle to render complex interfaces like Microsoft Planner.

5. Specific Display Issues and Solutions

Problem 1: Planner Hub Does Not Load Properly

If the Planner Hub does not load or displays incorrectly, it can prevent you from accessing your plans and tasks.

Solution: Try refreshing the page first. If the issue persists, clear your browser cache and cookies as described above. If this does not resolve the problem, consider using a different browser or checking for any available updates.

Problem 2: Tasks or Plans Are Missing from View

Sometimes, tasks or entire plans may not appear in the Planner interface, even though they exist and can be accessed from other devices.

Solution: Refresh the page to see if the missing tasks or plans reappear. If not, try accessing Planner from a different browser or device. Additionally, check your internet connection, as a slow or unstable connection might cause these elements to load incorrectly.

Problem 3: Misaligned or Overlapping Interface Elements

This issue can make it difficult to interact with certain parts of the Planner interface, such as task lists, buttons, or navigation menus.

Solution: First, try resizing your browser window or adjusting the zoom level (Ctrl + or - on Windows, Command + or - on Mac). If this does not resolve the issue, check for any browser extensions that might be affecting the display. Disable any such extensions and refresh the page.

Problem 4: Slow Performance and Laggy Interface

If Planner is taking too long to load or if the interface is lagging, it could be due to several factors, including network issues, browser problems, or heavy system resource usage.

Solution: Close any unnecessary tabs or applications running on your device to free up system resources. Ensure your internet connection is stable, and try refreshing the page. If the problem persists, consider clearing your browser cache or using a different browser.

6. Reporting Persistent Display Issues

If you have tried all the suggested solutions and the display issues persist, it might be time to report the problem to Microsoft.

Solution: Reporting the Issue to Microsoft Support

- Submit Feedback Through Planner: Microsoft Planner has a built-in feedback mechanism where you can report issues directly to the development team. Click on the settings gear icon in the top right corner, select "Give Feedback," and describe your issue in detail.

- Contact Microsoft Support: If you need more immediate assistance, you can contact Microsoft Support directly through their website or by calling their support line. Provide them with detailed information about the issue, including screenshots, if possible.

- Use the Planner Community: The Microsoft Planner Community is a valuable resource where you can post your issue and receive advice from other users and Microsoft experts. Often, other users may have experienced the same problem and can offer solutions that worked for them.

6.2 Planner Support Resources

When working with Microsoft Planner, it's essential to know where to find help and support, especially when encountering issues or when trying to optimize your workflow. Microsoft offers a variety of support resources that users can access to get assistance with Planner. These resources include direct support channels, community forums, and extensive online documentation. In this section, we will explore these resources in detail, starting with how to access Microsoft Support.

6.2.1 Accessing Microsoft Support

Accessing Microsoft Support is a critical step when you face issues that you cannot resolve through troubleshooting on your own. Microsoft offers several avenues for getting direct help, ranging from self-help resources to live support from experts. Understanding how to access and utilize these resources can save time and help you maintain productivity when using Microsoft Planner.

Self-Help Resources

Before reaching out for live support, Microsoft provides a wealth of self-help resources that are easily accessible online. These resources include:

- Microsoft Support Website: The official Microsoft Support website is a comprehensive hub where you can find answers to common issues, tutorials, and guides on using Microsoft products, including Planner. This website features a searchable knowledge base where users can type in keywords related to their problem and receive a list of relevant articles and solutions.

- Microsoft Learn: For users who prefer a more structured learning path, Microsoft Learn offers detailed, step-by-step courses on using various Microsoft products. Microsoft Planner is often included in broader courses on Office 365 or project management. These courses are free and can be taken at your own pace, making them a valuable resource for deepening your understanding of Planner.

- In-App Help: Microsoft Planner also includes built-in help features. Users can access help articles and tips directly from within the Planner application by clicking on the "Help" icon, usually represented by a question mark. This option provides quick access to relevant information without leaving the application.

Contacting Microsoft Support

If self-help resources do not resolve your issue, or if you encounter a complex problem that requires expert assistance, you can contact Microsoft Support directly. There are several ways to do this:

- Online Chat Support: Microsoft offers a live chat support option where you can speak directly with a support agent. This service is available 24/7, making it convenient for users in different time zones. To access chat support, visit the Microsoft Support website, navigate to the Planner section, and select the "Contact Support" option. You will be prompted to describe your issue, and then you will be connected with a support agent who specializes in Planner.

- Phone Support: For issues that require more detailed explanations, you can opt to speak with a support agent over the phone. Microsoft provides phone support for both individual and enterprise users. The phone numbers for support vary depending on your location, so you will need to select your country from the Microsoft Support website to get the correct contact information. Phone support is particularly useful for urgent issues that need immediate resolution.

- Email Support: If your issue is not urgent, or if you prefer written communication, you can submit a support request via email. Microsoft Support will respond to your inquiry, usually within 24-48 hours. Email support is ideal for non-critical issues or when you need detailed documentation of the support process.

Microsoft 365 Admin Support

For organizations using Microsoft 365, there is an additional layer of support available to IT administrators. Microsoft 365 Admin Support provides specialized assistance for managing and troubleshooting issues within the Microsoft 365 suite, including Planner.

- Admin Center: Microsoft 365 administrators have access to the Admin Center, a dedicated portal for managing all aspects of the organization's Microsoft 365 environment. From the Admin Center, IT administrators can access support resources tailored to their needs, including detailed logs, system health checks, and user management tools. The Admin Center also allows administrators to raise support tickets on behalf of users within the organization.

- Priority Support: Organizations with certain Microsoft 365 plans, such as Enterprise plans, may have access to priority support. This means faster response times and access to more experienced support agents who can handle complex issues that might arise with Planner and other Microsoft 365 tools.

- Service Requests: Within the Admin Center, administrators can create and track service requests for issues affecting the organization. This feature allows for detailed tracking and ensures that issues are resolved in a timely manner.

Microsoft Planner Support Forums

In addition to direct support channels, Microsoft maintains active support forums where users can ask questions and receive answers from both Microsoft employees and the broader user community. These forums are an excellent resource for troubleshooting unique or uncommon issues and for learning from the experiences of other users.

- Microsoft Community Forums: The Microsoft Community Forums are a large, active community where users can post questions and receive responses from other users and Microsoft Moderators. The forums are categorized by product, and there is a dedicated section for Microsoft Planner. These forums are searchable, allowing users to find previously answered questions that might relate to their issue.

- TechNet and MSDN Forums: For IT professionals and developers, the TechNet and MSDN forums offer a more technical discussion space. These forums are particularly useful for advanced users who need to integrate Planner with other Microsoft services or customize its functionality through APIs and scripts. The discussions here are often more in-depth and may involve troubleshooting complex technical scenarios.

Social Media and Online Communities

Microsoft also engages with users through various social media channels and online communities. These platforms are useful for staying updated on the latest Planner features and getting quick tips from other users.

- Twitter: The official Microsoft 365 Twitter account (@Microsoft365) often shares updates, tips, and links to useful resources related to Planner. Users can tweet their questions or issues and may receive a response or be directed to appropriate support resources.

- LinkedIn: Microsoft has a strong presence on LinkedIn, where they share articles, case studies, and user success stories related to Planner and other Microsoft products. Engaging with this content can provide insights into how other professionals use Planner and how to maximize its potential.

- Reddit: The r/Office365 and r/MicrosoftPlanner subreddits are popular places for users to discuss Microsoft Planner. These communities are user-driven, meaning that discussions are led by everyday users, which can lead to discovering creative solutions or workarounds for specific problems.

Microsoft Planner Documentation

Finally, Microsoft's official Planner documentation is a critical resource for users who want to dive deeper into the tool's capabilities or troubleshoot specific issues. This documentation is continuously updated to reflect the latest features and best practices.

- Planner Documentation: Available on the Microsoft website, the Planner documentation includes detailed guides on setting up and using Planner, integrating it with other Microsoft tools, and troubleshooting common issues. The documentation is divided into sections, making it easy to find information relevant to your needs. This resource is particularly valuable for users who want to explore advanced features or customize their Planner experience.

- API Documentation: For developers looking to extend Planner's functionality through custom applications or integrations, Microsoft's API documentation provides detailed information on how to use the Planner API. This documentation includes examples, code snippets, and best practices for working with Planner programmatically.

Conclusion

Accessing Microsoft Support for Planner is straightforward, thanks to the variety of options available. Whether you prefer self-help resources, live support, or engaging with a community of users, Microsoft offers multiple avenues to get the help you need. By leveraging these resources, you can ensure that your experience with Microsoft Planner is smooth and productive, allowing you to focus on organizing your work and achieving your goals.

6.2.2 Using the Planner Community

Welcome 6.2.2 Using the Planner Community

Introduction to the Planner Community

The Microsoft Planner Community is an essential resource for anyone looking to maximize their use of Microsoft Planner. It provides a platform where users from all over the world can connect, share experiences, seek advice, and contribute to discussions about the best practices, tips, and tricks for using Microsoft Planner. The community is not just for beginners but also serves as a valuable resource for advanced users and IT professionals who need to troubleshoot issues or explore advanced functionalities.

Participation in the Planner Community allows you to tap into the collective knowledge of thousands of users. Whether you're dealing with a specific issue, looking for new ways to enhance productivity, or simply want to stay informed about the latest updates and features, the Planner Community is the place to be.

Joining the Planner Community

To join the Microsoft Planner Community, you typically need a Microsoft account. The community is hosted on Microsoft's official platforms, and it is integrated with other Microsoft services, making it convenient for those who are already using products like Microsoft Teams, Office 365, or Azure.

1. Creating a Microsoft Account: If you don't already have one, the first step is to create a Microsoft account. This account will give you access to all Microsoft services, including the Planner Community. You can sign up for free, and the process only takes a few minutes.

2. Navigating to the Planner Community: Once your account is set up, navigate to the Microsoft Tech Community website. Here, you can find a dedicated section for Microsoft Planner. Bookmark this page for easy access in the future.

3. Setting Up Your Profile: After joining the community, set up your profile by adding a picture, filling out your bio, and linking any relevant social media profiles. A complete profile helps other users understand your background and expertise, which can facilitate more meaningful interactions.

4. Community Guidelines: Before participating, it's important to familiarize yourself with the community guidelines. These guidelines outline the dos and don'ts of the community, ensuring that discussions remain respectful, productive, and relevant. Adhering to these guidelines will make your experience in the community more enjoyable and beneficial.

Exploring Community Resources

The Planner Community offers a wealth of resources that can help you get the most out of Microsoft Planner. These resources include discussion forums, user-generated content, official Microsoft blogs, webinars, and more.

1. Discussion Forums:

- General Discussions: The general discussion forums are the heart of the Planner Community. Here, users post questions, share tips, and discuss various topics related to Microsoft Planner. Whether you're troubleshooting an issue or seeking advice on how to organize your tasks more effectively, the discussion forums are an excellent place to start.

- Feature Requests: This forum is dedicated to users who want to suggest new features or enhancements for Microsoft Planner. If you have an idea that you believe could improve the tool, you can post it here. Other users can upvote your suggestion, increasing the chances that Microsoft will take it into consideration in future updates.

- Bug Reports: If you encounter a bug or technical issue, the bug report forums allow you to share your experience with the community. By doing so, you not only help other users who might be facing the same issue but also bring it to the attention of Microsoft's support team.

2. User-Generated Content:

- Blogs and Articles: Many experienced users contribute to the Planner Community by writing blogs or articles. These pieces often provide in-depth insights into specific aspects of Microsoft Planner, such as advanced task management techniques, productivity hacks, or case studies from real-world applications.

- Video Tutorials: Some community members create and share video tutorials that demonstrate how to use various features of Microsoft Planner. These videos are particularly helpful for visual learners who prefer step-by-step walkthroughs.

- Templates and Tools: Occasionally, users will share custom templates or tools that they've developed to enhance their use of Microsoft Planner. These resources can be downloaded and adapted to fit your own needs.

3. Official Microsoft Resources:

- Microsoft Blogs: The official Microsoft blogs provide the latest news and updates about Microsoft Planner. Here, you can find announcements about new features, upcoming changes, and best practices directly from the Microsoft development team.

- Webinars and Live Events: Microsoft frequently hosts webinars and live events focused on Microsoft Planner. These sessions often feature product experts who provide insights into how to use the tool effectively, showcase new features, and answer questions from the audience.

- Support Documentation: While the community forums are great for user-to-user interactions, sometimes you need official documentation. The Planner Community often links to Microsoft's extensive library of support documentation, where you can find detailed guides on how to use every aspect of Microsoft Planner.

Engaging with the Community

Engagement is key to getting the most out of the Planner Community. By actively participating in discussions, asking questions, and sharing your own knowledge, you not only help others but also deepen your own understanding of Microsoft Planner.

1. Asking Questions:

- Crafting Clear Questions: When asking questions in the forums, make sure your queries are clear and concise. Provide as much detail as possible, including any steps you've already taken to resolve the issue. This helps others to provide more accurate and helpful responses.

- Following Up: After receiving responses, it's courteous to follow up by thanking those who helped and, if possible, sharing whether their advice solved your problem. This feedback loop encourages continued participation and improves the quality of the community.

2. Answering Questions:

- Sharing Your Expertise: If you see a question that you know the answer to, don't hesitate to share your knowledge. Helping others not only builds your reputation within the community but also reinforces your own understanding of the tool.

- Providing Resources: When answering questions, try to include links to relevant resources, such as documentation, blog posts, or video tutorials. This not only makes your answer more helpful but also enriches the community's overall knowledge base.

3. Participating in Discussions:

- Engaging in Conversations: Beyond asking and answering questions, participate in general discussions. Share your experiences, offer suggestions, or discuss the latest updates. Engaging in these conversations helps you stay informed and connected with the broader Planner user base.

- Respecting Diverse Opinions: Remember that the Planner Community is a global platform with users from diverse backgrounds and varying levels of expertise. Respect differing opinions and approaches, even if they differ from your own. Constructive dialogue often leads to new insights and solutions.

4. Contributing Content:

- Writing Blogs or Articles: If you have deep knowledge of Microsoft Planner or have developed a unique way of using the tool, consider writing a blog or article. Sharing your insights can help others and establish you as a thought leader within the community.

- Creating Tutorials: If you enjoy teaching, creating tutorials—whether written or video— can be a rewarding way to contribute. Tutorials that break down complex features or demonstrate best practices are always in demand.

- Developing Templates: If you've created a Planner template that has been particularly useful for you, share it with the community. Templates can save others time and provide inspiration for organizing their own plans.

Leveraging Community Feedback

One of the most valuable aspects of the Planner Community is the feedback you can receive from other users. Whether you're seeking advice on improving your workflow or need help troubleshooting an issue, the community's collective knowledge can provide you with new perspectives and solutions.

1. Requesting Feedback on Your Workflow:

- Posting Your Workflow: If you're unsure whether you're using Planner in the most efficient way, consider posting your workflow to the community and asking for feedback. Experienced users can offer suggestions on how to streamline your processes or better utilize Planner's features.

- Implementing Suggestions: After receiving feedback, try implementing the suggestions that seem most promising. Then, share your results with the community to close the loop. This not only helps you improve but also contributes to the community's collective learning.

2. Providing Feedback to Others:

- Constructive Criticism: When providing feedback to others, focus on being constructive. Point out what they're doing well, and offer suggestions for improvement in a supportive manner.

- Encouraging Experimentation: Encourage other users to experiment with different approaches and features within Planner. Sometimes the best solutions come from trying something new or unconventional.

3. Using Feedback to Influence Development:

- Participating in Feature Discussions: If there's a feature you think could be improved, or if you have an idea for a new feature, discuss it with the community. Engage in threads where Microsoft's development team is seeking user feedback. Your input could influence future updates to Microsoft Planner.

- Joining Beta Programs: Occasionally, Microsoft offers beta programs for upcoming features or updates. By joining these programs, you can provide direct feedback to the development team and help shape the future of Microsoft Planner.

Staying Updated Through the Community

The Planner Community is also a great way to stay updated on the latest news and developments related to Microsoft Planner. By regularly visiting the community and engaging with its content, you can ensure that you're always informed about new features, updates, and best practices.

1. Following Key Contributors:

- Identifying Experts: Within the community, certain users frequently contribute high-quality content and insights. Follow these users to keep up with their latest posts and discussions.

- Subscribing to Updates: Many community platforms allow you to subscribe to specific threads or users. By doing this, you'll receive notifications whenever there's new activity, ensuring you don't miss important discussions.

2. Participating in Webinars and Events:

- Attending Live Sessions: Keep an eye out for announcements about webinars, live Q&A sessions, and other events. These are excellent opportunities to learn from Microsoft experts and

ask questions in real-time.

- Watching Recordings: If you can't attend live events, look for recordings posted in the community. These are often made available shortly after the event and can be a valuable resource for learning at your own pace.

3. Reading the Latest Blogs and Articles:

  - Official Updates: Microsoft frequently posts official updates and announcements in the community. Make a habit of reading these to stay informed about upcoming changes and how they might impact your use of Planner.

  - Community Contributions: Don't overlook the wealth of knowledge shared by other community members. Regularly reading blogs and articles contributed by users can provide you with new ideas and insights.

Conclusion

The Microsoft Planner Community is more than just a support forum; it's a thriving ecosystem of users dedicated to helping each other succeed with Microsoft Planner. By actively participating in the community, you can not only solve problems and learn new skills but also contribute to the collective knowledge and success of others. Whether you're a beginner or an advanced user, the Planner Community offers endless opportunities for learning, collaboration, and growth.

6.3 Keeping Planner Up to Date

As a cloud-based application within the Microsoft 365 suite, Microsoft Planner continuously evolves, with new features, updates, and enhancements being rolled out regularly. Staying up to date with these changes is crucial for maximizing the benefits of Planner and ensuring that you are using the tool as efficiently as possible. This section will guide you through understanding and managing these updates and new features.

6.3.1 Understanding Updates and New Features

Microsoft Planner, like other tools in the Microsoft 365 ecosystem, is constantly updated with new features, enhancements, and bug fixes. These updates are designed to improve the user experience, introduce new capabilities, and ensure the security and stability of the platform. Understanding these updates is essential for maintaining an effective workflow and taking full advantage of the features Microsoft Planner has to offer.

The Importance of Staying Informed

In the fast-paced world of software development, tools are continuously evolving to meet the changing needs of users and businesses. For Microsoft Planner users, staying informed about updates and new features is critical for several reasons:

1. Maximizing Productivity: New features and updates often include tools or enhancements that can significantly streamline your workflow. By understanding and utilizing these features, you can work more efficiently and effectively.

2. Ensuring Compatibility: Updates often address compatibility issues with other Microsoft 365 tools or third-party applications. Staying updated ensures that Planner works seamlessly with the other software tools you rely on.

3. Enhancing Security: Security is a top priority for any cloud-based tool, and updates often include important security patches and improvements. Keeping Planner up to date is essential for protecting your data and maintaining compliance with industry standards.

4. Leveraging New Capabilities: Microsoft frequently introduces new features to Planner that can change the way you organize and manage tasks. By understanding these new capabilities, you can leverage them to improve your planning processes.

5. Avoiding Disruption: Major updates can sometimes change the user interface or alter how certain features work. By staying informed, you can prepare for these changes and minimize any potential disruption to your workflow.

How Microsoft Releases Updates

Microsoft typically releases updates to Planner through its broader Microsoft 365 update cycle. These updates can be categorized into several types:

1. Feature Updates: These are major updates that introduce new functionality to Planner. Feature updates are usually announced well in advance, giving users time to learn about the new capabilities and how they might impact their workflow.

2. Security Updates: Security updates are designed to address vulnerabilities and protect users from potential threats. These updates are critical and are usually rolled out automatically to ensure that all users are protected.

3. Bug Fixes: These updates address specific issues or bugs that have been identified by users or through internal testing. Bug fixes are typically smaller updates that improve the stability and reliability of Planner.

4. Performance Enhancements: Microsoft also releases updates aimed at improving the overall performance of Planner, such as faster load times, better integration with other Microsoft 365 tools, and more responsive user interfaces.

5. User Interface Changes: Periodically, Microsoft updates the Planner interface to improve usability or align with changes in design standards across the Microsoft 365 suite. These updates might include new layouts, navigation improvements, or changes to how information is displayed.

Where to Find Information on Updates

To stay informed about the latest updates and new features in Microsoft Planner, there are several resources you can rely on:

1. Microsoft 365 Message Center: The Message Center within the Microsoft 365 admin portal is the primary source of information for updates. Here, administrators can find detailed information about upcoming updates, including their expected impact and release dates.

2. Microsoft Tech Community: The Microsoft Tech Community is a valuable resource for staying up to date with Planner updates. This community forum includes announcements from Microsoft, as well as discussions and feedback from other users.

3. Office 365 Roadmap: The Office 365 Roadmap is an official Microsoft resource that provides a comprehensive list of upcoming features and updates across the entire Microsoft 365 suite, including Planner. Users can filter the roadmap by product to find information specifically about Planner.

4. Release Notes: Microsoft regularly publishes release notes for its updates. These notes provide detailed information about what's included in each update, including new features, bug fixes, and security improvements.

5. Planner Help and Learning Center: The Planner Help and Learning Center on the official Microsoft website is another useful resource for learning about new features. Microsoft often updates this site with tutorials and guides for new Planner features.

6. Email Notifications: For users who are Microsoft 365 administrators, email notifications can be set up to receive updates directly in your inbox. These notifications include information about upcoming changes and how they might impact your organization.

Exploring New Features

When a new feature is introduced to Microsoft Planner, it's important to take the time to explore and understand how it can benefit your workflow. Here's a step-by-step guide on how to approach new features:

1. Review the Feature Announcement: Start by reading the official announcement from Microsoft. This announcement will provide an overview of the feature, including its purpose, how it works, and any prerequisites for using it.

2. Access Tutorials and Guides: Microsoft often provides tutorials, guides, or even webinars to help users understand new features. These resources are invaluable for getting up to speed quickly and ensuring that you can use the feature effectively.

3. Experiment in a Test Environment: If possible, try out the new feature in a test environment before rolling it out to your entire team. This will give you the opportunity to experiment with the feature without impacting your ongoing projects.

4. Assess the Impact on Your Workflow: Consider how the new feature will fit into your existing workflow. Will it replace a current process, enhance an existing one, or introduce a completely new capability? Understanding the impact will help you plan for its adoption.

5. Train Your Team: If the new feature is something that will benefit your entire team, make sure to provide training or resources so that everyone can use it effectively. This might involve conducting a training session, sharing documentation, or creating a quick reference guide.

6. Monitor for Updates: After a new feature is released, Microsoft may continue to refine and improve it based on user feedback. Keep an eye on the update channels to ensure you're aware of any changes or enhancements to the feature.

Examples of Recent Features

To illustrate the importance of understanding updates and new features, here are a few examples of significant updates that Microsoft Planner users have benefited from in recent years:

1. Task Grouping by Progress: One of the more recent updates allowed users to group tasks by progress status (e.g., Not Started, In Progress, Completed) directly within the Planner interface. This feature has enabled teams to more easily track the status of their projects and prioritize tasks that need attention.

2. Integration with Microsoft Teams: The deepening integration between Planner and Microsoft Teams has been a major enhancement, allowing users to add Planner tabs within Teams channels and manage tasks without leaving the Teams environment. This integration has streamlined collaboration and task management for remote and hybrid teams.

3. New Labels and Color Coding: Microsoft introduced an update that expanded the number of labels available for tasks and added more color options. This update has provided users with greater flexibility in categorizing and organizing tasks, making it easier to manage complex projects.

4. Planner API for Automation: The introduction of the Planner API has opened up new possibilities for automation and integration with other tools. Users can now automate task creation, updates, and reporting by integrating Planner with Power Automate or custom applications.

5. Improved Reporting Capabilities: Microsoft has enhanced the reporting capabilities of Planner by integrating it more closely with Power BI. This allows users to create custom reports and dashboards that provide deeper insights into project progress and task management.

Preparing for Major Changes

While many updates to Microsoft Planner are incremental, there are times when a major change can significantly impact how you use the tool. Preparing for these changes is essential to avoid disruption and ensure a smooth transition. Here's how to approach major updates:

1. Stay Ahead of the Curve: Keep an eye on the Microsoft 365 Roadmap and other update channels to identify major changes well in advance. This will give you time to prepare and plan for the transition.

2. Understand the Impact: Take the time to thoroughly understand how the update will affect your workflow. Will it require changes to how you organize tasks, collaborate with your team, or integrate with other tools?

3. Communicate with Your Team: If a major update will impact your team's workflow, make sure to communicate the changes early. Provide clear instructions on what to expect and how to adapt to the new features or interface.

4. Plan for Training: Major updates may require additional training for your team. Plan for training sessions, whether they're formal or informal, to ensure everyone is comfortable with the new features and can use them effectively.

5. Test the Update: If possible, test the update in a controlled environment before it's fully rolled out. This will give you the opportunity to identify any potential issues or areas where additional training might be needed.

6. Provide Feedback: Microsoft values user feedback, and providing feedback on major updates can help shape future improvements. If you encounter issues or have suggestions for enhancements, be sure to share them with Microsoft through the appropriate channels.

Best Practices for Staying Updated

To ensure that you and your team are always using the latest and most effective version of Microsoft Planner, consider adopting the following best practices:

1. Regularly Check Update Channels: Make it a habit to regularly check the Microsoft 365 Message Center, Tech Community, and other update channels for news about upcoming Planner updates.

2. Set Up Notifications: Configure email notifications to alert you to important updates or changes in Planner. This will help you stay informed without having to manually check for updates.

3. Participate in Beta Programs: If you want to stay on the cutting edge, consider participating in Microsoft's beta programs, which allow you to test new features before they're widely released. This can give you a head start on understanding and implementing new capabilities.

4. Engage with the Community: Join the Microsoft Planner community forums and discussions to stay connected with other users. The community can be a valuable resource for learning about updates, sharing best practices, and troubleshooting issues.

5. Schedule Regular Review Sessions: Periodically review your use of Planner with your team to ensure that you're taking full advantage of all the latest features. This can be part of a broader review of your project management processes.

6. Document Changes: Keep a record of major updates and how they've been implemented in your workflow. This documentation can be useful for training new team members or revisiting processes as your team evolves.

By staying informed and proactive about updates and new features in Microsoft Planner, you can ensure that your team remains productive, secure, and ready to leverage the latest tools and capabilities that Microsoft has to offer.

6.3.2 Preparing for Major Changes

Microsoft Planner, like many other digital tools, undergoes frequent updates and changes to enhance functionality, improve user experience, and integrate new technologies. Staying prepared for these major changes is crucial for maintaining productivity and ensuring that your workflows remain uninterrupted. This section explores strategies and best practices for effectively managing and preparing for major changes in Microsoft Planner.

Understanding the Scope of Changes

1. Types of Major Changes

   - Feature Updates: These involve the addition of new functionalities or enhancements to existing features. Examples include the introduction of advanced analytics tools or new integration capabilities.

   - User Interface (UI) Overhauls: Significant redesigns or changes in the layout and navigation of Planner can affect how users interact with the tool.

   - Performance Improvements: Updates aimed at enhancing speed, reliability, and overall performance of the application.

   - Integration Changes: Modifications in how Planner integrates with other Microsoft 365 apps or third-party services.

   - Security Updates: Enhancements focused on improving the security and privacy of user data.

2. Identifying and Assessing Changes

- Release Notes and Update Announcements: Microsoft regularly publishes release notes and announcements detailing the changes in new updates. Reviewing these documents helps in understanding the scope and impact of the changes.

- Beta Features and Early Access Programs: Participating in beta programs or reviewing early access features can provide insights into upcoming changes and allow for early preparation.

Preparing for User Interface (UI) Changes

1. Training and Familiarization

- User Training: When significant UI changes are introduced, providing training sessions or workshops for users can help them adapt quickly. Ensure that the training covers new features, changes in navigation, and updated workflows.

- Documentation Updates: Update internal documentation, user guides, and tutorials to reflect the new UI. This ensures that users have access to current information and instructions.

2. Testing and Feedback

- Pilot Programs: Implement a pilot program where a small group of users test the new UI changes before a full rollout. Gather feedback to identify potential issues and make necessary adjustments.

- User Feedback Mechanisms: Create channels for users to provide feedback on the new UI. This can include surveys, feedback forms, or dedicated support teams.

Managing Feature Updates

1. Reviewing New Features

- Feature Assessment: Evaluate how new features align with your organization's needs and workflows. Determine if the features enhance productivity or require changes in current processes.

- Integration Testing: Test new features in a controlled environment to ensure they integrate seamlessly with existing systems and workflows.

2. Implementation and Rollout

- Phased Rollout: Implement new features in phases to manage the transition smoothly. Start with a small group of users before extending to the entire organization.

- Training and Support: Provide training and support resources to help users understand and utilize new features effectively.

Handling Performance Improvements

1. Monitoring System Performance

- Performance Metrics: Track performance metrics before and after updates to assess improvements. This can include response times, load times, and overall system reliability.

- User Feedback: Collect feedback from users regarding any changes in performance. Address any issues promptly to ensure continued efficiency.

2. Updating System Configurations

- Configuration Adjustments: Adjust system configurations to optimize performance based on the new updates. This may involve changes in settings or resource allocations.

Managing Integration Changes

1. Evaluating Impact

- Impact Assessment: Assess how changes in integrations affect your workflows and other connected applications. Identify any potential disruptions or benefits.

- Compatibility Checks: Ensure that Planner's new integrations are compatible with existing systems and tools.

2. Updating Integration Settings

- Configuration Updates: Update integration settings to accommodate new features or changes. Ensure that data flow between Planner and other applications remains seamless.

- Testing Integrations: Test integrations thoroughly after updates to confirm that they function as expected.

Addressing Security Updates

1. Understanding Security Enhancements

- Security Briefings: Review security updates and enhancements provided by Microsoft. Understand how these changes improve data protection and privacy.

- Compliance Checks: Ensure that security updates align with your organization's compliance requirements and standards.

2. Implementing Security Measures

- System Updates: Apply necessary updates to your systems and configurations to comply with new security measures.

- User Awareness: Educate users about new security features and best practices for protecting data.

Communicating Changes to Users

1. Change Management Communication

- Change Announcements: Communicate upcoming changes clearly and proactively to all users. Provide information on what to expect, how it will affect their workflows, and any required actions.

- Support Channels: Offer support through various channels, including help desks, online forums, and training sessions, to assist users during the transition.

2. Providing Resources and Support

- Guides and Tutorials: Create and distribute updated guides, tutorials, and FAQs to help users adapt to changes.

- Ongoing Support: Provide ongoing support and assistance to address any issues or concerns that arise during the transition.

Monitoring and Evaluating Post-Update

1. Post-Implementation Review

- Review Sessions: Conduct review sessions to evaluate the effectiveness of the changes and identify any issues that need to be addressed.

- User Feedback: Gather feedback from users on their experience with the new updates. Use this feedback to make any necessary adjustments.

2. Continuous Improvement

- Update Strategy: Develop a strategy for ongoing updates and improvements. Stay informed about future changes and continuously refine your approach to managing updates.

- Best Practices: Establish best practices for preparing for and managing updates to ensure that future changes are handled efficiently.

By following these strategies and best practices, you can effectively prepare for and manage major changes in Microsoft Planner. This proactive approach will help minimize disruptions, enhance productivity, and ensure a smooth transition during updates.

CHAPTER VII
Case Studies and Real-World Applications

7.1 Case Study: Microsoft Planner in a Marketing Team

7.1.1 Setting Up a Campaign Plan

In this case study, we'll explore how a marketing team can leverage Microsoft Planner to set up and execute a comprehensive campaign plan. Effective marketing campaigns require meticulous planning, clear task assignments, and efficient tracking of progress. Microsoft Planner is an ideal tool to facilitate these needs, providing a visual and collaborative platform to organize work and achieve goals.

Introduction to the Marketing Campaign

Before diving into the setup process, let's consider a hypothetical scenario. Imagine a mid-sized company, "TechWave," is planning to launch a new software product. The marketing team is tasked with creating and executing a multi-channel campaign to generate buzz, attract potential customers, and ultimately drive sales. The campaign will span various channels, including social media, email marketing, content marketing, and events.

Initial Planning and Goal Setting

The first step in setting up a campaign plan in Microsoft Planner is to outline the campaign's goals and objectives. The marketing team at TechWave convenes to discuss the overarching goals, such as increasing brand awareness, generating leads, and achieving a specific number of product sign-ups. These goals are then broken down into measurable objectives, such as:

- Increase social media followers by 20% in three months.

- Generate 500 new leads through email marketing.

- Achieve 200 product sign-ups from the campaign.

With clear objectives in place, the team can now proceed to set up the campaign plan in Microsoft Planner.

Creating the Campaign Plan

Step 1: Setting Up the Plan

The marketing team leader creates a new plan in Microsoft Planner and names it "New Software Launch Campaign." This plan will serve as the central hub for all campaign-related activities.

- Access Microsoft Planner: Log in to Microsoft Planner through Office 365 or the Planner app.

- Create a New Plan: Click on "New Plan," enter the name of the plan, and select the appropriate group (e.g., "Marketing Team").

- Set Privacy Settings: Choose whether the plan should be public or private. For this campaign, the team selects "Private" to ensure that only team members can access it.

Step 2: Defining Buckets

Buckets in Microsoft Planner are used to organize tasks into different categories. The marketing team defines buckets based on the key components of the campaign:

- Strategy and Planning: Tasks related to campaign strategy, goal setting, and planning.

- Content Creation: Tasks for creating blog posts, social media content, email newsletters, and other marketing materials.

- Social Media: Tasks specific to managing and executing social media activities.

- Email Marketing: Tasks for designing, scheduling, and sending email campaigns.

- Event Management: Tasks related to organizing webinars, live demos, and other events.

- Analytics and Reporting: Tasks for tracking campaign performance and generating reports.

Step 3: Adding Tasks

With the buckets defined, the team begins adding tasks to each bucket. Each task represents a specific action item that needs to be completed as part of the campaign.

- *Strategy and Planning:*

  - Conduct market research

  - Define target audience

  - Develop campaign messaging

  - Create campaign timeline

- *Content Creation:*

  - Write blog post on product features

  - Design social media graphics

  - Draft email newsletter

  - Create promotional video

- *Social Media:*

  - Schedule posts for Facebook, Twitter, LinkedIn

  - Engage with followers

- Monitor social media analytics

- *Email Marketing:*

  - Design email templates

  - Segment email list

  - Schedule email blasts

- *Event Management:*

  - Plan webinar details

  - Coordinate with guest speakers

  - Promote webinar on social media

- *Analytics and Reporting:*

  - Set up tracking in Google Analytics

  - Monitor campaign performance

  - Generate weekly progress reports

Step 4: Assigning Tasks

Each task is then assigned to specific team members based on their roles and expertise. Microsoft Planner allows for easy task assignment, ensuring accountability and clarity.

- Conduct market research: Assigned to Jane, the market analyst.

- Write blog post on product features: Assigned to John, the content writer.

- Schedule posts for social media: Assigned to Emily, the social media manager.

- Design email templates: Assigned to David, the graphic designer.

- Plan webinar details: Assigned to Sarah, the event coordinator.

- Set up tracking in Google Analytics: Assigned to Mike, the digital marketing specialist.

Step 5: Setting Due Dates and Priorities

To keep the campaign on track, each task is given a due date and priority level. High-priority tasks, such as defining the target audience and developing campaign messaging, are scheduled to be completed first. Tasks with dependencies, such as creating social media graphics before scheduling posts, are planned accordingly.

Step 6: Adding Task Details

Detailed descriptions, checklists, attachments, and comments are added to each task to provide clear instructions and resources for team members. For example:

- Task: Write blog post on product features

  - Description: Create a 1000-word blog post highlighting the key features and benefits of the new software product.

  - Checklist:

    - Research product features

    - Draft blog post

    - Review and edit

    - Publish on company blog

  - Attachments: Product feature sheet, images of the product

  - Comments: John can leave comments or questions for the team to review.

Monitoring Progress and Making Adjustments

As the campaign progresses, the marketing team regularly reviews the Planner board to monitor task completion and overall progress. Team members update the status of their tasks, add comments, and upload deliverables. The team leader conducts weekly check-ins to discuss any challenges, reassign tasks if necessary, and ensure that the campaign stays on track.

Collaboration and Communication

Microsoft Planner's integration with Microsoft Teams enhances collaboration and communication. The marketing team creates a dedicated channel for the campaign in Microsoft Teams, where they can:

- Discuss tasks and share updates in real-time.

- Access the Planner tab to view and update the campaign plan directly from Teams.

- Use video calls and meetings to brainstorm ideas and resolve issues.

Analyzing the Results

Once the campaign is complete, the marketing team uses Microsoft Planner's analytics and reporting features to evaluate the campaign's success. Key performance indicators (KPIs) such as social media engagement, email open rates, lead generation, and product sign-ups are analyzed. The team generates a final report summarizing the outcomes and lessons learned, which is then shared with stakeholders.

Final Thoughts

Setting up a campaign plan in Microsoft Planner enables the marketing team to organize their work efficiently, collaborate effectively, and achieve their goals. By leveraging Planner's features, the team can stay focused, meet deadlines, and deliver a successful marketing campaign that drives results for TechWave's new software product. This case study demonstrates the power of Microsoft Planner as a versatile tool for managing complex projects and achieving business objectives.

7.1.2 Task Assignment and Tracking

In any marketing team, managing tasks effectively is crucial to the success of campaigns. Microsoft Planner offers a robust platform for assigning tasks to team members, tracking progress, and ensuring that the team meets its goals on time. This section will explore how a marketing team can leverage Microsoft Planner to streamline task assignments and monitor the progress of various activities.

1. Understanding Task Assignment in Microsoft Planner

Task assignment in Microsoft Planner begins with creating tasks that align with the objectives of the marketing campaign. Each task represents a specific action item that needs to be completed as part of the larger plan. For instance, in a campaign to launch a new product, tasks may include creating promotional content, designing graphics, scheduling social media posts, and organizing launch events.

1.1 Creating and Naming Tasks

The first step in task assignment is creating tasks within the relevant plan. Each task should have a clear, descriptive name that immediately communicates the action required. For example, instead of simply naming a task "Social Media," it could be more specific, such as "Draft Social Media Content for Product Launch." This level of detail helps ensure that team members understand exactly what is expected.

When creating tasks, it's important to break down larger projects into manageable subtasks. This approach not only makes the workload more manageable but also provides a clearer overview of what needs to be done. In the context of the marketing team, subtasks for the "Draft Social Media Content for Product Launch" task might include writing captions, selecting images, and scheduling posts.

1.2 Assigning Tasks to Team Members

Once tasks are created, they need to be assigned to the appropriate team members. Microsoft Planner allows for easy task assignment with just a few clicks. The marketing manager can assign tasks based on each team member's strengths and workload. For instance, a content writer would be assigned tasks related to drafting blog posts or social media captions, while a graphic designer would handle tasks like creating promotional images.

It's essential to consider the current workload of each team member when assigning tasks. Overloading one person can lead to delays and decreased productivity, whereas distributing tasks evenly across the team ensures that work progresses smoothly. Microsoft Planner's interface displays each team member's assigned tasks, making it easy for the manager to see who is responsible for what and adjust assignments as necessary.

1.3 Setting Deadlines and Priorities

In marketing campaigns, timing is everything. Therefore, setting appropriate deadlines for tasks is critical. Microsoft Planner allows deadlines to be set for each task, ensuring that all components of the campaign are completed on time. Deadlines should be realistic, giving team members enough time to complete their tasks without unnecessary pressure, yet firm enough to keep the campaign on track.

Alongside deadlines, assigning priorities to tasks helps the team focus on the most important activities. Microsoft Planner enables the categorization of tasks by priority level—urgent, high, medium, or low. For example, tasks like "Submit Final Ad Copy to Media Outlet" might be marked as urgent, while "Brainstorm Future Campaign Ideas" might be a lower priority task that can be revisited later.

2. Tracking Task Progress

Tracking the progress of assigned tasks is a key aspect of project management in Microsoft Planner. The platform provides several features to help marketing teams monitor how work is progressing and identify any potential issues before they escalate.

2.1 Using Buckets to Organize Tasks

Buckets in Microsoft Planner serve as containers for grouping related tasks. For a marketing campaign, buckets might be organized by stages of the campaign, such as "Planning," "Content Creation," "Design," "Social Media," and "Post-Campaign Analysis." This structure allows team members to quickly find tasks related to their current phase of work.

Tasks within each bucket can be moved from one stage to another as they progress, offering a visual representation of the campaign's status. For example, a task in the "Content Creation" bucket may move to "Design" once the text is approved, and then to "Social Media" once the graphics are finalized. This workflow helps everyone on the team understand the current status of the campaign and what remains to be done.

2.2 Monitoring Progress with Task Labels

Microsoft Planner offers color-coded labels to help categorize and track tasks according to various criteria. In a marketing team, labels can be used to denote different types of content, such as "Blog Post," "Email Newsletter," or "Social Media." Alternatively, labels can indicate the current status of a task, such as "In Progress," "Pending Approval," or "Completed."

These labels provide at-a-glance information about the state of the campaign, making it easier to spot where attention is needed. For instance, if many tasks are labeled "Pending Approval," the manager knows to focus on reviewing and approving these tasks to keep the campaign moving forward.

2.3 Tracking Task Completion

Microsoft Planner tracks the completion of tasks in real-time, updating the status as team members mark their work as done. This feature is particularly useful for marketing managers who need to keep track of the campaign's overall progress without micromanaging every detail.

Tasks marked as complete move out of the main workflow, reducing clutter and helping the team focus on what still needs to be done. The platform also provides progress charts that visually represent the number of completed tasks versus those that are still in progress or overdue. These charts are valuable tools for managers to quickly assess whether the team is on track to meet campaign deadlines.

2.4 Setting Up Task Dependencies

In complex marketing campaigns, certain tasks may depend on the completion of others before they can begin. Microsoft Planner allows for the establishment of task dependencies, where one task is linked to another, ensuring that work proceeds in the correct sequence.

For example, the task "Design Promotional Banners" may be dependent on the completion of "Finalize Campaign Slogan." By setting up this dependency, Microsoft Planner will prevent the design team from starting work on the banners until the slogan is finalized. This feature helps to avoid bottlenecks and ensures that all aspects of the campaign are aligned.

2.5 Reviewing and Adjusting Task Assignments

As the campaign progresses, it may become necessary to adjust task assignments. This could be due to changes in team availability, unforeseen challenges, or shifts in campaign priorities. Microsoft Planner allows managers to reassign tasks quickly and easily, ensuring that the right people are working on the right tasks at all times.

For instance, if a team member falls behind due to an unexpectedly heavy workload, their tasks can be redistributed to others who have more capacity. This flexibility helps to keep the campaign on track and ensures that deadlines are met without overburdening any individual team member.

3. Collaborating on Tasks

Effective task management in Microsoft Planner is not just about assigning and tracking tasks but also about fostering collaboration among team members. Collaboration is essential in marketing teams, where different perspectives and expertise come together to create compelling campaigns.

3.1 Using Comments for Collaboration

Microsoft Planner's comment feature allows team members to discuss tasks directly within the platform. This functionality is particularly useful for marketing teams, where feedback and revisions are often required. For instance, a content writer might draft social media posts and then ask for feedback from the design team or campaign manager directly in the task comments.

Comments can be threaded, making it easy to follow conversations and keep track of decisions. This feature helps to ensure that everyone is on the same page and that important feedback is not lost in a sea of emails or messages.

3.2 Attaching Files and Resources to Tasks

Tasks in Microsoft Planner can also include attachments, such as documents, images, or links to external resources. This feature allows marketing teams to keep all relevant materials in one place. For example, a task for creating a promotional video might include a script document, design mockups, and links to video editing guidelines.

By attaching these resources directly to the task, team members can access everything they need without having to search through different platforms or communication channels. This integration streamlines the workflow and reduces the time spent on administrative tasks.

3.3 Integrating with Microsoft Teams

Microsoft Planner seamlessly integrates with Microsoft Teams, enhancing collaboration even further. Teams is a communication platform that allows for real-time discussions, video meetings, and file sharing. By integrating Planner with Teams, marketing teams can discuss tasks, share updates, and collaborate on projects without leaving the Teams environment.

For example, the marketing team can set up a dedicated Teams channel for a campaign, where all relevant tasks from Planner are displayed. Team members can then discuss tasks in the channel, hold virtual meetings, and share files, all while keeping everything organized and easily accessible.

4. Analyzing Task Performance

Beyond just assigning and tracking tasks, Microsoft Planner offers tools to analyze the performance of the marketing team's work. This analysis is crucial for understanding what went well, what could be improved, and how to optimize future campaigns.

4.1 Reviewing Task Completion Rates

One of the most straightforward metrics to analyze is the task completion rate. Microsoft Planner allows managers to see how many tasks were completed on time versus those that were delayed. This information is useful for identifying patterns in team performance and understanding where delays tend to occur.

For example, if the analysis shows that tasks related to content creation are often delayed, the manager might decide to allocate more time or resources to this area in future campaigns. Alternatively, they might look into whether bottlenecks are caused by external factors, such as waiting for approvals or resources from other departments.

4.2 Assessing Workload Distribution

Microsoft Planner's analytics tools also help managers assess whether tasks were distributed evenly among team members. If some team members were consistently overloaded while others had lighter workloads, this insight can inform better task assignment in the future.

A balanced workload is crucial for maintaining team morale and productivity. By analyzing past campaigns, the marketing manager can ensure that future task assignments are fair and aligned with each team member's capacity and skills.

4.3 Gathering Feedback for Continuous Improvement

Finally, after the completion of the campaign, it's valuable to gather feedback from the team on the task assignment and tracking process. This feedback can be collected through surveys, one-on-one meetings, or team discussions. Microsoft Planner's task comments and completion data can also be reviewed to understand where team members faced challenges or where the process could be streamlined.

This feedback loop is essential for continuous improvement. By regularly analyzing and refining how tasks are assigned and tracked, the marketing team can improve efficiency, reduce stress, and achieve better results in future campaigns.

Conclusion

Task assignment and tracking are critical components of successful marketing campaigns, and Microsoft Planner provides a powerful platform to manage these processes. By creating clear tasks, assigning them effectively, and utilizing Planner's tracking and collaboration features, marketing teams can ensure that campaigns run smoothly and achieve their goals. Moreover, analyzing task performance after each campaign helps the team continuously improve their processes, leading to even greater success in the future.

7.1.3 Analyzing the Results

In this section, we'll delve into how the marketing team uses Microsoft Planner to analyze the results of their campaign. Analyzing the outcomes is a critical phase in any project, as it helps the team understand what worked well, what didn't, and where improvements can be made. By utilizing the data and insights available in Microsoft Planner, the marketing team can draw valuable conclusions, refine their strategies, and enhance future campaigns.

Understanding the Data Available in Microsoft Planner

Microsoft Planner provides various tools and features that allow teams to monitor and analyze their progress. For the marketing team, this begins with reviewing the status of tasks, the completion rate, and any delays or issues encountered during the campaign.

- Task Completion Status: The marketing team can quickly assess how many tasks were completed on time, how many were delayed, and how many are still in progress. This information is easily accessible from the Planner's interface, where tasks are displayed with their respective statuses.

- Assignment Overview: By reviewing the assignments, the team can see which members were most productive, which tasks were re-assigned, and how workload was distributed. This can help in understanding whether the task assignments were efficient and if some team members were over or under-utilized.

- Time Tracking: Although Microsoft Planner itself does not include detailed time-tracking features, integration with other tools (such as Microsoft Teams or Power BI) can provide insights into the time spent on each task. This data is crucial for understanding how long tasks took compared to the initial estimates and identifying any bottlenecks.

Utilizing Planner's Built-In Charts and Visualizations

Microsoft Planner includes built-in charts that give a visual representation of the team's progress. These charts are particularly useful for a quick, high-level overview of how the campaign is progressing. The marketing team uses these charts to identify patterns and trends that may not be immediately obvious from looking at individual tasks.

- Bucket Progress: Each bucket represents a phase or a category in the campaign plan. By analyzing the progress of tasks within each bucket, the team can determine which phases were executed smoothly and which required more effort. For example, if the "Content Creation" bucket shows a significant number of overdue tasks, this might indicate issues in the content development process, such as a need for more resources or better planning.

- Task Status Distribution: The team can see the distribution of tasks across different statuses—Not Started, In Progress, Completed, and Late. This distribution helps the team understand how the campaign progressed over time and where they might have lost momentum.

- Team Member Contribution: Visualizations also show how many tasks each team member completed, allowing the team to recognize high performers and identify areas where some members may need additional support or training.

Incorporating Feedback into the Analysis

A crucial part of the analysis process involves gathering feedback from the team and stakeholders. Microsoft Planner facilitates this by allowing comments and notes on each task, where team members can provide insights or explain challenges they faced.

- Team Feedback: The marketing team reviews the feedback left in task comments to understand the challenges team members encountered. For instance, if several tasks in the "Social Media Promotion" bucket have comments about difficulties with reaching the target audience, the team knows this is an area to focus on in future campaigns.

- Stakeholder Feedback: Feedback from stakeholders, such as clients or department heads, is also considered. This feedback might include perceptions of the campaign's success, areas of concern, or suggestions for future improvements. By incorporating this feedback into their analysis, the team ensures that the campaign meets both internal and external expectations.

Identifying Successes and Challenges

Analyzing the results of a campaign is as much about recognizing successes as it is about identifying challenges. The marketing team uses Planner's data to highlight what worked well and what didn't.

- Successes: The team identifies tasks and strategies that led to successful outcomes. For example, if the "Email Marketing" bucket shows a high completion rate with tasks completed ahead of schedule and positive feedback in the comments, this would be recognized as a success. The team can then document the approach taken for email marketing as a best practice for future campaigns.

- Challenges: On the other hand, the team also looks at tasks that were delayed or not completed. For example, if the "Paid Advertising" bucket has several overdue tasks with comments indicating issues with budget approvals, this would be flagged as a challenge. The team can then explore ways to streamline budget approval processes or adjust their approach to paid advertising.

Using Insights to Improve Future Campaigns

The ultimate goal of analyzing results is to apply the insights gained to improve future campaigns. The marketing team uses the findings from Microsoft Planner to refine their strategies and optimize their workflow.

- Refining Task Assignment: If the analysis shows that some team members were consistently overburdened, the team can adjust future task assignments to ensure a more balanced distribution of work. This might involve reassigning certain types of tasks to team members who have demonstrated strengths in those areas.

- Optimizing Workflows: The team might discover that certain workflows were inefficient, such as approval processes or content reviews. Based on the analysis, the team can develop new workflows that reduce delays and improve efficiency. For example, they might decide to implement a more streamlined content approval process or introduce regular check-ins to keep tasks on track.

- Adjusting Timelines: The team can use the time-tracking data to adjust their timelines for future campaigns. If certain phases consistently took longer than expected, the team might extend the timeline for those phases in future plans, allowing for more realistic scheduling.

- Enhancing Communication: Feedback analysis might reveal communication issues that led to misunderstandings or delays. The team can then implement new communication protocols or tools to ensure that everyone is on the same page moving forward. For example, they might decide to increase the frequency of team meetings or use Microsoft Teams more effectively for real-time updates.

Documenting Lessons Learned

As part of their analysis, the marketing team documents the lessons learned from the campaign. This documentation serves as a valuable resource for future campaigns and helps to institutionalize knowledge within the team.

- Best Practices: The team creates a list of best practices based on the successes identified during the analysis. These best practices can be shared with other teams or departments within the organization to help improve overall campaign management.

- Areas for Improvement: The team also documents areas where improvements are needed. This might include recommendations for additional training, process changes, or resource allocation. By clearly outlining these areas, the team can focus on making targeted improvements in future campaigns.

- Actionable Insights: The team translates the analysis into actionable insights that can be implemented in future campaigns. For example, if the analysis showed that tasks were often delayed due to dependency issues, the team might implement a new task dependency tracking system in Planner.

Reviewing and Reporting the Results

Once the analysis is complete, the marketing team prepares a report summarizing their findings. This report is shared with stakeholders to provide a clear overview of the campaign's outcomes, successes, and areas for improvement.

- Executive Summary: The report includes an executive summary that highlights the key findings from the analysis, including overall campaign success, major challenges, and recommendations for future campaigns.

- Detailed Analysis: The report provides a detailed breakdown of the analysis, including data from Planner's charts and visualizations, feedback from team members and stakeholders, and a comparison of planned versus actual outcomes.

- Recommendations: The report concludes with a set of recommendations for future campaigns, based on the insights gained from the analysis. These recommendations are actionable and provide a clear roadmap for improving future marketing efforts.

- Presentation to Stakeholders: In addition to the written report, the team might prepare a presentation for stakeholders, summarizing the analysis and recommendations. This presentation is an opportunity to engage stakeholders in a discussion about the campaign's outcomes and future strategies.

Continuous Improvement

Analyzing the results of a campaign using Microsoft Planner is not a one-time activity but part of a continuous improvement process. The marketing team uses each campaign as an opportunity to learn and grow, applying the insights gained to improve their performance over time.

- Iterative Learning: Each campaign builds on the lessons learned from previous campaigns. The team continually refines their strategies, task management practices, and workflows, leading to progressively better outcomes.

- Feedback Loops: The team establishes feedback loops to ensure that insights from the analysis are fed back into the planning and execution of future campaigns. This ensures that the team is always learning from their experiences and making informed decisions.

- Long-Term Impact: Over time, the cumulative effect of these improvements leads to more successful campaigns, higher team productivity, and better alignment with organizational goals. The marketing team's use of Microsoft Planner as an analysis tool plays a crucial role in driving this long-term impact.

By thoroughly analyzing the results of their marketing campaigns, the team not only understands their performance but also gains valuable insights that help them achieve greater success in the future. Microsoft Planner's tools and features provide the foundation for this analysis, enabling the team to make data-driven decisions and continuously improve their approach to campaign management.

7.2 Case Study: Microsoft Planner for Event Management

7.2.1 Creating a Plan for Event Preparation

Event management is a multifaceted task that requires meticulous planning, coordination, and execution. Microsoft Planner serves as an invaluable tool in orchestrating all aspects of an event, from initial brainstorming to post-event wrap-up. This section delves into the process of creating an event preparation plan using Microsoft Planner, focusing on how to organize tasks, assign responsibilities, and ensure smooth communication among team members.

Understanding the Scope of the Event

Before diving into the technicalities of Microsoft Planner, it's essential to understand the scope of the event. Whether it's a corporate conference, a product launch, or a community gathering, the event's size, objectives, and target audience will influence how you structure your plan. Key questions to consider include:

- What is the event's main goal?

- How many attendees are expected?

- What is the timeline for the event, including milestones and deadlines?

- Who are the key stakeholders, and what are their roles?

Once you have a clear understanding of these aspects, you can begin translating them into a structured plan within Microsoft Planner.

Setting Up the Event Preparation Plan in Microsoft Planner

1. Creating the Plan

- Initiating the Plan: Start by creating a new plan in Microsoft Planner. Give it a descriptive name that reflects the event, such as "Annual Conference 2024 Preparation." This will make it easily identifiable among other plans.

- Adding a Description: Include a brief description of the event in the plan details. This should encapsulate the event's purpose, key dates, and any other critical information that team members need to know upfront.

- Choosing a Group: Decide whether the plan will be part of an existing Microsoft 365 Group or if you'll create a new one. If the event involves collaboration across different departments or external partners, a new group dedicated to the event might be more effective.

2. Structuring the Plan with Buckets

- Defining Key Stages: Use buckets to represent the major stages or workstreams of the event preparation. Common buckets for an event might include:

- Pre-Event Planning: Covers initial tasks such as budget approval, venue selection, and defining the event theme.

- Marketing and Promotion: Includes tasks related to advertising, social media campaigns, and press releases.

- Logistics and Operations: Focuses on vendor coordination, equipment setup, and attendee registration.

- Program Development: Involves curating content, scheduling speakers, and organizing breakout sessions.

- Post-Event Activities: Encompasses tasks like sending thank-you notes, conducting surveys, and financial reconciliation.

- Adding Tasks to Buckets: Within each bucket, create specific tasks that need to be completed. For instance, under "Marketing and Promotion," tasks might include "Design Event Flyer," "Launch Social Media Campaign," and "Send Invitations to VIP Guests."

3. Assigning Responsibilities

- Task Assignment: For each task, assign it to the appropriate team member or group of members. Microsoft Planner allows you to assign tasks to multiple people, which is particularly useful for collaborative efforts.

- Setting Due Dates: Assign realistic deadlines to each task to ensure the event preparation stays on track. The timeline should be based on the event date, working backward to identify when each task must be completed.

- Priority Levels: Use the priority feature to indicate the importance of tasks. High-priority tasks, such as securing the venue or confirming keynote speakers, should be clearly marked so the team can focus on these first.

Detailed Task Management

1. Task Descriptions and Checklists

- Providing Clarity: For each task, add a detailed description outlining what needs to be done. This could include specific instructions, expected outcomes, and any relevant links or attachments.

- Using Checklists: Many tasks in event planning are multi-step processes. For instance, "Secure Catering Services" might involve contacting vendors, reviewing proposals, and finalizing contracts. Use the checklist feature within tasks to break down these steps, ensuring nothing is overlooked.

- Attachments and Links: Attach relevant documents, such as contracts, design files, or schedules, directly to tasks. This centralizes information and makes it easily accessible to all team members.

2. Labels for Categorization

- Customizing Labels: Microsoft Planner allows you to create color-coded labels for tasks. Customize these labels to fit the event's needs, such as "Urgent," "In Progress," "Needs Approval," or specific categories like "Venue" or "Marketing."

- Applying Labels: Apply these labels to tasks to help quickly identify their status or category. For example, a task labeled "Urgent" might require immediate attention, while a "Needs Approval" label indicates that the task is awaiting a sign-off from management.

3. Tracking Progress

- Task Completion: Mark tasks as completed as they are finished. This not only helps in tracking progress but also gives a sense of accomplishment to the team.

- Progress Visualization: Use the built-in charts in Microsoft Planner to visualize the progress of the plan. This provides a quick overview of how many tasks are completed, in progress, or yet to be started.

- Daily or Weekly Reviews: Schedule regular check-ins using Planner's built-in calendar feature to review the progress of the event preparation. This ensures that any potential delays are identified early, and adjustments can be made to keep the event on schedule.

Collaboration and Communication

1. Team Communication

- Using Comments: Leverage the comments section within each task to facilitate communication. Team members can leave updates, ask questions, and provide feedback directly within the task. This keeps all discussions context-specific and easy to track.

- Integration with Microsoft Teams: If your organization uses Microsoft Teams, integrate Planner with Teams for seamless communication. You can create a dedicated channel for the event, linking the Planner plan to this channel so that updates and discussions happen in one place.

- Notifications and Alerts: Set up notifications to ensure that team members are aware of task assignments, approaching deadlines, and any changes to the plan. This keeps everyone informed and reduces the risk of tasks falling through the cracks.

2. Collaborating with External Stakeholders

- Inviting External Partners: If your event involves vendors, speakers, or other external partners, you can invite them to collaborate on the plan. Assign them specific tasks, provide them with necessary access, and include them in relevant communications.

- File Sharing and Permissions: Manage permissions carefully to ensure that external stakeholders have access only to the information they need. Use Microsoft 365's sharing options to control who can view or edit files linked to tasks.

- Real-Time Collaboration: Encourage real-time collaboration by using Microsoft Planner's real-time updates feature. This ensures that all changes, comments, and progress updates are immediately visible to everyone involved.

Ensuring a Smooth Execution

1. Risk Management and Contingency Planning

- Identifying Potential Risks: Use Microsoft Planner to identify potential risks to the event's success. Create a separate bucket labeled "Risk Management" where tasks related to risk assessment and mitigation can be tracked.

- Developing Contingency Plans: For critical tasks, develop contingency plans. For example, if the primary venue becomes unavailable, have a backup venue ready. These contingency tasks should be clearly marked and assigned so that they can be quickly activated if needed.

- Monitoring Critical Path: Track the critical path tasks—those that directly impact the event's timeline. Ensure these tasks are prioritized and monitored closely, as any delays here could jeopardize the entire event.

2. Final Preparations and Rehearsals

- Pre-Event Rehearsals: Schedule rehearsal tasks within Microsoft Planner, whether it's a run-through of the event schedule, testing equipment, or coordinating last-minute logistics. Assign team members to oversee these rehearsals and ensure all details are covered.

- Final Checklists: Create final checklists for each major area, such as venue setup, technology, catering, and attendee materials. These checklists should be completed and signed off before the event day to ensure everything is in place.

- Day-of-Event Tasks: Set up a separate bucket or even a new plan for day-of-event tasks. This could include tasks like "Venue Setup," "Speaker Coordination," and "Attendee Check-in." Having a clear plan for the day itself helps manage the chaos and ensures a smooth operation.

Post-Event Activities

1. Debrief and Feedback Collection

- Post-Event Review: Schedule a debrief meeting shortly after the event to review what went well and what could be improved. Use Microsoft Planner to create tasks related to feedback collection, such as sending out surveys to attendees or conducting internal reviews.

- Stakeholder Feedback: Assign tasks to gather feedback from key stakeholders, including sponsors, speakers, and team members. Their insights can be invaluable for planning future events.

- Analyzing Outcomes: Use the feedback to create a report on the event's success, highlighting key achievements and areas for improvement. This can be managed within Planner, with tasks assigned to different team members for data collection and report writing.

2. Financial Reconciliation and Reporting

- Expense Tracking: Use Planner to manage post-event financial tasks, such as reconciling expenses, processing vendor payments, and reviewing the budget. Assign specific tasks for each financial element, ensuring accuracy and accountability.

- Final Reporting: Task team members with creating a final event report that includes financial details, attendee numbers, and feedback analysis. This report serves as a record of the event and a guide for future planning.

3. Archiving and Knowledge Management

- Archiving the Plan: Once all tasks are completed, archive the event plan for future reference. Microsoft Planner allows you to keep a record of the entire planning process, which can be invaluable for future events.

- Creating a Knowledge Base: Use the lessons learned from the event to create a knowledge base or best practices document. Store this in a shared location accessible to all relevant team members, ensuring that the knowledge is retained within the organization.

Conclusion

Creating a plan for event preparation using Microsoft Planner provides structure, clarity, and accountability to the complex process of event management. By breaking down tasks, assigning responsibilities, and maintaining open lines of communication, you can ensure that every aspect of the event is meticulously planned and executed. Whether you're managing a small internal event or a large-scale conference, Microsoft Planner offers the tools needed to keep everything on track and deliver a successful event.

7.2.2 Collaborating with Vendors and Stakeholders

Effective event management requires meticulous coordination with a variety of external and internal parties, including vendors, suppliers, sponsors, and key stakeholders. Microsoft Planner is a powerful tool that facilitates seamless collaboration among these parties, ensuring that all tasks are aligned, progress is tracked, and communication is transparent. This section will explore the best practices and strategies for using Microsoft Planner to manage these collaborations, ultimately leading to a successful event.

Understanding the Role of Vendors and Stakeholders in Event Management

Before diving into the practical application of Microsoft Planner, it is essential to understand the roles that vendors and stakeholders play in the event management process:

- Vendors: These are third-party service providers that supply goods or services necessary for the event, such as catering, equipment rental, audio-visual services, and décor. Coordinating with vendors involves ensuring that they deliver their services on time, within budget, and according to the specifications outlined in the contracts.

- Stakeholders: Stakeholders include any individuals or groups who have an interest in the success of the event. They can range from event sponsors and investors to key employees and executives. Stakeholders often have specific goals and expectations for the event, making it crucial to keep them informed and engaged throughout the planning process.

Setting Up a Collaboration Framework in Microsoft Planner

To effectively manage collaboration with vendors and stakeholders, it is important to set up a structured framework within Microsoft Planner that facilitates clear communication, task assignment, and progress tracking.

1. Creating a Dedicated Plan for Vendor and Stakeholder Management: Start by creating a separate plan within Microsoft Planner dedicated solely to managing vendors and stakeholders. This plan should include all relevant tasks and deadlines, categorized into buckets that reflect different aspects of the collaboration, such as contract negotiations, logistics, communication, and reporting.

2. Defining Clear Responsibilities: For each task within the plan, clearly define who is responsible for completing it. This could be a member of the event planning team, a vendor, or a stakeholder. By assigning tasks to specific individuals, you ensure accountability and streamline communication.

3. Establishing Milestones and Deadlines: Milestones are critical in event management, especially when coordinating with multiple external parties. Use Microsoft Planner to set

specific deadlines for key deliverables from vendors and stakeholders. This helps to keep everyone on track and ensures that the event progresses according to the schedule.

Collaborative Task Management with Vendors

Vendors play a crucial role in the execution of an event, and managing their contributions effectively is key to success. Microsoft Planner offers several features that enhance vendor collaboration:

1. Assigning Tasks and Subtasks: Within the dedicated plan for vendor management, assign tasks to each vendor based on their scope of work. For example, the catering vendor could be assigned tasks such as menu finalization, food tasting, and delivery scheduling. Subtasks can be used to break down these tasks further, ensuring that each step of the process is clearly outlined.

2. Utilizing Labels for Vendor Categorization: Microsoft Planner's labeling feature can be used to categorize tasks by vendor type or priority. For instance, labels such as "Catering," "AV Equipment," and "Venue" can help in quickly identifying tasks related to specific vendors. Priority labels like "Urgent" or "High Priority" can also be applied to tasks that require immediate attention.

3. Tracking Vendor Deliverables: Use the progress tracking feature in Microsoft Planner to monitor the status of each vendor's deliverables. The status indicators (Not Started, In Progress, Completed) provide a quick overview of where each vendor stands in terms of fulfilling their contractual obligations. This real-time visibility allows you to address any delays or issues promptly.

4. Facilitating Communication with Vendors: Microsoft Planner integrates with Microsoft Teams and Outlook, enabling seamless communication with vendors. For each task, use the comments section to leave notes, updates, or requests for the vendors. You can also link Microsoft Planner tasks to Teams channels, where vendors can directly participate in discussions related to their tasks.

Engaging Stakeholders through Microsoft Planner

Stakeholders often require regular updates on the event's progress and may need to provide input or approvals at various stages. Microsoft Planner can be leveraged to manage these interactions efficiently:

1. Creating Stakeholder-Specific Buckets: Within the plan, create buckets that are specifically dedicated to stakeholder-related tasks, such as "Stakeholder Meetings," "Feedback Collection," and "Approval Requests." This organization helps to keep all stakeholder interactions in one place, making it easier to manage.

2. Scheduling Regular Updates and Meetings: Use Microsoft Planner to schedule and track regular updates for stakeholders. Set up recurring tasks for sending progress reports, holding status meetings, or requesting feedback. By assigning these tasks to appropriate team members, you ensure that stakeholders are kept informed throughout the event planning process.

3. Capturing and Addressing Stakeholder Feedback: When stakeholders provide feedback or request changes, it is important to capture these inputs systematically. Create tasks in Microsoft Planner to track each piece of feedback and assign team members to address them. Use labels like "Pending Feedback" or "Under Review" to categorize tasks that are awaiting stakeholder input.

4. Managing Approvals: Many aspects of event planning require stakeholder approvals, whether it's the budget, vendor contracts, or final event design. Microsoft Planner can be used to create approval tasks, which are then assigned to the relevant stakeholders. Set clear deadlines for these approvals to ensure that they are received on time, preventing any delays in the planning process.

Integrating Microsoft Planner with Other Tools for Enhanced Collaboration

To further enhance collaboration with vendors and stakeholders, Microsoft Planner can be integrated with other Microsoft 365 tools and third-party applications:

1. Microsoft Teams Integration: By linking your Planner plan to a Microsoft Teams channel, you can create a central hub for all communication related to vendor and stakeholder management. Teams allows for real-time chat, file sharing, and video conferencing, making it easier to collaborate and resolve issues quickly.

2. Outlook Integration for Scheduling: Integrate Microsoft Planner with Outlook to streamline the scheduling of meetings and deadlines. Tasks in Planner can be linked to calendar events in Outlook, ensuring that all involved parties are aware of important dates and can plan accordingly.

3. Using Microsoft Forms for Stakeholder Feedback: Collecting structured feedback from stakeholders can be streamlined using Microsoft Forms. Create a form for stakeholders to submit their feedback, and link the responses directly to tasks in Microsoft Planner for easy tracking and follow-up.

4. Power Automate for Workflow Automation: Automate repetitive tasks and notifications using Power Automate. For instance, you can set up a workflow that automatically sends a reminder email to vendors or stakeholders when a task's deadline is approaching. This reduces manual follow-up and ensures that everyone stays on track.

Case Example: Managing an Event with Multiple Vendors and Stakeholders

To illustrate the practical application of these strategies, consider the following scenario:

- Event: A corporate gala with multiple vendors, including catering, AV equipment, and venue services.

- Stakeholders: The event includes key sponsors, company executives, and an external marketing team.

Using Microsoft Planner, the event management team creates a dedicated plan with separate buckets for each vendor and stakeholder. Tasks are assigned according to each vendor's scope of work, with labels indicating the priority level. Regular updates are scheduled in Planner, with automatic reminders sent through Outlook. Stakeholders are kept informed through scheduled reports and approval tasks, while any feedback or changes are captured as tasks in Planner. Microsoft Teams is used to facilitate real-time communication, ensuring that any issues are quickly addressed.

Outcome: The event is successfully executed with all vendor services delivered on time and to the expected standard. Stakeholders are satisfied with the transparent communication and timely updates, contributing to a smooth planning process.

Best Practices for Vendor and Stakeholder Collaboration in Microsoft Planner

1. Consistent Communication: Maintain regular communication with vendors and stakeholders using the tools available in Microsoft Planner and its integrations. This helps to build trust and ensures that everyone is on the same page.

2. Clear Task Assignments: Always assign tasks to specific individuals to avoid ambiguity. Make use of subtasks to break down larger tasks into manageable steps, ensuring nothing is overlooked.

3. Regular Progress Reviews: Schedule regular progress reviews to ensure that all parties are meeting their obligations. Use the progress tracking features in Planner to identify any potential delays or issues early on.

4. Leverage Integration Tools: Take full advantage of Microsoft Planner's integration capabilities with other Microsoft 365 tools to create a seamless workflow. This not only enhances efficiency but also improves collaboration by providing a unified platform for all event-related activities.

5. Document Everything: Keep a detailed record of all communications, feedback, and approvals in Microsoft Planner. This documentation is invaluable in ensuring accountability and can serve as a reference in case of disputes or misunderstandings.

By following the strategies outlined in this section, event managers can leverage Microsoft Planner to enhance collaboration with vendors and stakeholders, leading to more organized, efficient, and successful events. This systematic approach not only streamlines the planning process but also ensures that all parties are aligned and working towards the common goal of executing a memorable and impactful event.

7.2.3 Managing Last-Minute Changes

Managing last-minute changes is a crucial skill in event management. Events are dynamic by nature, and unforeseen circumstances can often arise, necessitating adjustments to plans and schedules. Microsoft Planner, with its flexible and collaborative features, can significantly ease this process. This section will explore how to effectively handle last-minute changes using Microsoft Planner, ensuring your event remains successful despite any disruptions.

Understanding the Impact of Last-Minute Changes

Before diving into the specifics of managing changes, it is essential to understand their potential impact on your event. Last-minute changes can affect various aspects, including:

1. Schedules and Timelines: Adjustments to the schedule can cause delays, affecting the overall flow of the event.

2. Budget: Changes may lead to increased costs or require reallocating funds.

3. Resources: Last-minute changes can strain available resources, such as personnel, equipment, and venue arrangements.

4. Stakeholder Expectations: Modifications can impact the expectations of stakeholders, including attendees, sponsors, and vendors.

Recognizing these impacts helps in planning and executing effective strategies to manage changes smoothly.

Step-by-Step Guide to Managing Last-Minute Changes with Microsoft Planner

1. Communicate Changes Effectively

Effective communication is critical when handling last-minute changes. Use Microsoft Planner to streamline communication with your team and stakeholders:

- Update Tasks and Assignments: Immediately update relevant tasks in Planner. Modify task details to reflect the new requirements or changes. For example, if a vendor cancels, update the task assigned to them and assign a new task to the team member responsible for finding a replacement.

- Use Comments for Notifications: Utilize the comment feature within tasks to notify team members of the changes. Comments ensure that everyone involved is aware of the new developments and can respond accordingly.

- Send Notifications: Ensure that all relevant team members are notified of the changes. Microsoft Planner integrates with Microsoft Teams and Outlook, allowing you to send notifications and updates directly.

2. Reallocate Resources

Managing last-minute changes often involves reallocating resources. Microsoft Planner's task management features can help with this:

- Adjust Task Priorities: Modify task priorities based on the urgency of the change. For instance, if a key speaker cancels, increase the priority of tasks related to finding a replacement or rearranging the schedule.

- Reassign Tasks: If a team member's responsibilities change due to the new circumstances, reassign tasks to other team members who can handle them. Ensure that the reassignment is clearly communicated to avoid confusion.

- Update Resource Allocation: If the change affects resource allocation, such as equipment or venue space, update the corresponding tasks in Planner to reflect the new arrangements.

3. Revise Timelines and Deadlines

Adjusting timelines and deadlines is a common aspect of managing last-minute changes. Use Microsoft Planner to keep track of these adjustments:

- Modify Due Dates: Change the due dates for affected tasks to align with the new timeline. This ensures that everyone is aware of the revised deadlines and can plan their work accordingly.

- Update Milestones: If the change impacts key milestones, adjust them in Planner. Ensure that any changes to milestones are communicated to all stakeholders to keep everyone on the same page.

- Track Progress: Use Planner's progress tracking features to monitor how the adjustments are affecting the overall timeline. This helps in identifying any potential delays and taking corrective actions promptly.

4. Address Stakeholder Concerns

Handling last-minute changes often involves addressing the concerns of various stakeholders:

- Inform Stakeholders: Use Microsoft Planner to document and share updates with stakeholders. Ensure that all parties affected by the changes are informed in a timely manner.

- Provide Alternatives: If the change impacts stakeholders, offer alternatives or solutions to mitigate any negative effects. For example, if a venue change occurs, provide details about the new location and any additional information they need.

- Maintain Transparency: Keep communication open and transparent. Provide regular updates on how the changes are being managed and what steps are being taken to ensure a successful event.

5. Leverage Planner's Collaboration Features

Microsoft Planner's collaboration features are invaluable when managing last-minute changes:

- Create New Tasks: For any new requirements arising from the change, create new tasks in Planner. Assign these tasks to the appropriate team members and set deadlines for completion.

- Collaborate in Real-Time: Use Planner's integration with Microsoft Teams for real-time collaboration. Team members can discuss changes, share updates, and work together to address issues quickly.

- Review and Adjust Plans: Regularly review the updated plan in Planner to ensure that all changes are accounted for and that the event is on track. Adjust the plan as needed to address any new developments.

6. Document and Analyze

After managing the changes, it is important to document the process and analyze the outcomes:

- Document Changes: Use Planner to record all changes made during the event management process. This documentation can be valuable for future reference and for analyzing the effectiveness of your response.

- Analyze Outcomes: Evaluate how well the changes were managed and their impact on the event. Identify any lessons learned and areas for improvement. This analysis can help in refining your approach to handling last-minute changes in future events.

7. Prepare for Future Changes

Preparation is key to managing last-minute changes effectively. Use insights from your experience to prepare for potential changes in future events:

- Develop Contingency Plans: Create contingency plans for common issues that may arise. Having predefined strategies can help in managing changes more smoothly.

- Train Your Team: Ensure that your team is trained to handle unexpected changes. Familiarity with Microsoft Planner's features and effective communication strategies can enhance their ability to respond quickly and efficiently.

- Stay Flexible: Embrace flexibility in your planning and execution. Being adaptable and open to changes will enable you to manage disruptions more effectively.

Conclusion

Managing last-minute changes in event management requires a proactive and organized approach. Microsoft Planner's features, such as task management, real-time collaboration, and progress tracking, can significantly streamline this process. By effectively communicating changes, reallocating resources, revising timelines, addressing stakeholder concerns, and leveraging Planner's collaboration tools, you can navigate last-minute disruptions with greater ease and ensure a successful event despite any unforeseen challenges.

7.3 Real-World Examples

7.3.1 Using Planner in Education

Introduction to Microsoft Planner in Education

In an era where educational institutions are increasingly adopting digital tools to streamline operations and enhance learning experiences, Microsoft Planner stands out as a versatile and effective platform. While initially designed as a task management tool for business environments, its features have proven to be invaluable in the education sector as well. Microsoft Planner provides educators, administrators, and students with a centralized platform for organizing tasks, managing projects, and fostering collaboration. This section explores how Microsoft Planner can be effectively utilized in educational settings, including lesson planning, student project management, faculty collaboration, and more.

Organizing Lesson Plans and Curriculum Development

One of the primary applications of Microsoft Planner in education is for organizing lesson plans and curriculum development. Teachers can use Planner to create a structured outline of their teaching plan for the semester or academic year. Each lesson can be treated as a separate task within a plan, with detailed instructions, objectives, and resources attached. This not only helps teachers stay organized but also ensures that they can easily adapt their plans based on student progress and feedback.

For example, a high school history teacher might create a plan titled "World History Curriculum 2023-2024." Within this plan, each week's lessons can be organized into separate buckets, such as "Week 1: Ancient Civilizations," "Week 2: Middle Ages," and so on. Each bucket contains tasks that represent individual lessons, complete with due dates, resource links, and notes. This structure allows the teacher to maintain a clear overview of the curriculum, ensuring that all necessary topics are covered within the allotted time frame.

Moreover, Planner's ability to attach files and links directly to tasks means that teachers can easily share reading materials, worksheets, and multimedia resources with their students. By integrating Planner with Microsoft Teams, these resources can be accessed by students directly, making it easier for them to keep track of assignments and study materials.

Managing Student Projects and Assignments

Another significant application of Microsoft Planner in education is managing student projects and assignments. Group projects are a common aspect of education, especially in higher education and project-based learning environments. However, coordinating these projects can be challenging, particularly when students have to collaborate remotely. Microsoft Planner addresses this challenge by providing a platform where students can organize their tasks, set deadlines, and track progress collectively.

Consider a university setting where students are assigned to work on a marketing campaign project. The professor can create a plan titled "Marketing Campaign Project" in Microsoft Planner, and add all the students involved as members of the plan. The project can then be broken down into key phases, such as "Research," "Campaign Strategy," "Content Creation," and "Presentation." Each phase is represented as a bucket within the plan, with tasks assigned to specific students based on their roles within the group.

Students can use Planner to communicate within tasks by leaving comments, sharing documents, and updating task statuses. The professor, as an observer, can monitor the progress of the project, provide feedback, and ensure that deadlines are met. This setup not only improves the organization of the project but also fosters accountability among students, as their contributions are clearly visible to both peers and instructors.

Additionally, individual assignments can be managed through Microsoft Planner. For instance, in a literature course, the instructor might assign each student a task to submit a book review by a certain date. Each task can include guidelines for the review, submission instructions, and a grading rubric. This centralized approach simplifies the tracking of assignment submissions and grading, reducing the administrative burden on educators.

Facilitating Faculty Collaboration and Communication

Collaboration among faculty members is essential for the successful operation of educational institutions. Microsoft Planner can facilitate this collaboration by providing a shared space where faculty members can organize their collective tasks, manage departmental projects, and communicate efficiently.

For example, in a university department, faculty members often need to work together on tasks such as curriculum development, event planning, and accreditation processes. By creating a department-wide plan in Microsoft Planner, each faculty member can be assigned specific tasks related to these projects. Tasks such as "Draft Curriculum for New Course," "Organize Guest Lecture Series," or "Prepare Accreditation Documents" can be tracked within the plan, with each task assigned to the appropriate faculty member or committee.

Planner's integration with other Microsoft 365 tools, such as Outlook and Teams, further enhances collaboration. Meetings scheduled in Outlook can be linked to relevant tasks in Planner, ensuring that all participants are aware of the context and objectives of the meeting. Meanwhile, ongoing discussions in Microsoft Teams can be linked to Planner tasks, allowing faculty members to reference important conversations and decisions within their task management system.

Moreover, Planner's ability to set due dates, priorities, and labels helps faculty members prioritize their work and meet deadlines. This is particularly useful during busy periods, such as the beginning of a new semester or during accreditation reviews, where effective time management is crucial.

Enhancing Administrative Operations

Beyond the classroom, Microsoft Planner can also play a significant role in enhancing the administrative operations of educational institutions. Administrative staff can use Planner to manage a wide range of tasks, from enrollment processes to facility maintenance and event coordination.

For instance, during the student enrollment period, the admissions office can create a plan in Microsoft Planner to manage the various steps involved in processing applications. Tasks such as "Review Application Documents," "Schedule Interviews," and "Send Acceptance Letters" can be organized within the plan, with due dates and responsible staff members clearly identified. This approach ensures that the admissions process runs smoothly and that all tasks are completed on time.

Similarly, the facilities management team can use Planner to organize maintenance schedules, track work orders, and manage campus improvement projects. A plan titled "Campus Maintenance 2023" might include tasks such as "Repair HVAC Systems," "Renovate Classroom A101," and "Conduct Safety Inspections." Each task can be assigned to specific maintenance personnel, with updates and progress tracked in real-time.

Event coordination is another area where Microsoft Planner can be invaluable. For large-scale events such as graduation ceremonies, open days, or conferences, the events team can use Planner to manage all the logistical details. Tasks such as "Book Venue," "Arrange Catering," "Send Invitations," and "Coordinate Volunteers" can be tracked within a dedicated event plan, ensuring that nothing is overlooked.

Supporting Remote and Hybrid Learning

The shift towards remote and hybrid learning models, accelerated by the global pandemic, has highlighted the need for effective digital tools in education. Microsoft Planner is particularly well-suited to support these learning models by providing a platform where both students and educators can organize and manage their tasks, regardless of their physical location.

In a remote learning environment, where students and educators may be dispersed across different locations, maintaining a clear and organized workflow is essential. Microsoft Planner allows educators to assign tasks, set deadlines, and monitor progress remotely, ensuring that students remain engaged and on track with their studies.

For example, in an online course, the instructor can use Microsoft Planner to outline the course syllabus, with each week's lessons and assignments represented as tasks within a plan. Students can access these tasks, view due dates, and submit their work through linked platforms such as Microsoft Teams or OneDrive. The instructor can then provide feedback and grades, all within the same integrated system.

Hybrid learning, where students attend some classes in person and others online, presents unique challenges in terms of coordination and communication. Microsoft Planner can help bridge the gap between these two modes of learning by providing a consistent platform for task management. Educators can create plans that encompass both in-person and online components, ensuring that all students have access to the same resources and information, regardless of their attendance mode.

Promoting Student Accountability and Independence

One of the key benefits of using Microsoft Planner in education is its ability to promote student accountability and independence. By providing students with a clear structure for managing their tasks and responsibilities, Planner helps them develop essential time management and organizational skills that are critical for academic success and beyond.

In a self-paced learning environment, for example, students can use Microsoft Planner to create their own study plans. They can set goals, break down assignments into manageable tasks, and track their progress over time. This approach not only helps students stay on top of their work but also encourages them to take ownership of their learning process.

Moreover, the visual nature of Microsoft Planner, with its charts and progress tracking features, allows students to see how their work is progressing in real-time. This visibility can be a powerful motivator, helping students stay focused and motivated as they work towards their goals.

Educators can further support this by using Planner to provide regular check-ins and feedback. For instance, a teacher might create a recurring task in Planner to review students' progress on a weekly basis. This ensures that students receive the guidance and support they need, while also fostering a sense of responsibility for their own learning.

Conclusion

Microsoft Planner offers a wide range of features that can be effectively applied in educational settings, from organizing lesson plans and managing student projects to facilitating faculty collaboration and enhancing administrative operations. Its flexibility and integration with other Microsoft 365 tools make it an invaluable resource for educators, administrators, and students alike.

By incorporating Microsoft Planner into their workflows, educational institutions can not only improve the efficiency and organization of their operations but also create a more engaging and collaborative learning environment. Whether used for curriculum planning, student assignments, or faculty projects, Microsoft Planner provides the tools needed to achieve educational goals and support student success.

7.3.2 Planner for Personal Projects

In today's fast-paced world, balancing work, personal commitments, and leisure activities can be challenging. Organizing and tracking these activities effectively is crucial to ensuring that personal goals are met without feeling overwhelmed. Microsoft Planner, commonly recognized as a tool for team collaboration and project management, can also be an invaluable resource for managing personal projects. Whether you're planning a home renovation, organizing a family event, or working on a hobby project, Microsoft Planner offers a structured, visual approach to keep everything on track.

Setting Up a Personal Plan

The first step in using Microsoft Planner for personal projects is to set up a dedicated plan. Unlike professional or team-oriented projects, personal projects often have more flexibility and can vary greatly in scope and complexity. The beauty of Microsoft Planner lies in its adaptability, allowing you to customize your plan according to your needs.

- Define the Project Scope: Start by clearly defining what you want to achieve with your personal project. Are you planning a vacation, organizing your finances, or tackling a creative project? Understanding the scope will help you set realistic goals and timelines.

- Create a New Plan: Once you have defined the scope, create a new plan in Microsoft Planner. Name your plan based on the project, such as "Family Vacation 2024," "Home Office Renovation," or "Personal Fitness Goals." This will help you easily identify and access the plan later.

- Customize Buckets: Buckets in Microsoft Planner are used to categorize tasks. For personal projects, you can create buckets that align with the phases of your project. For example, if you are planning a vacation, you might have buckets like "Research Destinations," "Book Accommodations," "Prepare Itinerary," and "Pack and Prepare." Customizing buckets helps in breaking down the project into manageable sections.

Task Creation and Prioritization

With your plan set up, the next step is to start creating tasks. Each task represents an actionable item that needs to be completed to move your project forward.

- Creating Tasks: Add tasks under the relevant buckets. For instance, in a "Home Renovation" plan, tasks could include "Select Paint Colors," "Hire a Contractor," "Purchase Materials," and "Schedule Renovation Timeline." Break down larger tasks into smaller, more manageable ones to avoid feeling overwhelmed.

- Setting Due Dates: Assign due dates to tasks to keep yourself on track. Personal projects can often stretch out if not properly managed, so setting deadlines is essential. For example, if you're working on a fitness goal, you might set a due date for "Join a Gym" within the first week, and "Create a Workout Schedule" by the end of the second week.

- Prioritizing Tasks: Use Microsoft Planner's priority settings to differentiate between tasks that are critical and those that are less urgent. This helps you focus on what needs immediate attention. For example, when organizing a family reunion, tasks like "Send Invitations" may take higher priority than "Plan Menu."

Using Labels for Organization

Labels are a powerful feature in Microsoft Planner that can further help you organize and categorize tasks within your personal projects. Labels can represent anything that adds an extra layer of classification to your tasks.

- Color-Coded Labels: Microsoft Planner allows you to assign different colors to labels, which can be customized with your own text. For a home renovation project, you might use labels like "Budget," "Urgent," "Outsourced," and "DIY" to categorize tasks according to these themes. The visual cue of color makes it easy to scan your plan and understand the status or category of each task at a glance.

- Applying Labels to Tasks: Assign labels to your tasks based on their characteristics. For instance, in a vacation planning project, you could have labels like "Research," "Booking," "Packing," and "Activities." Tasks related to researching destinations can be tagged with "Research," while tasks like booking flights and hotels would fall under "Booking."

- Filtering Tasks by Labels: One of the most useful features of labels is the ability to filter tasks. If you want to see only the tasks related to your budget in a renovation project, you can filter by the "Budget" label. This helps you focus on specific aspects of your project without being distracted by unrelated tasks.

Tracking Progress and Staying Motivated

One of the most significant advantages of using Microsoft Planner for personal projects is the ability to track your progress visually. Seeing your tasks move from "Not Started" to "In Progress" to "Completed" can be incredibly motivating.

- Progress Tracking: As you complete tasks, mark them as "Completed" in Microsoft Planner. This not only gives you a sense of accomplishment but also helps you track what has been done and what still needs attention. For ongoing projects like fitness goals, you can use recurring tasks to keep track of daily or weekly activities.

- Using the Charts View: Microsoft Planner provides a "Charts" view that offers a visual representation of your progress. It shows you how many tasks are completed, in progress, or not started, and how they are distributed across your buckets. This is particularly useful for seeing how balanced your workload is and ensuring that no part of your project is neglected.

- Adjusting Plans as Needed: Personal projects can be fluid, and sometimes plans need to change. If you find that your original timeline is unrealistic or that some tasks need to be re-prioritized, don't hesitate to adjust your plan. Microsoft Planner's drag-and-drop interface makes it easy to move tasks between buckets, change due dates, or update priorities as your project evolves.

Collaboration on Personal Projects

While personal projects are often individual endeavors, there are instances where collaboration with family members, friends, or other stakeholders is necessary. Microsoft Planner makes it easy to involve others in your project.

- Sharing Your Plan: You can share your Microsoft Planner plan with others who are involved in your project. For example, if you're planning a family vacation, you can invite your family members to the plan so they can contribute to tasks like "Select Attractions to Visit" or "Book Accommodations."

- Assigning Tasks to Others: If certain tasks need to be handled by someone else, you can assign these tasks to them directly in Microsoft Planner. This ensures that everyone involved knows what their responsibilities are and can track their own progress.

- Using Comments for Communication: Each task in Microsoft Planner has a comment section, where you and your collaborators can communicate directly about that specific task. This is particularly useful for keeping discussions organized and ensuring that all relevant information is easily accessible.

Case Example: Planning a Personal Fitness Goal

Let's explore how you might use Microsoft Planner to manage a personal fitness goal. Assume your objective is to improve your overall fitness and health over the next six months.

- Step 1: Define the Plan

  Create a plan called "Fitness Goals 2024" with buckets that represent different aspects of your fitness journey, such as "Exercise," "Diet," "Mental Wellness," and "Tracking Progress."

- Step 2: Create Tasks

  Under the "Exercise" bucket, you might have tasks like "Join a Gym," "Create a Workout Routine," "Start Running Program," and "Weekly Yoga Sessions." In the "Diet" bucket, tasks could include "Consult a Nutritionist," "Create a Meal Plan," and "Track Caloric Intake."

- Step 3: Set Due Dates and Priorities

  Assign due dates for starting the running program or joining a gym. Prioritize tasks that are foundational to your plan, such as creating a workout routine or consulting a nutritionist.

- Step 4: Use Labels

Apply labels like "High Intensity," "Low Intensity," "Meal Prep," and "Mental Health" to categorize tasks. This helps in ensuring a balanced approach to your fitness goals.

- Step 5: Track Progress

As you complete each task, mark it as "Completed." Use the Charts view to monitor your overall progress. For instance, you might aim to have at least one task completed in each bucket every week.

- Step 6: Adjust and Stay Motivated

If you find that certain exercises are too challenging or that your diet needs tweaking, adjust your tasks and priorities. Use the comments section to note how you're feeling after workouts or to log any challenges you encounter.

Benefits of Using Planner for Personal Projects

Using Microsoft Planner for personal projects offers several key benefits:

- Organization: Planner provides a clear and structured way to organize personal projects, making it easier to manage multiple tasks and deadlines.

- Flexibility: You can tailor Planner to fit the unique needs of any personal project, from simple tasks to complex, multi-phase projects.

- Visualization: The ability to visualize progress through charts and task completion bars keeps you motivated and aware of your achievements.

- Collaboration: Planner's collaborative features make it easy to involve others in your personal projects, ensuring that everyone is on the same page.

- Accountability: By setting due dates and priorities, Planner helps you stay accountable to your personal goals, reducing procrastination and enhancing productivity.

Conclusion

Microsoft Planner is more than just a tool for professional project management; it's also a powerful resource for organizing and managing personal projects. Whether you're looking to renovate your home, achieve a fitness milestone, or plan a major life event, Planner's versatile features provide the structure and flexibility needed to succeed. By setting up detailed plans, creating and prioritizing tasks, and tracking your progress, you can transform your personal goals into actionable steps and achieve them with confidence.

7.3.3 Planner in Non-Profit Organizations

Non-profit organizations often operate with limited resources, which makes efficiency and effective management of tasks even more crucial. Microsoft Planner can play a pivotal role in helping these organizations streamline their operations, manage projects, and coordinate team efforts. This section will explore how non-profit organizations can utilize Microsoft Planner to enhance their workflow, improve collaboration, and achieve their mission-driven goals.

1. Organizing Volunteer Activities

Non-profits often rely heavily on volunteers to carry out their activities. Managing these volunteers efficiently is key to ensuring that events and initiatives run smoothly. Microsoft Planner can be used to create detailed plans for volunteer management, allowing non-profits to assign tasks, set deadlines, and track progress in an organized manner.

For instance, a non-profit organizing a community clean-up event can use Planner to create a plan that includes tasks such as recruiting volunteers, assigning roles, procuring supplies, coordinating with local authorities, and marketing the event. Each task can be assigned to different team members or volunteers, with deadlines set to ensure everything is completed on time.

2. Managing Fundraising Campaigns

Fundraising is a critical activity for non-profits, as it provides the necessary funds to support their causes. Microsoft Planner can help non-profits manage their fundraising campaigns by creating detailed plans that outline each step of the process.

A fundraising campaign plan might include tasks such as identifying potential donors, crafting fundraising messages, organizing fundraising events, and tracking donations. By using Planner, non-profits can ensure that all aspects of the campaign are covered, deadlines are met, and team members are held accountable for their tasks. This level of organization can significantly increase the chances of a successful campaign.

3. Coordinating Outreach Programs

Outreach programs are another vital aspect of non-profit work, as they help raise awareness about the organization's mission and engage the community. Whether it's organizing educational workshops, health clinics, or community support services, Microsoft Planner can be an invaluable tool in coordinating these efforts.

For example, a non-profit focused on mental health awareness might use Planner to organize a series of workshops. The plan could include tasks such as booking venues, preparing materials, promoting the workshops, and coordinating with guest speakers. By using Planner, the non-profit can ensure that all these elements are managed efficiently, leading to a well-organized and impactful outreach program.

4. Enhancing Collaboration Among Teams

Non-profits often have teams that work on different projects or initiatives, sometimes across various locations. Microsoft Planner can help these teams collaborate more effectively by providing a centralized platform where all tasks and plans are visible to everyone involved.

For instance, a non-profit working on both a food drive and a literacy program can use Planner to manage both projects simultaneously. Teams can easily switch between plans, update task statuses, and communicate with each other through comments. This transparency and ease of communication can lead to better coordination and more successful outcomes for the non-profit.

5. Tracking Grant Applications and Compliance

Many non-profits rely on grants to fund their operations. The process of applying for grants, managing the funds, and ensuring compliance with grant requirements can be complex and time-consuming. Microsoft Planner can be used to manage these processes more effectively.

A non-profit applying for multiple grants might create a separate plan for each grant application. These plans could include tasks such as researching grant opportunities, writing proposals, gathering required documentation, submitting applications, and tracking application statuses. Once a grant is awarded, Planner can be used to manage compliance tasks, such as reporting on the use of funds and meeting any other requirements set by the grantor.

6. Streamlining Internal Processes

Non-profits, like any other organization, have internal processes that need to be managed efficiently. Whether it's onboarding new employees, managing finances, or conducting board meetings, Microsoft Planner can help streamline these processes.

For example, a non-profit could create a plan for onboarding new staff members, with tasks such as setting up email accounts, providing training, and assigning initial responsibilities. By using Planner to manage these tasks, the non-profit can ensure that new employees are onboarded smoothly and are quickly integrated into the team.

7. Planning and Executing Events

Events are a common way for non-profits to engage with their communities, raise funds, and promote their causes. Whether it's a gala, a charity run, or a virtual conference, organizing these events requires careful planning and coordination.

Microsoft Planner can be used to create detailed event plans that cover every aspect of the event. For example, a non-profit organizing a charity run might create a plan that includes tasks such as securing a venue, coordinating with local authorities, managing registrations, promoting the event, and arranging for refreshments. Each task can be assigned to a specific team member, with deadlines set to ensure that everything is completed on time.

8. Managing Program Delivery

Non-profits often run programs that deliver services directly to their target populations. Whether it's a food distribution program, a literacy initiative, or a health clinic, managing these programs effectively is crucial to their success.

Microsoft Planner can be used to create detailed plans for program delivery, with tasks such as coordinating with partners, scheduling service delivery, managing logistics, and tracking outcomes. By using Planner, non-profits can ensure that their programs are delivered efficiently and that they meet their objectives.

9. Reporting and Accountability

Accountability and transparency are critical for non-profits, especially when it comes to reporting to donors, grantors, and other stakeholders. Microsoft Planner can help non-profits track their activities and generate reports that demonstrate their impact.

For example, a non-profit could create a plan for its annual report, with tasks such as gathering data, writing sections of the report, designing the layout, and distributing the report to stakeholders. By using Planner to manage this process, the non-profit can ensure that the report is comprehensive, accurate, and delivered on time.

10. Integrating Planner with Other Tools

Non-profits often use a variety of tools to manage their operations, from CRM systems to accounting software. Microsoft Planner can be integrated with these tools to create a more seamless workflow.

For instance, a non-profit might use Microsoft Teams for communication, SharePoint for document management, and Dynamics 365 for donor management. By integrating Planner with these tools, the non-profit can create a more cohesive system where tasks are automatically updated across platforms, and team members can easily access the information they need.

11. Leveraging Planner for Strategic Planning

Strategic planning is essential for non-profits to ensure that they are working towards their long-term goals. Microsoft Planner can be used to create and manage strategic plans, with tasks that break down the organization's goals into actionable steps.

For example, a non-profit with a five-year strategic plan might use Planner to create annual plans that align with its long-term goals. These plans could include tasks such as conducting needs assessments, setting annual objectives, developing new programs, and evaluating progress. By using Planner, the non-profit can ensure that it stays on track with its strategic goals and adapts to changing circumstances.

12. Engaging with Stakeholders

Stakeholder engagement is crucial for non-profits, as it helps build trust and support for their work. Microsoft Planner can be used to manage stakeholder engagement efforts, with tasks such as scheduling meetings, preparing reports, and organizing events.

For instance, a non-profit might create a plan for its annual stakeholder meeting, with tasks such as sending invitations, preparing presentations, and gathering feedback. By using Planner, the non-profit can ensure that its stakeholders are engaged and informed about its work.

13. Customizing Planner for Non-Profit Needs

One of the strengths of Microsoft Planner is its flexibility, which allows non-profits to customize it to meet their specific needs. Whether it's creating custom labels for categorizing tasks, setting up recurring tasks for ongoing activities, or using different views to manage complex projects, Planner can be tailored to fit the unique requirements of non-profits.

For example, a non-profit focused on disaster relief might create custom labels for different types of disasters (e.g., hurricanes, wildfires, earthquakes) and use these labels to organize its response efforts. By customizing Planner, the non-profit can create a system that works best for its specific operations.

14. Measuring Impact and Success

Non-profits need to measure their impact to demonstrate the effectiveness of their work and to secure ongoing support from donors and grantors. Microsoft Planner can help non-profits track their progress towards their goals and measure their success.

For example, a non-profit working on a literacy program might use Planner to track the number of students served, the completion of program activities, and the achievement of learning outcomes. By using Planner to manage these tasks, the non-profit can easily gather data and generate reports that showcase its impact.

15. Scaling Operations with Planner

As non-profits grow, they need tools that can scale with them. Microsoft Planner is well-suited for non-profits of all sizes, from small organizations with a few staff members to large organizations with multiple programs and teams.

For example, a non-profit that starts with a single program might eventually expand to offer multiple programs across different regions. By using Planner, the non-profit can create separate plans for each program, with tasks and timelines tailored to the specific needs of each initiative. This scalability ensures that the non-profit can continue to operate efficiently as it grows.

Conclusion

Microsoft Planner is a powerful tool that can help non-profit organizations manage their operations more effectively, improve collaboration among team members, and ultimately achieve their mission-driven goals. By using Planner to organize volunteer activities, manage fundraising campaigns, coordinate outreach programs, enhance collaboration, track grant applications, streamline internal processes, plan and execute events, manage program delivery, report to stakeholders, and measure success, non-profits can maximize their impact and make a difference in the communities they serve.

The flexibility and scalability of Microsoft Planner make it an ideal solution for non-profits, allowing them to customize the tool to meet their specific needs and grow with the organization. Whether a non-profit is just getting started or is well-established, Microsoft Planner can help them stay organized, focused, and effective in their work.

Appendix

Appendix A: Keyboard Shortcuts for Microsoft Planner

Microsoft Planner is a versatile tool that allows users to manage tasks, collaborate with teams, and track progress on various projects. While the graphical interface of Planner is user-friendly, learning and utilizing keyboard shortcuts can significantly enhance your efficiency. This section provides an in-depth guide to the keyboard shortcuts available in Microsoft Planner, covering various functions from navigation to task management and customization.

A.1 Navigation Shortcuts

Navigating through Microsoft Planner using keyboard shortcuts allows for quick access to different sections of the interface, enabling users to move between plans, buckets, and tasks without needing to rely on the mouse. Below are some essential navigation shortcuts:

A.1.1 Accessing the Planner Hub

The Planner Hub is the central location where all your plans are listed. From here, you can quickly access any plan, view charts, and monitor overall progress.

- Alt + H: This shortcut brings you directly to the Planner Hub, where you can see all your active plans.

- Tab: Use the Tab key to cycle through the different elements on the Planner Hub screen, such as the list of plans, charts, and the "New Plan" button.

- Enter: After highlighting a plan with the Tab key, press Enter to open that plan.

These shortcuts make it easier to quickly jump into a specific plan, especially when managing multiple projects.

A.1.2 Moving Between Buckets and Tasks

Buckets are used in Microsoft Planner to categorize tasks within a plan. Efficiently moving between buckets and tasks is crucial for quick task management.

- Ctrl + Left Arrow / Right Arrow: These shortcuts allow you to move between different buckets within a plan. Use the Left Arrow to move to the previous bucket and the Right Arrow to move to the next one.

- Up Arrow / Down Arrow: Once you're inside a bucket, use the Up Arrow to move up the list of tasks and the Down Arrow to move down.

- Tab: When on a specific task, the Tab key can be used to cycle through the task's details, such as the title, due date, and labels.

- Shift + Tab: This shortcut allows you to move in reverse order, cycling back through the task details.

These navigation shortcuts streamline the process of organizing tasks within buckets and ensure that you can quickly find and manage specific tasks.

A.1.3 Opening and Closing Task Details

Task details provide crucial information such as descriptions, due dates, attachments, and comments. Efficiently accessing and closing these details can save time.

- Enter: Highlight a task and press Enter to open the task details. This shortcut allows you to view and edit task information without having to click on the task.

- Esc: Press the Escape key to close the task details and return to the main plan view. This is especially useful when you need to quickly return to the broader view of your plan after updating a task.

Using these shortcuts enhances the speed at which you can interact with individual tasks, allowing for quick edits and updates.

A.2 Task Management Shortcuts

Managing tasks effectively is at the heart of using Microsoft Planner. The following keyboard shortcuts help you create, assign, and update tasks with greater efficiency.

A.2.1 Creating Tasks

Creating new tasks is a frequent activity in Microsoft Planner. Keyboard shortcuts can make this process quicker and more streamlined.

- N: Pressing the "N" key in the plan view opens the task creation window, allowing you to immediately start typing the name of your new task.

- Tab: After entering the task name, press Tab to move to the next field, such as assigning a team member or setting a due date.

- Enter: Once all necessary details are entered, pressing Enter will save the task and add it to the selected bucket.

These shortcuts ensure that task creation is a seamless process, especially when adding multiple tasks in quick succession.

A.2.2 Assigning Tasks to Team Members

Assigning tasks to team members is essential for collaboration and ensuring that work is distributed appropriately.

- Alt + A: When a task is selected, press Alt + A to open the "Assign To" field.

- Tab: Cycle through the list of team members using the Tab key.

- Enter: Select a team member by pressing Enter. If multiple members need to be assigned, repeat the process.

These shortcuts facilitate quick assignment, allowing you to distribute tasks without having to navigate through the interface manually.

A.2.3 Setting Due Dates and Priorities

Setting due dates and priorities helps ensure that tasks are completed on time and according to their importance.

- Alt + D: Use this shortcut to open the due date field for a selected task. You can then enter a date using your keyboard.

- Alt + P: This shortcut opens the priority selection menu, where you can choose between Low, Medium, High, or Urgent priorities using the arrow keys and Enter.

Efficiently setting due dates and priorities helps in managing deadlines and ensuring that critical tasks are addressed promptly.

A.3 Customizing Your Planner View

Customizing the view in Microsoft Planner allows users to organize their workspace according to their preferences, making it easier to focus on the most relevant tasks.

A.3.1 Expanding and Collapsing Buckets

Depending on the number of tasks and buckets, it may be necessary to expand or collapse buckets for a cleaner view.

- Alt + E: Pressing Alt + E expands the selected bucket, displaying all tasks within it.

- Alt + C: This shortcut collapses the selected bucket, hiding its tasks and providing a more streamlined view.

These shortcuts are particularly useful when dealing with large projects that contain many tasks, as they help declutter the interface.

A.3.2 Adjusting Task Priorities

Adjusting task priorities on the fly allows for dynamic management of workload based on changing circumstances.

- Alt + Shift + Up Arrow / Down Arrow: These shortcuts allow you to increase or decrease a task's priority directly from the main view. The Up Arrow increases the priority, while the Down Arrow decreases it.

These adjustments can be made quickly without needing to open the task details, making it easier to respond to urgent changes.

A.3.3 Switching Between Different Views

Microsoft Planner offers different views, such as Board, Charts, and Schedule, each providing unique insights into your plan.

- Alt + 1: Switch to the Board view, which is the default Kanban-style layout.

- Alt + 2: Move to the Charts view, where you can see progress visualizations such as pie charts and bar graphs.

- Alt + 3: Switch to the Schedule view, which displays tasks on a calendar.

These shortcuts allow you to quickly toggle between views depending on your needs, providing a more versatile planning experience.

A.4 Task Interaction and Editing Shortcuts

Beyond just creating and navigating tasks, interacting with and editing tasks is a regular part of using Microsoft Planner. These shortcuts make such interactions quicker and more intuitive.

A.4.1 Adding Labels to Tasks

Labels are color-coded tags that help categorize tasks for better organization.

- Ctrl + L: With a task selected, press Ctrl + L to open the label selection menu. Use the arrow keys to navigate between different labels and press Enter to apply a label.

- Ctrl + Shift + L: This shortcut allows you to apply multiple labels in one go by keeping the selection menu open after each label is applied.

Labels enhance the visibility of task categories, making it easier to identify tasks by their associated labels.

A.4.2 Commenting on Tasks

Adding comments to tasks is essential for collaboration, providing a space for discussion and updates.

- Alt + C: Open the comment field for a selected task by pressing Alt + C. This shortcut allows you to start typing a comment immediately.

- Enter: After typing your comment, press Enter to save it and add it to the task.

These shortcuts facilitate quick communication with team members directly within the task interface.

A.4.3 Attaching Files and Links

Attaching files and links to tasks provides additional context and resources necessary for task completion.

- Alt + T: Open the attachments menu by pressing Alt + T. From here, you can attach files from your computer or add links to relevant online resources.

- Tab + Enter: Use Tab to navigate through the options (e.g., attach a file, attach a link) and press Enter to select your desired option.

This quick method of attaching resources to tasks ensures that all necessary information is easily accessible to team members.

A.5 Managing Multiple Plans with Shortcuts

For users managing multiple projects, switching between plans and keeping them organized can be time-consuming. Keyboard shortcuts help streamline these processes.

A.5.1 Switching Between Plans

Switching between different plans is a common task, especially when managing several projects simultaneously.

- Ctrl + Tab: Use Ctrl + Tab to cycle between open plans. This is particularly useful when you have multiple plans open in separate tabs in your browser.

- Alt + O: Opens the "My Plans" menu, allowing you to select a different plan to open.

These shortcuts allow you to move between plans without having to navigate back to the Planner Hub.

A.5.2 Creating New Plans Quickly

Creating new plans for different projects is a frequent task for project managers and team leads.

- Ctrl + N: This

shortcut opens the "New Plan" dialog, where you can immediately start typing the name of your new plan and set its privacy settings.

- Tab: After entering the plan name, use Tab to move through additional fields like "Add Members" or "Select Group."

- Enter: Press Enter to create the plan and automatically open it.

These shortcuts speed up the creation process, allowing for quick setup of new projects.

A.5.3 Organizing Plans with Groups and Filters

Grouping and filtering plans can help manage larger workloads by organizing projects into more manageable sections.

- Alt + G: Opens the group selection menu, where you can organize tasks by groups such as "Completed," "In Progress," or custom labels.

- Alt + F: Opens the filter menu, allowing you to filter tasks based on criteria like due date, priority, or assigned team member.

Efficient use of groups and filters through these shortcuts helps maintain clarity and focus, especially in complex projects.

A.6 Advanced Shortcuts for Power Users

For users who are well-versed in Microsoft Planner, advanced shortcuts can further enhance productivity and enable more complex task management.

A.6.1 Bulk Editing Tasks

Managing multiple tasks simultaneously is often necessary when making changes to large projects.

- Shift + Click: Select multiple tasks by holding Shift and clicking on them. Once selected, you can apply bulk changes like assigning tasks to a member, changing due dates, or updating priorities.

- Ctrl + Click: Allows for non-contiguous selection, where you can pick and choose tasks across different buckets or plans.

These bulk editing shortcuts save time by enabling simultaneous updates to several tasks.

A.6.2 Automating Repetitive Tasks

For repetitive tasks that occur regularly, automation through keyboard shortcuts can simplify your workflow.

- Alt + R: Opens the "Recurrence" menu for a selected task, allowing you to set up a recurring schedule (e.g., daily, weekly, monthly).

- Ctrl + C / Ctrl + V: Copy and paste tasks within a plan or between different plans, retaining the task details but allowing for quick duplication.

Automation shortcuts reduce the manual effort needed to manage recurring tasks, freeing up time for other important activities.

A.6.3 Integrating with Other Microsoft Tools

Microsoft Planner integrates seamlessly with other Microsoft tools such as Outlook, Teams, and To Do. Keyboard shortcuts can facilitate these integrations.

- Alt + M: Opens the "Move to Outlook" menu, allowing you to convert a Planner task into an Outlook task or calendar event.

- Alt + S: Share a task or plan directly to a Microsoft Teams channel using this shortcut, facilitating team collaboration.

These integrations help streamline your workflow across multiple Microsoft applications, ensuring that Planner remains a central hub for project management.

By mastering these keyboard shortcuts, users of Microsoft Planner can significantly enhance their productivity, streamline their workflow, and manage tasks more efficiently. Whether you are a novice or an advanced user, these shortcuts provide valuable tools for optimizing your use of Microsoft Planner and achieving your goals with greater ease and speed.

Appendix B: Microsoft Planner Glossary

Understanding the terminology used within Microsoft Planner is essential for making the most out of its features and functionalities. This glossary provides definitions and explanations of key terms and concepts you'll encounter when using Microsoft Planner.

Buckets

Buckets are used to organize tasks within a plan. Think of buckets as categories or stages in your workflow. For example, in a project management plan, you might have buckets labeled "To Do," "In Progress," and "Completed." Buckets help you to visually separate tasks and streamline the management process.

Card

A card in Microsoft Planner represents an individual task. Each card can contain details such as a description, assigned members, due dates, attachments, and comments. Cards are the primary units of work within a plan.

Charts

Charts in Microsoft Planner provide a visual representation of your plan's progress. These can include graphs and pie charts that show task distribution, completion status, and more. Charts help you to quickly understand how your plan is progressing and where attention is needed.

Checklist

A checklist is a set of sub-tasks or steps within a task. Checklists help in breaking down a task into smaller, manageable parts, making it easier to track progress and ensure all components of the task are completed.

Comments

Comments allow team members to communicate and collaborate directly within a task. This feature supports real-time communication, enabling users to provide updates, ask questions, or give feedback without leaving the task card.

Due Date

The due date is the deadline by which a task should be completed. Setting due dates helps in prioritizing tasks and managing time effectively. It ensures that all team members are aware of the timeline for task completion.

Filters

Filters in Microsoft Planner allow you to sort and view tasks based on specific criteria such as due dates, assigned members, labels, and priority. Filters help you to focus on tasks that are relevant at any given moment, improving productivity.

Group

A group in Microsoft Planner is a collection of users who can access and collaborate on plans within that group. Groups are often associated with Office 365 Groups, enabling seamless integration and communication across various Microsoft tools.

Labels

Labels are color-coded tags that can be applied to tasks for categorization and identification. For instance, you might use labels to denote task priority, department, or project phase. Labels provide a quick visual reference for task status and context.

Members

Members are users who have been added to a plan. Each member can be assigned tasks, add comments, and contribute to the plan's progress. Managing members effectively ensures that everyone involved in the project is informed and engaged.

My Tasks

"My Tasks" is a view that consolidates all tasks assigned to an individual across all plans. This feature helps users to focus on their responsibilities and manage their workload efficiently by providing a centralized view of all their tasks.

Notifications

Notifications keep team members informed about updates and changes within a plan. These can include notifications for new task assignments, comments, due dates, and task completions. Notifications ensure timely communication and awareness.

Planner Hub

The Planner Hub is the main dashboard where you can view all your plans in one place. It provides an overview of the status of each plan, allowing you to navigate between different projects and manage them efficiently.

Priority

Priority indicates the level of importance of a task. Microsoft Planner allows you to set tasks as "Urgent," "Important," "Medium," or "Low." Prioritizing tasks helps in focusing efforts on the most critical activities first.

Plan

A plan in Microsoft Planner is a collection of tasks organized to achieve specific goals. Plans can be created for various projects, teams, or personal objectives. Each plan consists of buckets, tasks, and other elements to manage and track progress.

Progress

Progress in Microsoft Planner refers to the status of a task, which can be marked as "Not Started," "In Progress," or "Completed." Tracking progress helps in monitoring task completion and identifying any potential delays or issues.

Task

A task is an individual unit of work that needs to be completed. Tasks are the building blocks of plans in Microsoft Planner. Each task can include details such as a title, description, due date, assigned members, and attachments.

Task Details

Task details encompass all the information related to a task, including its title, description, checklist, labels, attachments, and comments. Reviewing task details ensures that all necessary information is available to complete the task efficiently.

Team

A team in Microsoft Planner refers to a group of individuals working together on a plan. Teams are typically aligned with organizational structures or projects, facilitating collaboration and communication.

Template

A template in Microsoft Planner is a pre-defined plan structure that can be reused for similar projects or workflows. Templates save time and ensure consistency by providing a standard format for new plans.

View

Views in Microsoft Planner determine how tasks are displayed. Common views include Board view, which shows tasks organized by buckets, and Charts view, which provides visual progress indicators. Choosing the right view helps in managing tasks more effectively.

Board View

Board view is the default view in Microsoft Planner, displaying tasks organized by buckets in a Kanban-style board. This view helps in visualizing the workflow and moving tasks through different stages of completion.

Assignments

Assignments refer to the process of designating tasks to specific team members. Assigning tasks ensures clear accountability and ownership, helping team members understand their responsibilities within the plan.

Collaboration

Collaboration in Microsoft Planner involves team members working together on tasks, sharing updates, and providing feedback. Effective collaboration enhances productivity and ensures that everyone is aligned with the plan's goals.

Integration

Integration refers to the ability of Microsoft Planner to connect with other Microsoft tools and third-party applications. Integrations enhance functionality and streamline workflows by allowing seamless data sharing and automation.

Milestone

A milestone is a significant point or event in a project that indicates progress. While Planner doesn't have a specific milestone feature, tasks can be used to represent milestones, helping teams to track major achievements and deadlines.

Recurrence

Recurrence in Microsoft Planner allows tasks to be repeated at regular intervals. This feature is useful for ongoing activities or routine tasks that need to be completed periodically.

Resource Allocation

Resource allocation involves assigning the necessary resources, such as team members or time, to tasks. Proper resource allocation ensures that tasks are completed efficiently and project goals are met.

Schedule

The schedule in Microsoft Planner refers to the timeline for task completion, including due dates and deadlines. Managing the schedule is crucial for staying on track and ensuring timely delivery of project objectives.

Status

Status in Microsoft Planner indicates the current condition of a task, such as "Not Started," "In Progress," or "Completed." Monitoring task status helps in understanding progress and identifying any issues early on.

Sub-tasks

Sub-tasks are smaller tasks within a larger task, often represented by a checklist. Sub-tasks help in breaking down complex tasks into manageable steps, making it easier to track and complete each component.

Tag

A tag in Microsoft Planner is a keyword or label used to categorize and identify tasks. Tags enhance organization and allow for quick searching and filtering of tasks based on specific criteria.

Timeline

The timeline in Microsoft Planner provides a chronological view of tasks, highlighting start and due dates. While Planner doesn't have a built-in Gantt chart, the timeline helps in understanding task sequences and dependencies.

Workflow

Workflow refers to the sequence of processes and steps involved in completing tasks within a plan. Defining and optimizing workflows in Microsoft Planner helps in improving efficiency and productivity.

Workload

Workload management involves distributing tasks among team members to ensure balanced and manageable workloads. Effective workload management prevents burnout and ensures that all tasks are completed on time.

Planner Integration

Planner integration refers to connecting Microsoft Planner with other tools, such as Microsoft Teams, Outlook, SharePoint, and Power Automate. Integrations enhance functionality and streamline workflows, making it easier to manage tasks across different platforms.

Planner Mobile App

The Planner mobile app allows users to access and manage their plans and tasks on the go. Available for both iOS and Android, the mobile app provides flexibility and ensures that you can stay productive from anywhere.

Planner Notifications

Notifications in Microsoft Planner keep users informed about updates, task assignments, due dates, and comments. Notifications can be customized to suit individual preferences, ensuring that important information is always received in a timely manner.

Planner Permissions

Permissions in Microsoft Planner control who can view, edit, and manage plans and tasks. Setting appropriate permissions ensures data security and controls access based on user roles and responsibilities.

Planner Templates

Templates in Microsoft Planner are pre-designed plans that can be used as a starting point for new projects. Templates save time and provide consistency, ensuring that best practices are followed across different plans.

Planner Hub

The Planner Hub is the central dashboard where users can view and manage all their plans. It provides an overview of the status of each plan, making it easier to navigate and prioritize tasks.

Task Dependencies

Task dependencies refer to the relationship between tasks that determines the order in which they need to be completed. While Microsoft Planner doesn't have a built-in feature for dependencies, understanding and managing task sequences is crucial for project success.

Task Prioritization

Task prioritization involves determining the order in which tasks should be completed based on their importance and urgency. Setting priorities helps in focusing on critical tasks and managing time effectively.

Task Tracking

Task tracking in Microsoft Planner involves monitoring the progress and status of tasks to ensure they are completed on time. Tracking tasks helps in identifying any delays or issues early

on, allowing for timely interventions.

Project Timeline

A project timeline in Microsoft Planner provides an overview of key milestones, deadlines, and task sequences. While Planner doesn't have a built-in Gantt chart, understanding the project timeline helps in managing tasks and resources effectively.

Project Management

Project management in Microsoft Planner involves planning, executing, and monitoring tasks and resources to achieve specific project goals. Planner provides the tools to organize tasks, collaborate with team members, and track progress, making it an essential tool for project managers.

Project Collaboration

Project collaboration in Microsoft Planner refers to team members working together to complete tasks and achieve project goals. Effective collaboration ensures that everyone is aligned and contributes to the success of the project.

Project Goals

Project goals in Microsoft Planner are the specific outcomes or objectives that a project aims to achieve. Setting clear goals helps in defining tasks, allocating resources, and measuring success.

Project Dashboard

The project dashboard in Microsoft Planner provides an at-a-glance view of the project's status, including task completion, upcoming deadlines, and key metrics. The dashboard helps in making informed decisions and staying on track with project objectives.

Microsoft 365 Integration

Microsoft Planner integrates seamlessly with other Microsoft 365 tools such as Teams, Outlook, SharePoint, and Power Automate. This integration enhances functionality and allows for a unified approach to managing tasks and projects.

Collaborative Planning

Collaborative planning in Microsoft Planner involves team members working together to define tasks, set deadlines, and allocate resources. Collaborative planning ensures that everyone is involved in the decision-making process and that the plan reflects the team's collective goals.

Appendix C: Troubleshooting and FAQs

In this appendix, we'll delve into common troubleshooting issues users may encounter while using Microsoft Planner and provide clear, actionable solutions. We'll also address frequently asked questions to help you optimize your use of the tool.

C.1 Troubleshooting Common Issues

C.1.1 Syncing Issues

One of the most common challenges with Microsoft Planner is syncing issues. These can arise when updates made on one device don't immediately appear on another or when changes made by team members are not reflected in real-time.

Possible Causes:

- Internet Connectivity: Microsoft Planner relies on a stable internet connection to sync changes. A slow or intermittent connection can delay syncing.

- Outdated App Version: Using an outdated version of Microsoft Planner may cause syncing problems as updates often contain critical fixes.

- Browser Issues: If you're accessing Planner through a web browser, issues such as cache buildup or browser version incompatibility might hinder syncing.

Solutions:

- Check Your Connection: Ensure you have a stable and fast internet connection. Consider restarting your router or switching to a more reliable network.

- Update Your App: Regularly check for updates in the Microsoft Store or through your Office 365 portal. Keeping your app up-to-date ensures you have the latest fixes and features.

- Clear Browser Cache: If using a browser, clear your cache and cookies regularly. Ensure your browser is up-to-date or try switching to another supported browser such as Microsoft Edge or Google Chrome.

C.1.2 Task Assignment Issues

Sometimes, users may face difficulties when assigning tasks to team members. This issue might manifest as the inability to assign tasks or team members not receiving notifications about their assignments.

Possible Causes:

- Insufficient Permissions: The person assigning the task may not have the necessary permissions to assign tasks to other team members.

- User Not in Plan Group: The individual you're trying to assign a task to may not be added to the Plan's group, which is required for task assignments.

- Notification Settings: If a user has disabled notifications, they may not receive alerts when tasks are assigned to them.

Solutions:

- Check Permissions: Ensure you have sufficient permissions to manage tasks and assign them to others. You may need to request higher access from the plan's owner or administrator.

- Add Users to the Plan Group: Before assigning tasks, confirm that the intended assignee is part of the plan group. If not, add them to the group.

- Verify Notification Settings: Ask the team member to check their notification settings in Planner and ensure they have not disabled task assignment alerts.

C.1.3 Display and Interface Issues

Display problems can disrupt the user experience, such as tasks not appearing in the correct order, the Planner board not loading correctly, or UI elements being misaligned.

Possible Causes:

- Browser Cache or Cookies: Cached data may cause Planner to load outdated or incorrect information.

- Screen Resolution: Certain screen resolutions might not display Planner's interface optimally, leading to misaligned or overlapping elements.

- System Glitches: Occasional bugs in the Planner application might lead to display issues.

Solutions:

- Clear Cache and Cookies: Regularly clearing your browser's cache and cookies can prevent display issues. This step is particularly important if you frequently switch between different plans or accounts.

- Adjust Screen Resolution: Check your display settings and adjust the screen resolution to a level that is compatible with Microsoft Planner, usually 1920x1080 or higher.

- Refresh or Restart: If you encounter a display issue, try refreshing the browser or restarting the app. This often resolves minor glitches.

C.1.4 Issues with Notifications

Sometimes users may not receive notifications for task assignments, due dates, or comments, which can lead to missed deadlines or communication breakdowns.

Possible Causes:

- Disabled Notifications: The most common cause is that notifications have been disabled either within Planner or in the user's Outlook settings.

- Email Delivery Problems: Notifications sent via email might end up in the spam/junk folder or be blocked by corporate firewalls.

- Mobile App Issues: If you're using Planner on a mobile device, notification issues might stem from app settings or mobile OS configurations.

Solutions:

- Enable Notifications: Go to the Planner settings and ensure notifications are enabled for task assignments, due dates, and comments. Also, check the settings in Outlook to make sure Planner notifications are allowed.

- Check Email Settings: Regularly check your spam/junk folder to ensure Planner notifications are not being filtered out. Consider adding the Planner notification email address to your safe senders list.

- Adjust Mobile Settings: On mobile devices, check that Planner is allowed to send notifications. This can be managed in your device's settings under "Notifications" or a similar menu.

C.2 Frequently Asked Questions

C.2.1 How Do I Recover Deleted Plans or Tasks?

Recovering deleted plans or tasks in Microsoft Planner can be a challenge because Planner does not have a built-in "trash" or "recycle bin" feature. However, there are a few strategies you can employ:

For Tasks:

- Check the Task History: If a task was accidentally marked as complete instead of deleted, you can find it under the "Completed Tasks" section of the Planner board. Simply reopen the task.

- Look in Microsoft Teams: If your plan is associated with a Microsoft Teams channel, you may be able to recover some task details or conversations through Teams' activity logs.

For Plans:

- Check with the Administrator: If a plan was deleted, it might still be recoverable by a global administrator within the Office 365 admin center. Administrators can often recover deleted groups (which include the Planner) within 30 days.

- Recreate the Plan: If recovery is not possible, consider recreating the plan using the information available in emails, task assignments, or other records.

C.2.2 What Should I Do If Microsoft Planner is Not Syncing with Outlook?

When tasks or due dates from Microsoft Planner do not sync with Outlook, it can disrupt personal and team workflows. Here's what you can do:

Verify Sync Settings:

- Check Connection: Ensure that Planner is correctly connected to your Outlook calendar. You can do this by selecting the "Add to Outlook" option in Planner.

- Update Permissions: Make sure you have granted the necessary permissions for Planner to integrate with Outlook. This can be adjusted in your Office 365 account settings.

Troubleshoot Sync Delays:

- Manual Sync: Try manually refreshing the sync between Planner and Outlook by re-adding the calendar link.

- Clear Cache: If you're experiencing persistent issues, clearing your Outlook app's cache may resolve sync delays.

- Contact Support: If these steps don't work, consider contacting Microsoft support for further assistance.

C.2.3 How Can I Export Data from Microsoft Planner?

Exporting data from Microsoft Planner is essential for reporting, analysis, or record-keeping. While Planner doesn't have a direct export feature, you can still export data using several methods:

Exporting via Excel:

- Use Microsoft Graph API: If you are familiar with APIs, Microsoft Graph API allows you to export Planner data into an Excel file. This method is more advanced and requires some technical knowledge.

- Copy and Paste: Manually copy tasks and details from Planner into an Excel spreadsheet. This is a straightforward but time-consuming method for smaller plans.

Third-Party Tools:

- Use Power Automate: Microsoft Power Automate can be used to set up a flow that exports Planner tasks to an Excel file or another database automatically.

- Planner Extensions: Some third-party tools and extensions are designed to help export Planner data. Research and select a reputable tool that fits your needs.

C.2.4 How Can I Improve Performance in Microsoft Planner?

Performance issues in Microsoft Planner can hinder productivity, especially when dealing with large plans or numerous tasks. Here's how to optimize Planner's performance:

Manage Plan Size:

- Archive Old Plans: Keep your active plans lean by archiving or deleting completed or obsolete plans. This reduces the load on Planner and improves responsiveness.

- Limit the Number of Tasks: Try to limit the number of tasks in a single plan. Break down large projects into multiple smaller plans to avoid overloading the Planner interface.

Optimize Task Views:

- Use Filters and Views: Instead of displaying all tasks at once, use filters to view only those that are relevant. This reduces loading times and makes Planner more manageable.

- Update Regularly: Keep your Microsoft Planner and related Office 365 apps updated to ensure optimal performance and benefit from the latest improvements.

C.2.5 How Can I Automate Task Management in Microsoft Planner?

Automation can significantly streamline task management in Microsoft Planner. Here are some ways to automate your workflow:

Using Microsoft Power Automate:

- Set Up Automated Reminders: Power Automate allows you to create flows that send automatic reminders for upcoming task deadlines.

- Automate Task Creation: You can also automate task creation based on certain triggers, such as a new email or form submission.

Integration with Other Apps:

- Connect with Outlook: Automate the syncing of Planner tasks with your Outlook calendar to keep track of deadlines effortlessly.

- Use Third-Party Tools: Some third-party automation tools, such as Zapier, can help connect Microsoft Planner with other apps and automate repetitive tasks.

C.3 Contacting Microsoft Support and Further Resources

C.3.1 How to Contact Microsoft Support

If you encounter issues that you cannot resolve with troubleshooting, contacting Microsoft Support is your next step. Here's how to reach out:

Through the Planner App:

- Help and Feedback: Within the Planner app, navigate to the "Help & Feedback" section to access support resources or submit a request directly to Microsoft.

- Microsoft 365 Admin Center: If you're an admin, you can open a support request directly from the Microsoft 365 Admin Center.

Via Microsoft Website:

- Support Portal: Visit the Microsoft Support website and search for Planner-related articles or submit a support ticket.

- Community Forums: Engage with the Microsoft Planner Community Forum, where you can ask questions and get answers from Microsoft experts and other users.

C.3.2 Utilizing Online Resources

In addition to official support, there are numerous online resources where you can learn more about Microsoft Planner, troubleshoot issues, and connect with other users:

Microsoft Learn:

- Official Tutorials: Microsoft Learn offers a wide range of tutorials and courses on using Planner effectively.

- Certifications: Consider pursuing a certification in Microsoft Office 365 or related fields to deepen your expertise.

YouTube and Blogs:

- Video Guides: Many YouTube channels provide step-by-step guides for using Planner, resolving issues, and maximizing productivity.

- Tech Blogs: Follow tech blogs and forums that regularly publish articles about Microsoft Planner updates, tips, and best practices.

Thank you

As you reach the end of "Microsoft Planner Essentials: Organize Your Work, Achieve Your Goals," we hope this guide has provided you with the knowledge and tools to effectively harness the power of Microsoft Planner. From setting up your first plan to mastering advanced features, Microsoft Planner is a versatile tool designed to help you streamline your tasks, collaborate with your team, and ultimately achieve your goals.

Whether you're managing projects at work, organizing personal tasks, or anything in between, the strategies and best practices covered in this book are intended to help you get the most out of Microsoft Planner. Remember, productivity is not just about getting things done—it's about getting the right things done, in the right way, and at the right time. Microsoft Planner is your ally in this pursuit.

As you continue to use Microsoft Planner, keep exploring its features and refining your approach. With each plan you create and each task you complete, you are building a more organized, efficient, and successful workflow.

Acknowledgments

Thank you for purchasing and reading "Microsoft Planner Essentials: Organize Your Work, Achieve Your Goals." Your decision to invest in this book reflects a commitment to improving your productivity and enhancing your ability to manage tasks effectively.

Writing this book has been a journey of exploration and discovery, and it's a privilege to share that journey with you. We hope that the insights and instructions provided here will serve as a valuable resource in your daily work and personal projects.

Your support and interest in Microsoft Planner are greatly appreciated. If this book has helped you in any way, we encourage you to share your thoughts and feedback. Your experiences and suggestions are vital in helping us improve future editions and resources.

Once again, thank you for choosing this book. May your plans be successful, your tasks well-managed, and your goals achieved. Happy planning!

www.ingramcontent.com/pod-product-compliance
Lightning Source LLC
LaVergne TN
LVHW081331050326
832903LV00024B/1116